Into the Wild

Into the Wild
The Making of an Explorer

LUCY SHEPHERD

MICHAEL JOSEPH

PENGUIN MICHAEL JOSEPH

UK | USA | Canada | Ireland | Australia
India | New Zealand | South Africa

Penguin Michael Joseph is part of the Penguin Random House group of companies whose addresses can be found at global.penguinrandomhouse.com

Penguin Random House UK,
One Embassy Gardens, 8 Viaduct Gardens, London SW11 7BW

penguin.co.uk

First published 2026

001

Copyright © Lucy Shepherd, 2026
Map illustration © Jamie Noble
All other illustrations by Lucy Shepherd

The moral right of the author has been asserted

This book reflects the personal experiences and views of its author, and does not represent the views of any sponsors or affiliated companies

No part of this book may be used or reproduced in any manner for the purpose of training artificial intelligence technologies or systems. In accordance with Article 4(3) of the DSM Directive 2019/790, Penguin Random House expressly reserves this work from the text and data mining exception

Set in 13.2/16pt Garamond Premier Pro
Typeset by Six Red Marbles UK, Thetford, Norfolk
Printed and bound in Great Britain by Clays Ltd, Elcograf S.p.A.

The authorized representative in the EEA is Penguin Random House Ireland, Morrison Chambers, 32 Nassau Street, Dublin D02 YH68

A CIP catalogue record for this book is available from the British Library

ISBN: 978–0–241–77553–0

Penguin Random House is committed to a sustainable future for our business, our readers and our planet. This book is made from Forest Stewardship Council® certified paper.

For Mum and Dad,
who gave me the courage to roam freely and walk my own path.

And for Ian Craddock,
who lit the path ahead.

Contents

Map	x
Foreword	1
Prologue	3

The Making of An Explorer

1	My Roots	9
2	The Pit	15
3	The Start of a Lifetime	21
4	Ian Craddock	31
5	Stair Club	39
6	Tim	45
7	Ian's Gift – 2020	51
8	Are You Lucy Shepherd?	54
9	Two Become Six	61
10	Water Dog	65
11	The Whistle	71
12	The Great Idea	79
13	Summer Shock	82
14	Carrying the Flame	86
15	Anders	91
16	Planning	99

The Big One

17	Make Good Decisions	105
18	Assemble	113
19	Go Time	121
20	The Capsize	140
21	Insertion Point	146
22	Going Commando	154
23	Routines	160
24	Sufferfest	164
25	The Land of the Giants	171
26	Wolf Fish	175
27	The Invisible Danger	183
28	Bushmaster	189
29	Bamboo	196
30	Setting Sail	208
31	Balata Bleeders	212
32	Marksmen	216
33	Bush Cow	227
34	Roses	230
35	Wap Killer	233
36	Bush Dai Dai	240
37	Aaron	246
38	Resupply Two	252
39	Peccary	256
40	Mosquito Worm	268
41	Cheerfulness in the Face of Adversity	283
42	Forest Family	289

Epilogue — 300
Afterword — 306
Acknowledgements — 308

Into the Wild

Foreword

There are still places in this world where the map grows vague. Places where nature breathes in its fullest form. Places that are untamed, unpredictable and – perhaps most remarkably, as a result of us discovering more and more – still unknown. Still wild.

This is a story from one of those places.

In the heart of South America lies a stretch of wilderness that few have entered.

It is a land where jaguars roam unseen and ancient mountains rise from rainforest. It's a place where every step forward is a step into mystery. It's here, in the Kanuku Mountains of Guyana, that I led a small team on a journey deep into the unknown.

Exploration, contrary to what some might think, is not dead. In fact, it's *very* much alive and it's more exciting than ever. The more we discover, the more we realize just how much we *don't* know. Exploration is part of what makes us human. Without it we stagnate.

This realization drives me. Adventure is often overlooked as being indulgent, a personal thrill, but it's a catalyst for so much. It reminds me how vital it is to protect these last wild spaces, not just with laws and boundaries, but by rekindling a feeling we've perhaps lost along the way: awe for this planet.

That's what nature gives me: awe, perspective. A sense of

being small in the best possible way yet part of something so much bigger too. I believe we all need a bit more of that. I believe it can change how we treat the world and, more important than ever right now, treat each other.

And so this isn't just an expedition log. As much as it's a story about a remarkable wilderness, this is a story of shared humanity, a story of connection, friendship and people – their limits, resilience and humour. It's about the sting of sweat in your eyes, the stillness of just 'being', the battered feet and the unspoken bonds that form when you're weeks from help, surrounded by life that doesn't care whether you make it out or not.

This is also a story about the jungle. Not as a hostile force to *conquer*, but as a teacher. To re-learn what we've lost. And, perhaps more than anything, it's a call to remember what's at stake – Because these last wild places are vanishing. Fast. Stories are powerful, they can remind us to care. And if we don't keep telling these stories, we may lose them before we've even truly heard them.

So this is mine. A record of this journey. The story so far . . . into the wild.

Prologue

Our boat slices through the calm and silent waters of the Essequibo River, but I can see that things are about to change. The crashing white rapids are ahead of us.

Anders looks at the camera and with a half-grin he says, 'Don't try this at home.' I sense some nerves in his voice but at least the rapids mean that we are nearing our drop-off location, where we can finally begin the expedition on foot.

We slow down as our boat captain, Neville, calls the bow boy back to the engine to take control. Jenson, who is in front of me, follows the order and moves past me to the back of the boat. I don't know if I like the idea of the younger and less-experienced man taking charge, but I guess that means these rapids can't be that bad, and maybe Neville sees it as a training opportunity.

We slow down as the engine changes hands. I have one hand tightly gripped to the boat and the other is on my phone, filming. I'm smiling, getting myself ready for an adrenaline rush.

We're about thirty metres away, but the engine slows down and suddenly it cuts out. I'm not sure if that was Jenson's fault or not but, surely, we should be taking this on just as aggressively as the rapids itself. The engine crackles on again but the noise is overcome by the pummelling white water.

As we get closer it's revealed that the rapids are bigger than they seemed. There's a large rock on the left that was at first hidden. The water pounds it and there's a threatening whirlpool that swirls around next to the rock. There's also a sudden drop. The water crashes down into the rock, becomes a whirlpool that then spits out the water on the other side of the rapids.

This doesn't look right. Would Neville have handed the reins to Jenson, had he seen what was in store for us?

Either way, we're committed now, and we've just got to go for it.

We go straight; I hope to God that Jenson has spotted the whirlpool. We take it on and the long, dented aluminium boat flies up into the air. It happens in slow motion. We slam down on the other side, but we haven't passed it. We've got just the bow through the rapid and the rest of the boat is stuck.

'Come on!' I yell.

I look around: we are genuinely stuck. The engine can hardly be heard as the water hammers the boat. We're not moving at all.

The water is rushing fast past us. I look to see the whirlpool and menacing rapids are just behind. If we don't free ourselves quickly, the boat is going to head straight for them.

I'm not smiling any more. Anders looks terrified and Neville is scanning all around to see what he can do. My team mate Mikey moves to the front of the boat with Jenson as Neville takes back control of the engine.

Mikey and Jenson push and pull the front of the boat. They're trying to get more weight at the front to free the back. *Maybe this is a trick that they always use to free the boat?* I think. *Or maybe this is just a last port of call.*

Mikey and Jenson continue rocking the boat side to side. It's not working. We can't manoeuvre it forward. Instead, we are slowly edging backwards towards the deadly vortex. I've been

PROLOGUE

filming this whole time but something in my gut tells me to stop now. I quickly put the phone into my zipped trouser pocket.

I can tell what's about to happen.

The water thrashes the boat – we are becoming free, but in the wrong direction. Backwards. The engine is simply not powerful enough to deal with the current and this pressure of water. We suddenly lose our alignment and, as soon as we aren't parallel to the current, the boat is caught and flips to the right. Without notice, the boat catapults us out as it upturns. We all go under.

The Making of an Explorer

1. My Roots

I WAS BORN WITH A FERAL STREAK. Growing up as an only child in coastal Suffolk, I had vast fields, as far as my legs could run, a gang of animals to talk to and trees that felt more familiar than the kids at school. I loved the feeling of dirt under my nails, calluses on the palms of my hands and the breeze in my hair.

In my younger child years, I suppose you could call me a tomboy. I was just more interested in wild things than dolls or what shoes were cool.

I was lucky to have a vivid imagination. My mum used to praise it, urging me to hold on to that creativity. I really took that advice to heart. I lived in my mind and it became my escapism. My rich imagination was something I cherished and I'd love nothing more than spending hours daydreaming, coming up with all sorts of magical things in my head. I'd dream up everything from what it would be like to live with wild animals to going on adventures through mountains and jungles.

My childhood, it seems idyllic: the sprawling countryside, frequent tree-climbing adventures, and even an oak tree that later became home to my very first (and only) treehouse.

It wasn't always like that, however. Until I was eight, I lived in a house in Reydon, a small village a mile from the sea and next to what is now the picturesque town of Southwold. Back then, Southwold wasn't quite the same gentrified Londoner retreat that it is now. The population demographic then leaned more on the older side, and the high street and shops were traditional and needed some sprucing up. During those early years, it was only Mum with a job, as a doctor for the local surgery.

Mum and Dad had met in Turkey. They were sailing on separate flotillas, both on separate solo holidays, but thankfully, their paths crossed. They spent two weeks together, connecting each evening in various ports, and quickly fell in love.

Mum was born in Aden, Yemen, one of five (seven if you include her half-siblings), and when she was just three the family lived in Ibadan, Nigeria. She spent a number of years in Nigeria before moving to Edinburgh when she was ten. Her dad, Peter Cockshott, was a Professor of Radiology at the medical school; Una, her mother, also a doctor, spent her time investigating magical medicine, analysing the work of the witch doctors.

My explorer gene probably originates from my grandmother. Una is a bit of a legend in our family. Her roots run deep in the wilds of Scotland: born in Applecross on the remote west coast, her family came from the tiny island of Scarp (now uninhabited) in the Outer Hebrides, and she was raised in the Black Isle. She grew up in a strict religious household, daughter of the manse, which – perhaps unsurprisingly – steered her firmly towards atheism later in life. Unlike me, Una was incredibly academic. She left remote Scotland to study medicine in Edinburgh, was top of her year and earned several PhDs. After meeting Peter, my grandfather, who sadly died before I got to know him, she moved to Africa. It was there that the party life stepped up a notch. She led a vibrant life filled with lavish parties, diverse companions, and daring adventures. It was during her time in Nigeria that she met her second husband, the late John Mackintosh, the Labour MP for Berwick and East Lothian.

When I hear stories of Una's antics, all I can think is that they deserve to be made into a film. She was one of a kind and ahead of her time in a lot of ways, although perhaps she stepped over the line with her rebellion on occasions. She wasn't afraid to do things her way and that's something I try to do myself.

Dad grew up in less exotic surroundings. He was one of three boys, growing up in a working-class area in Harlow New Town, with a father who we later discovered was far more coercive and abusive – both emotionally and physically – to his children and to my grandmother, Sybil, than we'd ever realised. I get the impression that Dad has always had a get-up-and-go attitude. I massively respect him for that. He keeps himself busy, is a problem solver and more sensitive than he often lets on.

When Mum and Dad met, Dad lived in Suffolk. Returning to their homes after their Mediterranean meeting, Dad made the journey to Edinburgh to visit Mum and just three weeks after their initial meeting, he proposed. Sounds romantic, right? Well, I guess it is, but not so much when I tell you where he proposed . . . in a busy pub, while they were half standing and without a ring. I think they were eager to get a move on as they were in their late thirties.

Mum made the move to Suffolk because Dad was involved with a small wholesale fish business – but not long after she'd left vibrant Edinburgh for sleepy Lowestoft, the job vanished. Whoops. Just like that. The local depot shut down due to a drop in fish landings. Technically, Dad could've gone back to the main depot in Hertfordshire, but they'd just relocated and got married. With Mum settling into her new job as a GP, he decided it was best to stay put in Suffolk.

Dad was without any qualifications, so it was up to Mum to hold the fort and she worked tirelessly for many years. Dad was, for that period, effectively a house husband. Mum encouraged him to do an access course at the local college, which led to him going on to university and subsequently becoming a teacher. Maybe that's where I get my independence from. Although not outdoorsy or world-changing, Mum has always been a leader in her own life, fiercely taking control when needed. And Dad, he's always been project-driven, eager to complete things and move on to the next, and has an admirable open mind. I see that in myself, too.

Very soon after my parents' marriage, Mum fell pregnant with twin boys but, sadly, they were born premature and died within a few minutes. Mum very quickly fell pregnant again, this time with triplets. However, I would be the only one to survive. Born via Caesarean four weeks early and weighing just four pounds, my birth was nearly fatal for both me and my mum. Even in those critical days, she was pragmatic, instructing my dad on how to change nappies and how exactly to care for me should the worst happen. Although she has never shown any interest in doing any risk-taking expeditions herself, I think her natural no-flapping, logical attitude would be ideal in those intense situations. Thankfully, Mum made a full recovery. It's surprising to a lot of people when they find out that I am an only child through those circumstances, yet still my parents never bubble-wrapped me, and have always supported my somewhat risky endeavours and career choice.

Over the years, we had a steady rotation of Labradors and German Shepherds, always at least one of each. I felt a profound connection with the German Shepherds in particular; their loyalty was unmatched. We had Pippa, Lucky, and, towards the end of my childhood, Cleo . . . and now Sheps.

Then there were the cats. Embarrassingly we went through a lot of cats – too many, really. Some went rogue, a few had genetic problems and more than one got flattened on the country lanes, despite the nearest road being some distance away. We weren't bad pet owners but we seemed to be cursed when it came to cats.

When Dad took up smallholding, on the side of his teaching job, things got even more chaotic. We had pigs, chickens, ducks, bees and then sheep. Lots of sheep. Bottle-feeding lambs became the norm because the young, dopey mothers constantly rejected them. They'd come inside the house, we'd curl them up in towels by the log burner and feed them milk. They would wag their little stringy tails like happy puppies.

Henry was my favourite lamb, even though you're not supposed to have favourites. He'd follow me around the garden, skipping after me like a needy sidekick. It's hard not to romanticize those memories of walking down the lane with Henry the lamb, Fidget the cat, Sidney the Labrador, Lucky the German Shepherd – oh, and there was even Jemima the duck. It must have been a ridiculous sight!

But lambs grow up, and when Henry got bigger, he changed. The testosterone kicked in and suddenly he was charging and becoming a bit of a bully to anyone who came near him. He'd charge at me and harass his twin brother, whom I had ingeniously named 'Sad Face' for obvious reasons – he had a sad face. Despite not raising him indoors like Henry, I grew quite fond of Sad Face. Unlike his aggressive twin, Sad Face was the black sheep – literally and figuratively – and his demeanour was as different as his colour. He would quietly approach me for attention and cuddles, perhaps jealous of the affection we had lavished upon Henry as a young lamb.

This charming story becomes a little less lovely and takes a bittersweet turn when, after my dad endured one too many of

Henry's aggressive rams, he made the decision that it was time for Henry to do what he was born to do: become dinner.

One day, I came home and found Dad in the kitchen.

'He's too much, Lucy,' he said. 'I can't have him knocking me or you over. It's time.'

My stomach sank.

'You don't mean Henry?' I asked, though I knew exactly what he meant.

'And Sad Face too,' he added, almost under his breath.

'What? No! Why Sad Face?'

Dad didn't have a good answer. I now think it was just practicality. I protested . . . I properly protested, but it didn't make a difference and the next day Henry and Sad Face's fate was met and they became lamb chops.

I didn't eat lamb for a year after that. Not because I suddenly went vegetarian, but because I was terrified I might end up eating a bit of Henry or Sad Face.

2. The Pit

OUTDOORS, I WAS OUTGOING AND COMFORTABLE. But at school, it was a different story. For most of my years at all those different schools, I was the quiet one, often labelled shy – a label I despised. I didn't see myself as shy. I simply had nothing to say in the uninspiring confines of a classroom where daydreaming was punished. No thank you. I much preferred being outside, living out the adventures I'd conjured up in my mind.

I'm told that I was bullied at middle school, but honestly, those memories are foggy. I think I blocked it out as a form of self-protection. I was never traditionally what you'd call 'cool' and would find it hard to slot into the different 'gangs', whatever age. However, I did find it easy and far more rewarding to build friendships one to one, and found I was able to get on with pretty much anyone in that way.

Secondary school is where I hold the most memories, a state school in Framlingham called Thomas Mills High School. I tend to bump into a few of my peers from there even now, and so many of them went on to lead really interesting lives. During my time there I hovered around the average mark, but outside of school my life felt more unique. It was me, my parents and our menagerie of pets; it sometimes felt like half of Noah's Ark.

I always had an adventurous spark, though that's hardly unique among children. There's a bit of an explorer in every kid. I relished the freedom of the outdoors, from hiding in ditches to scaling the tallest trees and ropes. My hands were permanently callused, my knees and elbows always scraped. Climbing so high that I could hear the anxious voices of adults below was thrilling. 'Oh, Lucy!' a friend's mum would say, covering her eyes. 'I can't watch!' It was then that I knew: I'd found my 'thing'.

Whenever I got new gear, like a waterproof jacket or trainers, the first thing I'd do was go to the woods with my best friend, Harry, and make sure they looked well-used. I couldn't bear the idea of brand-new clothes. I'd drag them through mud or slide down the muddiest hill I could find, much to my mum's dismay!

I'd climb trees to sit at the top and imagine I was in the Amazon, but my adventurous spirit often led to accidents and mishaps. Besides being known as shy, I was also considered accident-prone. Whether it was burns from campfires or broken bones, I seemed to collect injuries. Aged eight, I broke both my arms trying to mimic the cool boy at school who had managed to stand on top of the monkey bars. I followed him, with a strange sense of quiet confidence that I still remember to this day. I stood up proudly . . . and lasted about half a second before crashing down to the ground, both arms broken in several places, twisted into 'S' shapes.

But these incidents never deterred me. On the contrary. They fuelled my determination to find local adventures. It wasn't long before I discovered bivouac sacks; a type of waterproof cover that fits over a sleeping bag, which means you can go without a tent or tarpaulin and enjoy the fresh outside air.

THE PIT

I spent my weekends with Harry, so naturally he was the first person I shared a bivvy adventure with. Our parents were the best of friends – the Shepherds and the Jellicoes, known affectionately as 'Sheps and Jellies' – so we spent a lot of time together. Harry and I would constantly be playing make-believe games, constructing dens or making movies – which started at aged ten with my dad's camcorder.

When we were growing up, I remember feeling this subtle, unspoken envy. Not of Harry, but of what the world seemed to promise him. We were partners-in-crime, climbing trees, getting muddy, making dens and grand plans, but deep down I sensed that his adventures didn't have an expiry date. He was a boy; it felt like he could carry that wildness straight into adulthood without anyone questioning it. For me, it felt more complicated. There was this quiet fear that growing up would mean growing out of the things that made me feel most alive – as if adventure was something boys naturally continued, while girls were expected to smooth out their rough edges and settle down. I didn't have the language for it back then, but I know now that part of me was already fighting for the right to keep my wildness. And thank God I did.

I don't know where I first heard about the bivvy, maybe a book or something on telly, but the idea of sleeping outside (properly outside) without a tent felt so exciting, and so wild and freeing. I was probably about twelve or thirteen. I remember showing Harry this bit of basic kit, just an orange waterproof sack, and his face was confused. 'So . . . we sleep in that?' he asked. Clearly he was sceptical, but up for the adventure.

The first night we tried it we chose the field behind my house. Mum wasn't too sure, but she'd learned by then not to question my weird adventure ideas too much. We wandered off into the field and took sleeping bags, head torches and even dragged the dogs along too, although they didn't end up staying all night (clever dogs) and bounded over to greet us in the early hours of the morning when they were let out by my dad, bewildered as to why we'd chosen to spend the night away from comfort. I loved sleeping outside, come rain or shine – it felt like we were getting away with something, that we'd found a secret adventure on quite literally our doorstep.

We did that over and over again in other fields, random ditches and 'The Pit', which was basically a big dip of land near some woods that filled with water in winter and dried out in summer. The Pit was my little wild overgrown world. It felt hidden and remote. Harry and I would lie there in our bivvy bags, and even if it didn't rain, we'd still be soaked by the morning as they were not breathable at all.

We'd guess what animals we could hear. Most of the time it was probably just a vole or a mouse rustling through the grass, but sometimes it was more exciting, like the heavy thud of a deer's hooves or the eerie bark of a fox in the distance. Occasionally, an owl would screech overhead, making us grip our sleeping bags tighter. We'd freeze and whisper, 'Did you hear that?' Even just the question would freak us out, as of course we'd be absolutely certain it was something enormous and deadly.

I convinced more and more friends to join me for overnight stays outdoors in The Pit, no matter the weather. I think it was then that I started to get a reputation for taking adventure that bit further.

These experiences made me feel alive; there was a thrill in enduring the night. I seemed to love doing something a bit different, thriving by being a little cold and wet, and even thriving on being a bit scared . . . only to wake up to the light coming through the trees and the sound of the English countryside birds cheeping. It gave me a taste of what real adventure could feel like and I guess it also proved that we didn't have to go far to find it. All I had to do was venture off the beaten path.

Despite my growing passion for the wild, I never imagined I could turn it into a career. Even now, when people ask what I do and I respond with 'explorer', I get it – it sounds somewhat pretentious. I would be lying if I said I haven't squirmed when saying it before. For the first ten years of doing expeditions, I called myself an 'adventurer' but felt it didn't quite do some of expeditions I'd been on justice – so a few years ago, I decided it was time to claim the title for myself.

It seems a shame to consign such a vibrant term to history, reserved only for legendary figures like Percy Fawcett or Shackleton. I'm not claiming to be in their league, in fact the opposite. They are the giants of adventure. But exploration is very much alive and isn't there magic in that? If I had known that modern explorers still existed when I was younger, it might have given me a bit more peace of mind, knowing such a path was possible.

Around the age of fourteen, I briefly toyed with the idea of joining the forces. I devoured all the BBC 'on the frontline' documentaries I could find, enamoured with the rigorous training, discipline, camaraderie and travel. The only bit I wasn't sold on was the reason you're doing all of those things . . . the fighting.

At about the same age, inspired by TV shows fronted by the likes of Bruce Parry, Ben Fogle, Steve Backshall and of course Bear Grylls, I began to think and dream bigger. I was realizing just how vast, rich and layered the world was. It went beyond me simply observing and enjoying the visuals; it was more that watching those shows actually made my heart ache. There was something truly physical about the feeling it stirred up in me. Envy . . . well maybe, but not in a bitter way. I simply wanted to be them. I could see myself doing what they did, be where they were.

Even when Ben Fogle was shivering in sub-zero temperatures in the South Pole or Bear Grylls was covered in mud, eating whatever he could find, I didn't pity them . . . I envied them. I just thought, what a lucky guy. He was doing it. Then there was Bruce Parry, with his access to people and places all over the world – what a fantastic job! It gave me this overwhelming urge: I *have* to do that. Not just for the adventure, but for the connection, and so I suddenly felt the shortness of life, and wanted to get out there and experience the things that can't be replicated in books or classrooms.

These shows also made me realize that exploration wasn't confined to history. It's something I still find myself having to prove: that there's exploration to be done now, in modern times. Back then, I never stopped to ask why it was always men on screen – maybe because my imagination was strong enough to put myself there anyway. Fortunately, I grew up never being told that I couldn't do something because I was a girl. What I did notice was the way adults around me couldn't quite picture *me* doing it when I was older though; they likely thought I'd grow out of it. I definitely didn't *look* like the people on TV, but maybe, in some quiet way, that made me want it even more.

3. The Start of a Lifetime

My first ever expedition was to the Arctic of Svalbard when I was the young age of eighteen. It was one of those things where the stars really did align.

Spurred on by the adventure shows, upon leaving school I was eager to take a year out. I couldn't wait to leave Suffolk. Don't get me wrong, Suffolk is a beautiful part of the world, but I was itching to see more. I'd been led to believe that this was the one time in our lives where we got to be truly free and could work abroad. I waitressed, then did ski instructing in New Zealand, backpacked there afterwards, followed by travels through Australia and Asia – and then the one adventure that I had been eagerly awaiting and fundraising for during the whole of my final year at school.

A few years before, at fifteen years old, I had felt that my usual adventurous self, or identity if you want to call it that, was beginning to fade. I was trying hard to fit in with the crowd, caring what others thought and straying away from what was viewed as normal was terrifying – or was something I'd do in secret, like my movie-making. But then, I suddenly felt the need to reconnect with the outdoors and risk-taking version of myself. I couldn't pretend to show the same enthusiasm for a new music video or the latest trend in clothes. I craved freedom and adventure, and could feel there was more out there than simply hanging out in fields drinking blue WKD.

That's when I discovered the Ridgway Adventure school in the remote Scottish Highlands, an establishment born from the legacy of John Ridgway, a paratrooper turned Atlantic rower. His daughter, Rebecca, now runs the school and maintains its rigorous, almost military-like discipline, known as the toughest of its kind. I headed there for two weeks in the summer of my sixteenth birthday and it was a transformational experience. Sure, I'd done Duke of Edinburgh and enjoyed it, but this was a whole other level. Expectations of us were high. We'd be exercising before breakfast, cleaning up, and were taught climbing, kayaking and survival skills. It was where I was introduced to the term 'expedition' as we went on a number of mini expeditions over the course of the two weeks. We were completely self-sufficient as we went on a three-day kayaking journey and multi-day mountain hikes. The feeling of climbing these dramatic, severe-looking mountains and going days without seeing anyone but our group of people was bliss. I thrived in that environment and lapped up every second of it.

I learned that I loved having a purpose and enjoyed being in physically demanding situations with good people around me. I found my confidence again and realized that to really be happy, I needed to surround myself with similar driven-minded people in nature and with goals. I came away from there eager to do more expeditions and not long after, my mum found an advert in the paper.

It read: *British Schools Exploring Society (BSES) – 10-Week Arctic Expedition – 18–25 year olds wanted for 2011.* The words jumped out at me. I would be eighteen in 2011: this advert was for me.

THE START OF A LIFETIME

It was like a lightning bolt hit me the moment I read it. I applied, had interviews to see if I was suitable, went to weekend training camps, learned how to fundraise for the charity, and before I knew it, it was April 2011 and it was time to embark.

Svalbard is a Norwegian-owned archipelago located in between Norway and the North Pole. In fact, it's only a few hundred miles from the North Pole, making it home for a large number of polar bears. In the months I was there, April through to June, we had twenty-four-hour sunlight and were present for the winter to spring period. Temperatures started below minus twenty but we were witness to the 'slush flow', which is when the ice melts and large amounts of water rush through the land. We camped out for the entire time, moving through the terrain with skis, pulling pulks (sleds) containing all of our belongings. We climbed mountains, conducted science projects related to climate change and biodiversity changes, and mapped out ice caves. The expedition had real jeopardy and lessons, and I found such a great connection and friendship with my fellow team mates.

We were trained by former military dudes, and that same discipline I'd learned at the adventure school in Ardmore came into play in Svalbard. However, it all came crashing down when I returned to what was considered 'normal life' and I struggled. I'm not saying I was like a soldier coming back from war or anything, I was simply a young person struggling to find my place in life and felt more familiarity being in the wilderness. One day I was skiing through a whiteout pulling a pulk in −20°, feeling more myself than I ever had, and the next, I was standing in a supermarket aisle, paralyzed by choice. The fluorescent lights. The bland conversations. I remember staring at twenty types of peanut butter and just . . . freezing.

I was lost when I came back. No one told me how weird it

would feel to come home. Everyone was saying, 'What a once-in-a-lifetime experience!' To me, that felt like a punch in the stomach. Why should it only be once? Why should the best, most alive version of myself be a fluke?

At first, I tried to fit back in. I smiled when people asked about the adventure, nodded politely when they called it 'amazing'. But inside, I felt completely disconnected and knew they couldn't possibly know how much this experience had affected me. I wasn't built for this version of life: one without real adventure, without meaningful relationships and living alongside the wild world. I wanted more, but I didn't know how to get it.

To combat these feelings, I turned to something a lot of teenage girls and young adults turn to: I controlled my eating and my exercising. As soon as I was back from the Arctic, I discovered this newfound fitness that I'd never had before: 54 kg of pure, lean muscle. I took up running and those runs got longer and longer and longer. I counted my calories, feeling like I didn't need as much because I 'wasn't on expedition'. All of this, of course, led to me becoming dangerously underweight. This lasted a couple of years – controlling the one thing I could: my body. That control spiralled into disordered eating, a distraction from how lost I felt. I was visibly shrinking, in more ways than one. It wasn't until later that I realized if I wanted to live the life I dreamed of, the one that would allow me to go to wild places with a clear mission and purpose, I had to fight for it. No one was going to hand it to me and I couldn't starve my way into strength.

Following Svalbard, I went to study film and television production at the University of York. After all, filmmaking was my other love. I'd always struggled to communicate what I was thinking – maybe that stems from being an only child – but with film I found a way to articulate what was in my imagination. I was able to visually convey my ideas and would get such a thrill from seeing people watch the films that I had made from nothing. I realized that I could evoke emotions with my storytelling, and recognized that there was great power in it. I was good at it too.

I won dozens of awards by simply finding a loophole. I'd realized that there were small young-filmmakers competitions, all around the country, but no one was entering them. Often they'd have prize money attached and I'd regularly win £250, £500 – once I even won £2,000. This all went into a pot, which would later go towards my early expeditions.

But I felt different at university. The expedition had opened a door to a world I didn't know existed – now I couldn't close it, and no way did I want to either!

I needed to find a way to spend more time doing these high-impact expeditions. The only thing was, I still had no interest in joining the military, nor did I want to become an outdoor guide. I didn't even fancy myself as a camera person producing nature documentaries; I loved all that but it was not quite what was in my head. These were the paths that I could see to that life but I wanted to forge my own, and early on I had a vision of what that looked like, the vision of what I am doing now, and no one was quite doing it the way I had in mind . . . which made it even more attractive.

I learned about the Royal Geographical Society (RGS) as a result of the expedition to Svalbard, because the BSES was based in the same building and had ties to it. I was captivated by the RGS. Founded in 1830, it started as a sort of dining club for gentlemen explorers planning routes into the unknown. Over the decades it became the beating heart of British exploration, backing journeys from Shackleton's Antarctic expeditions to Livingstone's African travels.

I realized pretty quickly that this was the place to be and learn how to do exploration full time. The grand, historic building is in South Kensington, close to the Natural History Museum and Royal Albert Hall. It has an impressive amphitheatre, which I'd later spend many evenings at, both listening in awe to other explorers sharing their tales of adventure and having the privilege of sharing my own. If you look above the amphitheatre, there are names of historical explorers printed on the wood panels and photographs dating back to Shackleton's time.

Aged nineteen, I'd catch the train from York to London just to be near it: the Royal Geographical Society. I'd walk through the doors like I belonged, but inside, I felt like a total fraud, trying my best to not look like a kid in a candy store. Everyone there looked like they had many prestigious expeditions under their belt, or at the very least a PhD and an expensive watch that they'd been given by the watch company itself. I had neither.

I continued to hover in the corridors, trying not to look out of place while secretly hoping someone might notice me, but also terrified they actually would. What would I say? I'd be ready to introduce myself and then get cold feet. I knew that I needed the courage to begin conversations.

Once, I was lingering in the corridor when the 'world's greatest living explorer' walked right past me, briefcase in hand. I froze, just watching as he sat down at a desk nearby, calmly opened his case and pulled out papers, probably working on his next bestseller. I remember standing there, clutching my notebook, half wanting to go over and speak to him, half terrified he'd wonder what on earth this kid was doing loitering in the halls of the RGS.

I am of course talking about Sir Ranulph Fiennes. Being in his company should've inspired me, but back then, mostly it made me feel small. What the hell was I doing here? I hadn't

THE START OF A LIFETIME

summited Everest or sailed around the world. I'd just come back from the Arctic with big dreams, a dodgy tan line and no idea what I was doing next.

But even with that bubbling 'imposter syndrome', something kept pulling me back. Although I didn't fit in yet, I felt that this was a place that one day I would fit in; these could become my walls too. I didn't feel ready, but I wanted to be. I didn't know what I was doing, but I knew I had to try.

It wasn't until I met Neil Laughton at the RGS that I began to figure out how. I was told that Neil was an adventurer, a former Marine and SAS man and had a number of expeditions under his belt. He'd completed the Explorer's Grand Slam (climbed the seven summits, skied to the North and South Pole), flown a car from London to Timbuktu, led the first para-jet expedition over Everest – the mad list goes on. I was also told that he was very good friends with a figure I'd grown up watching: Bear Grylls. I approached Neil with the help of a friend, Ed, one of my team mates from Svalbard. Ed nudged me forward. 'Neil, this is Lucy.'

Neil turned to me with a curious nod. 'Ah, you're just back from Svalbard, right?'

'Yeah,' I said, feeling a bit awkward under his gaze. 'I hear you do expeditions too.'

He gave a small laugh. 'Yeah, a fair few over my years.'

I smiled. 'I'd love to do more myself . . . properly, I mean.'

He reached into his pocket and handed me his card. 'Drop me an email. Let's have a chat.'

'Thank you,' I said, taking it, trying not to look too eager.

'Good to meet you, Lucy,' he said with a nod, before turning back to his conversation.

I sent the email and before I knew it, we met at the esteemed tea room of the RGS. A place where many expeditions have been conjured up. I can't remember the exact conversation but I remember asking a lot of questions. I must have made some sort of impression on him though, because a few months later, I received an email from him inviting me on his next expedition.

> Hi Lucy,
>
> Rough plan of action: My next expedition is reenacting the Heroes of Telemark across their exact route on the Hardangervidda.
>
> How's your telemark cross-country skiing?
>
> Neil

An expedition across the Hardangervidda Plateau, in Norway, re-enacting the Heroes of Telemark story – an arduous winter journey in 1943 made by a group of saboteurs to blow up a Nazi-controlled heavy water plant. This was, basically, a factory that was making heavy water, which is a special type of water used to help produce nuclear weapons. The Nazis were trying to build an atomic bomb and the saboteurs' mission was to stop that happening.

The other team members were also ex-Special Forces. I'd be the youngest by a long way and the only female, but I didn't give it a second thought – I jumped at the chance.

It was during our training week in Scotland that I met the rest of the team. It was early January and snow was on the ground, but that didn't hold us back from swimming in the lochs, running up mountains and yomping (the Royal Marine word for hiking with weight on the back) for miles on end. It was day one when we were going through safety drills that I overheard some of the team taking Neil aside to talk about me. I could hear

THE START OF A LIFETIME

them whispering just out of earshot, but their words carried in the cold air.

'Why's she here anyway?' one of them muttered. 'She'll just slow us down.'

Another snorted softly. 'Look at her, she's tiny. She'll get cold before we've even got our skis on . . .'

Clearly they were going off appearances alone. I was a nineteen-year-old blonde girl who was very thin and deemed 'fragile'. I remember feeling pretty hurt that they were pushing back on Neil's decision, but then I heard Neil's reply: 'Just trust me. She's got what it takes.' That was all I needed to hear. Someone believed in me. Not just anyone: ex-SAS, seven-summiteer, high-flying entrepreneur and explorer, and Bear's good friend, Neil Laughton. It didn't matter what anyone else thought; Neil had faith in me.

The expedition went better than I had ever imagined. I kept up with them every step of the way, sometimes even overtaking as we skied across the plateau for hours with a pulk dragging behind us. I set up camp in −20°C without complaint, melted snow for water before dawn while they were still getting out of their sleeping bags. I didn't try to be tougher than them; I just quietly got on with it. When they pushed the pace uphill, I pushed past them. I excelled and held my own and earned the respect of these men.

Now, we were flying home. We all bundled into a flight back to London, gear stowed below, cheeks still wind-burned from the icy plateau.

I was sat next to Neil, I remember that clearly. The others were scattered throughout the plane, already nodding off, enjoying the flight food or flicking through magazines. The hum of the engines filled the silence, which was fine. I was just sat there, quietly smiling inside with that post-expedition high, which is a combination of exhaustion, pride and excitement to get home. Neil turned to me mid-flight, calm as ever, and declared: 'You could be the female Bear Grylls.'

I blinked at him. I wasn't expecting that and he'd said it like it was nothing.

He looked ahead again, as if he hadn't just dropped a bombshell into my brain. I needed to let it sink in. This wasn't someone who threw compliments around lightly. Neil knew Bear personally, had been on expeditions with the man himself. He'd done more expeditions than I could count, led teams, flown cars, done all the mad things you only ever see on documentaries. And here he was, saying that I could be the female Bear Grylls?

It felt . . . mighty, that's the only word for it. Like he'd just opened a door I was too shy to approach.

That line stuck. Not because I had any intention of becoming famous by hanging off helicopters – but because of *who* it came from. And because it told me that he really saw something in me. Not just potential, but proof.

At least all the proof I needed. Others would later say the same thing. It was maybe an easy way to try to summarize what I did, but it was different coming from Neil.

Sometimes all it takes is one sentence from someone you respect to tip the scales. One sentence that hits right when you need it and steers the direction of your life.

On the Hardangervidda, I proved that I was competent and my experience in Svalbard put me in a great position to operate alongside military-type guys.

Later on, other expeditions would also end up involving team mates with some sort of military background too. I felt comfortable teaming up with them, loved their ethos and I know it was reciprocated. One in particular would have a tremendous impact on what came next.

4. Ian Craddock

I FIRST CAME ACROSS IAN CRADDOCK'S Jungle Bushmaster courses online. Ian's website was no-nonsense. Just the name alone, Bushmasters, was enough to stop me scrolling. Named after the largest venomous snake in the Americas, of course it was. Ian's company takes novices, as well as military and film and TV crews, out into the jungle, and teaches them how to survive.

The tone of the website was exactly what I'd been looking for. It was unapologetically simple and tough, intimidating even. I researched some more into Ian, in that way you do, and I clocked a link: Ian knew Neil Laughton. Both of them were in the Special Forces . . . That was enough for me.

I'd been doing expeditions for three years by this point. I'd been working as a waitress to save up and had been a few more times on expedition above the Arctic Circle and begun mountaineering, but had never tackled a jungle adventure, nor planned one that sounded suitable – where skills were taught but then put to the test. Getting to the jungle for real expeditions and learning when you're not in the military is not straightforward.

Ian and I exchanged a few emails. His were short and blunt,

but not at all unkind. Just straightforward. He suggested that if I really wanted to master new jungle skills, then after the survival course, he could set me up with some local indigenous Amerindian guys who were heading out on a hunting trip.

So that was that: I booked my flight to Guyana.

Guyana is a small country on the northern coast of South America, mostly covered in dense rainforest and often overlooked by travellers – but to me, it sounded like pure, raw adventure. Guyana is the only English-speaking country in South America. It is a result of its history as a British colony, which began in the early nineteenth century.

I made it to the capital, Georgetown and, in the hotel, that's where I met Ian.

'You must be Lucy,' he said, barely standing to shake my hand. His grip was firm. 'Bloody good you made it. Drink?'

And just like that, it was done.

No big intro, no sizing me up. No deep questions about what I'd done or why I was there; he had all he needed to know from our emails. Just instant inclusion, like we were picking up mid-conversation.

Although short in stature, he made up for it in sheer presence. Ian gave off a legend persona immediately. From the first few hours, I could see how people either worshipped or detested/clashed with him. He was full-on. Direct, opinionated and fucking hilarious when he wanted to be . . . but oh *so* brutal when he didn't. He didn't take any bullshit, he didn't suffer fools and he definitely didn't care for sugar-coating.

Being British, he'd had to adapt to the laid-back Guyanese culture, but after over twenty years here, he'd earned every bit of the massive respect he received.

But with me? There was something slightly . . . different. It was like he had a vested interest. Respect, maybe? Or curiosity about me? Maybe I was different to the other people who wanted to do his course.

He didn't treat me like a student and he didn't do that jokey testing thing that I saw him do with others. I don't know what I did to earn that. Maybe it was knowing Neil. Or maybe it was how I carried myself? Though I doubt it; I was twenty-two years old and a total novice in the jungle. Maybe it was just instinct on his part. I don't know.

But whatever it was, I was in.

'Right,' he said, without any preamble. 'Tomorrow we're heading out at first light. You'll meet Harold and Lionel then too. They're the real deal. Amerindian hunters. You'll learn more from them in a month than most people do in a lifetime.'

I nodded, trying to look unfazed as I sipped the rum.

He looked at me sideways, a smirk playing on his lips. 'But listen, the jungle . . . it doesn't give a shit who you are. If you don't listen to it, it'll chew you up and spit you out.'

He turned back to the bar, already raising his hand to order another drink. 'You want to stand out?' he added, his voice casual but with that razor edge. 'Just fucking do it.'

That was Ian. No padding. Just action.

I remember stepping into the jungle for the first time. It was like being swallowed whole. The air was thick and heavy with moisture, filled with the scent of damp earth and rotting leaves. It's like something sweet but rancid all at once. There was the constant whine of insects and the sudden screeches of hidden birds or monkeys. Not being able to see far in front was claustrophobic: everything was so dense and tangled. It felt like stepping on to another planet. There was no feeling of peace or romantic connection. It was raw and I felt completely out of my comfort zone. I wasn't thinking about exploring it further or coming back. I was just thinking: *how the hell do I survive in this place?*

The survival course proved so valuable. I learned how to make fire in the waterlogged jungle, learned the nuances of jungle fishing, and foraged for food from the likes of palm or the more exotic: Kukrit grubs. These grubs are protein-rich, and live inside the hard shell of a fallen Kukrit nut. You crack open the nut and there they are, wriggling inside. When eaten raw, they've got this creamy, nutty taste from the Kukrit itself. It's not as tasty as it sounds. Put them over the fire and they crisp up on the outside, a bit like bacon or cashew. I like to think of it as the jungle's mini protein bar.

When the two-week course came to an end, I readied myself for the adventure I'd been waiting for. Lionel had always been Ian's number one and he had a great way of communicating the delights of the jungle. Harold was more on the quiet side, but a master with the bow and arrow.

Our hunting trip was planned to last for one month. We'd leave Surama village in a boat and make our way deeper and deeper into the jungle. Every night we'd fish and then smoke our catches so they would keep. The idea was to essentially bring as much food back to their wives as possible, to fill the pantry.

The day before leaving for the interior, I was stopped by a young guy, a westerner who'd just come out of the jungle himself. He was keen to talk with me about the jungle's darker side even though he could see how excited I was to finally be in the rainforest.

'Have you heard about the big cats?' he asked.

Big cats? I thought. I hadn't considered them a problem, surely they would just get out of the way. *If you see them . . . take a picture!* I had been more focused on the creepy crawlies: snakes, the spiders, that sort of thing.

'Oh no,' he said. 'The cats have been going senile. They've been taking livestock as big as cattle, they've been snatching children from their villages!'

This was news to me. I knew there were jaguars and pumas, but I had figured that as long as I wasn't crouched down for the loo or fetching water from a stream, I wouldn't be prey. It felt like this guy was purposefully raining on my parade. I'd been so excited to come to the jungle and here he was trying to spook me out. Was he mansplaining, deliberately trying to make me nervous? Was he genuinely trying to help? I couldn't tell.

He went on to tell me the characteristics of jaguars. They are the third largest cat, after tigers and lions, and are fearsome, stealthy predators. Looking like a bigger, stronger leopard, the jaguar's form is a masterclass in predatory design. It moves gracefully and invisibly with its beautiful golden-and-black rosette coat, distinguishable from a leopard's by the spot in the middle of each. It's also robust and lethal. They have powerful jaws, equipped with sabre-like teeth and, unlike most cats, they don't go for the throat; they creep up from behind, go for the back of the head and easily puncture the skull, killing their prey instantly.

You might have seen the nature programmes that show jaguars dragging huge black caiman out of the water by the head. Oh yes, like tigers, they are masters at swimming, too.

This all sounded like excellent knowledge to take in, and I tried to stop and thank this guy and be on my way, but he was persistent and kept going.

'They have this very specific noise they make. It's not really like a roar, a bit more like a leopard.' He goes to play the recording he has on his phone. It causes the hair on the back of my neck to stand up. The growl-like purr vibrates from the phone, similar to what I imagine a dinosaur would sound like. It's a deep and resonant snarl, made up of a series of hoarse, thirsty coughs and roars that resemble a saw cutting wood. The jaguars make these to communicate when they feel threatened or to mark their territory.

That was the end of our interaction. I thanked this stranger, and went to meet Lionel and Harold.

During the first night in the jungle on the hunting trip, I was exhausted. We'd spent a few hours hiking to the boat and the rest of the day making our way down the river.

As I lay in my hammock I felt so proud of myself. It had been a childhood dream to be in the jungle, especially on an adventure with guys who live and breathe it. *There's so much to learn from them*, I thought.

It was as I was drifting off to sleep that it happened. I awoke to an odd sound. I brushed it off as a frog but then I heard it again. And then again. *That isn't a frog.* I started to panic, but when I shouted to Lionel and Harold, I got nothing back. Nice gentlemen that they are, they had decided that for my first day it was best to respect my privacy, and so had placed their hammocks quite a distance from mine. I was on my own.

The noise continued. I couldn't help but think it sounded like the noise I'd been made to listen to by the stranger just hours before. *It can't be*, I thought.

The noise came closer, moved further away, then came closer again. It was circling me. I was now really starting to freak out and no longer had the ability to scream – I was too scared. I realized I didn't have anything to defend myself with; my bow and arrow and machete were outside of my hammock. But then I remembered I had a small Swiss army knife in my shirt chest pocket that my grandma Una had given me when I was just a child.

Very carefully I reached for it, conscious not to move the

hammock too much – if this creature was what I thought it was, then the movement of the swinging hammock would be like teasing a cat.

I took the penknife, opened it up and raised the knife above my head. Why? Well if it was what I feared, then all I could do was try to poke it in the mouth as it went for my skull.

I gripped the knife tightly as sweat dripped down my temple and I prayed to the universe: *Please don't let me die tonight.*

Time went on and on, and this snarling continued to move around my vicinity. My forearms hurt from holding the weapon so tightly.

After what felt like hours, there was a huge kerfuffle beneath my hammock. I felt something brush against my back and bum, but remained as still as I could. This went on for a few seconds, then whatever it was leapt into the bushes, and then – silence. No more noises and I didn't feel like I was being watched any more.

Before I knew it, the sun came up, illuminating the canopy floor. I sheepishly went over to Lionel and Harold to tell them what happened. Harold, who's a very silent man, came over to my hammock area, looked down at the ground, then looked up at me and simply nodded as he said, 'Jaguar.'

That was the first night – I was here for a whole month! To say I was frightened would be an understatement.

We later assessed the area and found the carcass of an armadillo. The jaguar hadn't been stalking me but the poor armadillo. It had sought shelter underneath me and the big cat had been playing with it, ghost-like up until the moment it struck.

That was a baptism of fire and it took a lot for me to keep my head up for the rest of that adventure, especially during the night.

*

On a number of occasions I'd be woken up by the guys, and would find myself running through the jungle, behind them, after a bird or small mammal, often wearing only Crocs on my feet and trying to keep up with my agile friends. I felt like a giraffe learning to walk as I clumsily battled through the undergrowth but I made it clear that I wasn't ready to be left at camp while they went hunting.

But I made it through and upon arrival into civilization again, I called my dad at the first opportunity I had comms.

'Lucy! So great to hear from you!' he said. 'How did it go?!'

'I don't think the jungle is for me. Everything out there seems to want to kill you . . . or at least, it felt that way.'

I think I said that to justify the fear I had experienced and how I felt I hadn't really excelled in the jungle environment.

After that harrowing ordeal, I naturally focused more on high altitude and cold expeditions, thinking that the jungle was too untamed, too dangerous for me. But a few years later, it was this exact wilderness that attracted me back.

5. Stair Club

I REMEMBER THE PRECISE MOMENT it all clicked. The moment I knew without a doubt, this – being an explorer – was what I wanted to do with my life. And that I'd do whatever it took to make it happen.

It was 2015, a few months after my first jungle trip. I'd been living in London for just six months, quietly convincing myself that the big expeditions were behind me. Time to grow up, get a proper job. I was working as a production assistant on a kids' animated show and trying to settle into city life. But then . . . I got dumped. With that, everything cracked open. It suddenly made sense.

Somewhere along the way in that relationship, I'd lost myself. I'd lost my identity. I'd lost the thing I loved most: adventure. It hit me. I needed to get out. Out of the job, out of the city, out of this life I didn't recognize. I felt trapped. I *needed* a rucksack on my back. To be self-sufficient. To trust myself again. To move. To walk. For miles. I didn't have much money, just enough for a plane ticket to Spain. I picked a route through the Picos de Europa, a remote and mountainous area.

I arrived with a rucksack stuffed with food and a tent and my trusty compass. I was totally expecting to meet other hikers along the way. I was so wrong. Turns out everyone goes to Spain to walk the famous Camino de Santiago, not remote trails in the mountains. I went days without seeing a soul. I hitchhiked when I had to, stumbled into villages where nobody spoke English and found myself in wild, breathtaking places, whistle in mouth, shouting 'Bear!' when I saw the warnings for European brown bears.

There was one particular morning that I won't forget, where I *felt* it. I was trudging uphill. It was early, cool and silent. I'd been hiking for a few hours already when a song came on my headphones: 'My Silver Lining' by First Aid Kit. I'd heard it before, but this time I *really* listened. I urge you to do the same. It's about the fear we all have of wasting time and of looking back with regret, but instead of dwelling, it's important to move forward and break free from anything holding us back. To take the harder path if that's the one that leads you to where you're meant to be.

It resonated. This was exactly how I felt. It hit something deep. What mattered most to me was freedom and adventure gives me that freedom. I wanted others to also feel that, to care for this planet. I didn't want to waste my time doing something I didn't love. I wanted to take risks. To try. To dare. Even if it sounded ridiculous. I didn't want to wait around any more. I wanted to *be* an explorer.

When I got home, I knew I had to say it out loud. I was in the kitchen with my parents. Nervous. It was right there on the tip of my tongue.

'Mum, Dad . . . I think I know what I want to do with my life.' Gosh it sounded so dramatic. Like a spotlight was on me.

They looked up. 'Yes, darling?'

I hesitated. It was going to sound like I'd lost my mind trekking 500 miles across Spain. But after one deep breath, I said it anyway.

'I want to be an explorer.'

I braced myself, waiting for them to laugh. But they didn't.

'OK,' they said, calm as anything. 'Tell us how you're going to do that. How you're going to make it your living.'

Wow. They weren't dismissive. They just wanted a plan. Wanted to know I'd thought it through. And I had. I told them I wasn't going to copy the people already on TV, but I *would* learn from them and model parts of my future career on them. I knew it would take time. I wasn't suddenly going to be an explorer. I knew it would be hard. But I was ready.

Saying it out loud was the first real step. That break-up, that trek, that song, it all led me to this. And I've been *keeping on* ever since.

Working in the TV and film industry was always where I saw myself career-wise while growing up. It seemed only natural since I'd been making movies. I always had it in the back of my mind to bring my two loves of film and adventure together, but I wanted to do it my way and didn't fancy myself working on the adventure shows where someone else got to have all the fun. In a way, I was always saving it up for the real thing.

During my years working in the TV industry, I gradually became more and more certain that it was adventure I wanted to do full time – being a professional explorer to be exact.

I worked for five years at ITN Productions and built strong working relationships with my colleagues. I'd originally met with Chris Shaw, head of the company at the time, back in 2015. He'd watched my early YouTube videos of me out in the Amazon, the same trip I met Ian, and wanted to develop a TV pitch to present to broadcasters. It was the first step of seeing my dream profession come to life. We made a taster tape with my existing material and filmed more too. Dan Grabiner led the development team then and plugged it to all the commissioners at the time. We received positive feedback but no one wanted to commit and risk new talent, as much as they repeatedly said they wanted a female in adventure on screen. And apparently, I smiled too much. I didn't have that stereotypical 'serious explorer' aura. This would become a theme in the following years. Looking back, I was nowhere near ready then and remember Dan saying to me, 'Keep doing what you're doing, it will happen.' I clung to those words. I longed to make money in the adventure field and change the way adventure storytelling was done.

I stayed on at ITN as a production coordinator, which allowed me to gain vast production experience, from live studio shows to true crime documentaries. I had a very supportive manager, John Keyes, who knew what my real goal was: to do exploration professionally. He gave me the freedom I needed, as long as the work got done. And I'm eternally grateful for that freedom. I got paid enough to save, which I'd then spend on expeditions and kit. The freelance nature of my job meant I could leave the country after a TV project for months at a time and just hope that there was a job to return to when I got back from whichever wild place in the world I had been.

I got a reputation for always coming to work with rucksacks or kit. I'd regularly leave work at 5 p.m. and get a train to the countryside, bivvy outside for the night and be back at the office for the next day. Or I'd disappear from my desk while I found a deserted room to practise my public speaking in, or would run out of the office at lunchtime to have meetings with someone from agents to sponsors. I continued to work with the ITN development team and Chris Shaw in pitching ideas, and even went on expedition to Greenland for a project they funded, but nothing significant really took.

I was good at my job and got it done, but had those tabs open on my desktop all the while, planning expeditions. I was offered promotions but didn't take them as it would take my focus away from what I was really aiming for.

Since those first days at ITN, my focus was to gain more experience in my exploration profession and just get on with it. With the lack of action from the broadcasters it meant I was going to have to do it myself and prove that this – me fronting adventure shows, real adventure shows that weren't glossy or fake – could work, and I knew in my heart that this was the expedition to prove it. I also knew that this Amazon expedition marked the moment in my life that was perhaps the biggest risk of all – leaving my somewhat secure freelance job at ITN and becoming a full-time explorer. During recent years I'd been paying more and more of my bills through talking gigs, brand partnerships and guiding in the Arctic for my friend Liv Engholm's (expert Norwegian polar guide) company. If I stayed with any more roots at ITN I wasn't sure I would be able to make the real leap I needed to. It was time to put all my eggs in this adventure basket, so with this expedition, that's exactly what I did. No plan B. I wasn't going back to freelance life: I was working for myself, for my company, and I had to make it work.

We human beings are a resilient bunch. Every one of us is; we wouldn't be here if we weren't. As we grow older, it's important to remind ourselves of just how far we can go. How can we do this? Well, on an expedition it's fairly straightforward. Every hour, something new is thrown our way, testing us and topping up our resilience. But in our modern, twenty-first-century lives, it's about actively putting ourselves in uncomfortable situations regularly. Resilience is like a muscle; you have to train it so it doesn't weaken. This might mean adding a little spice, basically small hardships to your day, like taking a cold shower in the morning (never nice!) or choosing the stairs over the lift. It's all about taking the path less travelled and thriving on it.

By being self-aware and choosing the more uncomfortable option, you get used to pushing past those barriers, which are so often just in our minds. I always try to add these little challenges to my daily life. For instance, while working at ITN, I really struggled with sitting in an office all day; I'd get lethargic, and my brain would trick me into thinking I was tired. This scared me, so I decided I needed to take immediate action to break this pattern before it became my identity. I was doing all the right things before and after work: cycling there, taking the stairs, hitting the gym – but it was that eight-hour period during the day that felt damaging.

The office was on the top floor of a skyscraper, so every day I set three alarms on my phone for 11:00, 12:30 and 15:30. When they went off, I'd stop whatever I was doing, get up from my desk, and run down to the basement and back up. It took about three minutes in total. I'd return to my desk refreshed, heart pounding, blood flowing and full of energy. It's somewhat counterintuitive: it takes energy to get energy. A few colleagues started wondering where I was going and why I returned looking so alert. They wanted to give it a try too. Before I knew it, I'd started 'Stair Club'. John Keyes was one of the earliest members. Our alarms would go off, I'd lead the charge, and we'd sneak out for three minutes. We returned refreshed every single time, and we'd feel a bit smug sitting back at our desks. And of course, the first rule about Stair Club was . . . you don't talk about Stair Club.

6. Tim

I LEARNED VERY QUICKLY HOW TO ORGANIZE expeditions on the cheap because that was the only way I could continue to do it. I'd arrange them myself, which meant I needed to have full understanding of every aspect of the adventure, something I thrived on. I went on various solo walking and winter adventures across Norway, Corsica and Spain, learning to navigate and rely on myself each day. I learned the kindness of strangers and that there was a certain magic to having these types of adventures alone, but soon, with the help of communities within the RGS and Scientific Exploration Society, I found other likeminded people I could go with.

In September 2015 – just a few months after I had declared to my mum and dad that I wanted to be a professional explorer – I met Tim at The Explorers Club in London. The club is mainly based in the States but was trying to branch out into the UK. Neil had invited me along as I'd reached out to him asking if he knew and could recommend anyone that might want to be the fourth team mate for an expedition in Patagonia.

'I'm heading to The Explorers Club tomorrow night,' he said. 'It's at Gaucho in Soho. Shackleton's granddaughter's going to be there, plus a bunch of RGS bigwigs. Come along.'

'It sounds a bit . . . prestigious,' I said, trying to hide my nerves.

'There'll be red wine and dinner. You can be my guest.'

That clinched it.

When the following night rolled around, I nearly bailed. I was lying on my bed, staring at the ceiling, knackered and doubting whether I'd find anyone useful there. But something in me got me out of that mindset. Something pulled me and said, '*Get up – go.*'

I walked into Gaucho and was led downstairs into a dim, glamorous basement buzzing with voices and wine glasses clinking. It was packed and there was energy. I loved that everyone in here had some connection to adventure. Neil was right: this was where I'd find my people. Neil spotted me straight away.

'Shepherd!' he boomed, arms wide, everyone in his vicinity taking notice. 'You've arrived. Right, you *have* to meet Shane.'

He turned to a woman beside him. 'Shane Winser, this is future television star Lucy Shepherd. Lucy, this is Shane. Shane runs expeditions for the Royal Geographical Society. You *need* to know each other.'

I blinked. *What?* OK, this was already worth getting out the house for.

Shane extended her hand. 'It's so lovely to meet you, Lucy Shepherd,' she said warmly.

'And, Shane,' Neil added, still in full showman mode, 'you need to make her a fellow.'

My jaw nearly hit the floor. A fellow of the RGS? Me? I was twenty-three and still felt like I was faking it half the time. Fellowships were for PHD old-timers, no?!

'Well,' Shane said, smiling, 'Neil's recommendation certainly carries weight. Why don't you come by my office at the RGS tomorrow? Neil, you come too. We'll all talk and see if you qualify.'

TIM

'Yes. Absolutely,' I said, probably too quickly.

Just like that, it felt like a new door had opened, which it had. I felt so welcomed into this world.

As the evening rolled on, I found myself in great company. Everyone had fascinating and inspiring stories. I was mid-conversation, enjoying the wine, when someone grabbed my arm.

'Lucy, I need to introduce you to someone.'

It was Shane. No explanation and no apologies. She didn't even really know me but was eager for me to meet this person, so whisked me away from the group, practically throwing me in front of two tall men. One of them, suddenly face to face with me, had piercing eyes that I clocked immediately.

'Lucy, this is Tim Taylor,' Shane announced. I was listening. 'He's just got back from an RGS-backed expedition in Pakistan. We didn't even know they made it out alive, but they did! He's a brilliant photographer, a Royal Marine reservist, mountaineer and even used to be a semi-pro mountain biker.'

Tim's eyes struck me, I don't know how else to say it. Everything slowed for a second and something about him just felt . . . familiar. I felt completely at ease in his company. He radiated warmth but at the same time confidence and capability. Shane hadn't even finished speaking when I found myself saying, without a second thought: 'Would you like to come to Patagonia with me?'

Ridiculous, I know . . . but that was the point of the night and why I was there, wasn't it? Shane's résumé of him ticked every box I needed. Plus, granted just a bonus, he was also incredibly good-looking.

Tim smiled. 'Well . . . yeah.'

He didn't flinch, nor did he run for the door. He just said yes.

I of course assumed he was being polite. But we ended up

continuing the conversation and sat opposite one another all night, talking over steak, red wine flowing, Shackleton's granddaughter next to us and Tim's friend Tom at the table too. It felt easy and electric all at once.

At the end of the night, neither Tim nor Tom had a place to stay in London, so they came back to mine.

That night kickstarted a whirlwind of planning and prepping from that moment on. Tim and I were pretty much inseparable and yes, we did go to Patagonia!

Turned out, just a few days earlier on his flight back from Pakistan, Tim and his team mate had talked about what they wanted most when they got home. Tim had apparently said: 'I want good red wine and steak, to go to Patagonia . . . and to meet a pretty blonde girl.' Somehow, all three arrived at once. We both found what we were looking for.

After Patagonia, Tim and I were a team. We began doing more and more expeditions together. I'd organize them and then we'd train for them alongside each other. Long weighted yomps, hill sprints, practising crevasse rescues in the Alps, Patagonia, Argentina, Iceland and then it was time for Denali.

Denali was done independently with just me, Tim, our good friend Matt Schulman and Will Shepherd (not related). Denali is the highest peak in North America and one of the seven summits. It's often referred to as the coldest mountain in the world and is no stranger to fierce storms. It didn't disappoint. Halfway up the mountain, we experienced one of those storms ourselves. At 14,000 feet, the mountain unleashed its fury. A violent storm swept in and didn't let up. The snow fell, our tents shaking under the weight of 90 m.p.h. winds and temperatures plummeting to −40C. For a whole fourteen relentless days we were trapped in our tents, leaving only to dig ourselves out or to brave the bitter cold for a toilet trip . . . although most of those were done inside. We got used to the awkward shuffle of a shared space and pee bottles. Tim and I huddled in one tent, Matt and Will in the other. On some nights, we zipped up our sleeping bags not knowing if we'd wake up in the morning. It is a dangerous cold there.

It was brutal. But we'd planned well. The only reason we were able to continue up the mountain once the storm had finally passed, after two weeks, was because we'd packed extra food and fuel.

Matt and I did the planning for that expedition independently, which always cuts out high costs that companies charge (of course with companies you also get a guide and access to kit, etc.). Matt lives in America so it was a constant stream of messages at all hours of the day.

Tim and I met Matt in the strangest of ways. It was 2016 and we were in Argentina after attempting the Patagonian Expedition Race in Chile. We'd tried to get permits to climb Aconcagua but were refused because it was too late in the season, so instead, we hitched a ride to a much lesser-known range, the Cordón del Plata. We were dropped off and hoped to get a ride back a month later. This mountain was remote: no basecamp or facilities, just miles and miles of rugged mountain terrain – just the way we like it.

We thought we were the only ones on the mountain, but after ten days of ferrying kit up and down the peak, we met Matt and Bahram. We bonded instantly with these charismatic, kind and physically fit early-twenties Americans. Bahram referred to Matt as being a beast in everything he put his mind to and he was entirely right. We kept in touch with Matt and Bahram, and met them on a number of occasions when they visited London.

INTO THE WILD

Matt had just finished his studies and was working for Facebook in San Francisco when he put the idea of climbing Denali to us. We were in instantly. Any time with Matt is worth spending and an adventure was even better. After Denali, we ski mountaineered across the High Sierras in California, which to this day is probably my favourite adventure. After that, Matt set up a business, and long story short, it became a unicorn and Matt, who wasn't even thirty yet, was founder and CEO of a very successful company. He couldn't be more deserving and, also, I'm not at all surprised. He is, like Bahram said, a beast and one of my favourite people in the world. There are definitely more adventures to be had with him.

Further expeditions followed to Tajikistan and Greenland, but I began to feel that something was missing.

I had recently begun to get paid for my public speaking – just a small amount, but it felt important for the direction I was headed. I soon realized that I was being a little bit of a hypocrite. I'd share stories with the aim to encourage the audiences to get outside their comfort zone and face their fears, but there was something that *I* wasn't facing: the jungle. My first adventure in Guyana had left me rattled and overwhelmed. I needed to improve my competence and confront my fears. The jungle held so many possible adventures – and something was now drawing me to it.

7. Ian's Gift – 2020

I REACHED OUT TO IAN.
   It wasn't the first time we'd been in contact since my first jungle adventure. We'd met a couple of times, his usual brand of encouragement. Ian didn't sugarcoat things or dress advice up in fancy words. He just said it how it was. Always blunt, always honest, but somehow still warm. I liked that about him. It was a breath of fresh air and proved you could think differently.

'You want to make a mark on the world?' he'd said once, as he sat with a pint in a pub. 'Then just do it.' He shrugged.

That was Ian in a nutshell. Where most people would be hesitant, or spiral into pros and cons, Ian cut all that out.

'But the big expeditions cost so much,' I'd said. I knew the expeditions I was wanting to do next were far out of reach.

'Put it on a credit card,' he replied, deadpan. It was like he was saying it was just free money and, hey, the bank could wait.

Ian had an answer for everything, always delivered with confidence and conviction. He wasn't someone who said things for no reason either. Ian *knew* people. He had been around. He'd helped make expeditions happen for Bruce Parry, for Steve Backshall. He was part of the world I was slowly edging my way into and that meant something. Just like Neil, Ian's belief in me carried weight and he was providing me with a different way of thinking. I was inspired at every sentence.

Then came the call . . . or maybe it was an email. Whichever way it came, I remember how it felt.

It was late 2019 and Ian told me he had something for me, an idea to get me back to the jungle. He told me about trying to go across the largely unexplored, rugged Kanuku Mountains in southern Guyana, a journey from south to north. He'd tried to do it himself once but hadn't managed to complete it. Successfully crossing such a remote and difficult path would put any explorer's name on the map. It was the kind of journey that could cement you as one of the elite. The terrain was unforgiving, food hard to come by. But here he was, offering it to me.

It felt like a gift and I guess that's what it was: a passing of the baton. Adventurers and explorers don't just give away ideas like this. Ian could've held on to it, tried again, or given it to someone with more credentials or a famous name, but he didn't. He offered it to me without hesitation, like a natural next step. He didn't present it as a test or a challenge, just an opportunity. 'Give it a go,' he said. 'And don't be afraid to fail.'

It was like he was saying: *I trust you with this, so go see what you can do with it.* He'd help me plan it and be there, in a small way, cheering me on.

Ian and I both naturally kept the expedition low profile. We weren't going to make it a big, flashy thing. There was no press release, no huge film crew. It would make it easier to just go and do it and avoid unwanted attention, plus, I wanted a real stripped-back adventure – this was about me returning to the jungle. Just a simple A to B idea that I was able to get sponsored for by the Scientific Exploration Society, and a journey through

Climbing high and never stopping.

Little Lucy, early explorations. Every child is an explorer – even turning over a rock to see what's underneath is exploring. Many of us lose that curiosity as we grow up.

Teacher's Comment
Lucy has taken an interest in explorers this term.

Name Lucy Shepherd   Autumn Term, 1997
Subject Science

Lucy thinks long and hard before she reacts. She observes things around her and makes comparisons. Lucy has a strong awareness of the world around her, interest and concern for all things in it. She is beginning to impart her knowledge and question.

School reports.

Playing in Scotland. There was always something so enticing about a bow and arrows!

Mum, Dad and me outside the home I did most of my growing up in.

Climbing ropes has always been my thing – even in my PJs.

My grandmother, Una, dancing in her home in Nigeria.

Weekends playing with my dog, Lucky.

Teenage me with camera in hand and best friend Harry, after we'd finished filming our version of Bear Grylls' *Man vs Wild!*

On my first ever expedition, crossing a glacier in Svalbard, 2011.

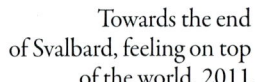

Towards the end of Svalbard, feeling on top of the world, 2011.

Ian Craddock in his element, Guyana, 2014.

Harold and me during my baptism of jungle survival training, 2014.

That beautiful smoky light in Guyana, 2014.

Me starting to get into jungle life, 2014.

In the Picos de Europa mountains, during my solo 500-mile hike across Spain, after promising myself that I was going to give everything I had to make adventure a career, 2015.

Another solo trek across Corsica's GR20, in 2015. I kept things cheap and this was my sleeping arrangement!

Me, Matt Schulman, Will Shepherd (not related!) and Tim Taylor: our independent team climbing Denali, 2017. The expedition where we got caught in a storm and were stuck in our tents for two whole weeks in -40°C and 90mph winds!

Joe (map man), Eggy, Guy, Aaron, Bento and me once we finished our south to north Kanuku mountain crossing, 2020.

Me, Tim and Sami.

dense jungle and largely unknown terrain. The biggest thing, though, was that I had Ian's backing.

I don't think I realized at the time just how important Ian's confidence in me was. How rare it is for someone to see your potential and then actually hand you the tools, or in this case, the map, and say go for it. He did. And it would shape everything that came next.

8. Are You Lucy Shepherd?

I HADN'T BEEN ABLE TO MEET IAN once I arrived in Guyana for this expedition, but I hoped to catch him on the other side.

Before setting off to the on-foot start point – a village called Sand Creek, further south – I was finishing my preparations in Lethem, a small border town near Bonfim, Brazil. It was the last real hub of civilization and I was feeling slightly out of my depth. Ian had given me minimal instructions, in his classic Ian way. All I had to do, apparently, was 'get to Sand Creek'. I liked that though: the responsibility was on me. He was in no way doing any babysitting – just simple guidance at the start, leaving me to figure out the rest.

That evening in Lethem, as I was packing, there was a knock at my guesthouse door. I wasn't expecting anyone. Unlocking and opening it, I was greeted by two very angry-looking Amerindian men, their arms crossed, brows furrowed.

'Are you Lucy Shepherd?' one asked in their pidgin-English Caribbean tone.

'Yes,' I replied, puzzled.

'We've heard you've come to cross the Kanuku Mountains.'

'That's right.'

The men's eyes looked me up and down, arms still crossed. 'Well, what gives you the right to cross mountains that we've lived in the shadow of our entire lives?'

They had a point. What did give me the right? The mountains had held a mystical allure for me; I'd been drawn to them ever since Ian first told me about his failed attempt. They'd taken hold of my imagination. But now I fully realized in that moment that I'd never stopped to think how that might feel to someone from here. These men clearly weren't just annoyed; they were passionate and possibly even hurt. Perhaps the mountains meant something deeper to them, sacred or personal? Or maybe they just wanted the chance to explore them for themselves. Maybe they, too, had that pull to adventure.

'We've always wanted to be the ones to make this journey,' one of them said, his brow still furrowed. 'But now *you* are here to do it before us.'

I was taken aback. I felt as though I was standing on stage in a theatre surrounded by darkness with just a spotlight on me. How could I have been so self-absorbed? I was an outsider and I'd made the assumption that I could come here, attempt this journey and not ruffle feathers. It hadn't occurred to me that someone else might be waiting for their shot as well.

I felt uncomfortable. It wasn't malicious but it was naive, and so in that moment, I felt it. A punch in my stomach: had I stepped into someone else's dream?

I didn't know what to say but I had to do something.

To diffuse the tension I quickly asked, 'Coke?' Their confusion was evident. I went on, 'Coca-Cola? Let me buy you one and we can talk.'

As we walked to the common area, I learned their names: Guy and Eggy. They were brothers and they had travelled across the savannah on a borrowed motorbike just to come and confront me. I left them on the sofas as I went to buy the ice-cold Coca-Colas as a peace offering from the bar. As a lady went to get the drinks, doubts swirled in my mind. Could I trust Guy and Eggy? Were they here to stop the expedition? Despite Ian's and my attempts to keep a low profile, word had clearly spread that I was here.

Returning with the drinks, I began to tell them about my plans, which I was going to be filming, as always. I wanted to really put my filmmaking skills to the test on this expedition.

I hoped that showcasing the expedition's genuine intent might disarm them a little and show that my reason to be here was genuinely innocent.

'I'd actually love to film our chat now,' I said, gently testing the waters. 'Would you mind?'

They looked a bit surprised but thankfully also curious. There was a long pause. Guy tilted his head. 'Why you want to film us?'

'Because it's part of the story,' I said. 'You've lived in the shadow of these mountains your whole lives. Your voices matter. I want to show why this journey matters, not just to me, but to the people who actually live here.'

Eggy smirked, shrugged. 'So we'll be in your movie?'

'If you're happy with that, yeah.'

He laughed and leaned back in his chair, visibly loosening. 'All right, then. You better get my good side.'

That seemed to shift something and their initial frostiness started to thaw. A little pride crept into their posture and, with it, the tone of the whole conversation started to soften.

They leaned over the map, fingers tracing rivers and ridge lines as if they knew them like old friends. I watched their expressions light up.

'You know, this bit here,' Guy said, tapping a thin, blue line, 'once you get past that bend, there's nothing. No trails. No people. Just forest and mountains and more forest.'

'You get sick out there,' Eggy added, 'no one's coming for you. No helicopter. No boat. You're on your own.'

'Oh I know,' I said, a little more defensive than I meant to sound. 'I know the risks. I've been working with Ian Craddock on this one.'

Guy gave a slow nod. 'Oh, big man Ian. I know Ian. We all know Ian. He's a good man, but still . . .' Guy didn't look convinced. 'People think they know. But trust me, even locals avoid it.'

Eggy gave me a sideways look. 'Animals aren't the only thing to worry about. There's jungle spirits in there.'

I gestured to the map again. 'You guys have thought about this a lot. I'd love to hear any tips you've got?'

They sat up a little taller.

'All right then,' Guy said. 'You don't move past 3 p.m., it's too dangerous. And the animals, they behave differently in these mountains – be on guard.'

'Keep checking below your hammock with your torch at night,' Eggy added. 'Snakes like to curl underneath at nighttime.'

'OK, OK!' I said. 'This is good stuff . . . Keep going!'

And they did: not just warnings, but stories. Hints of their own adventures, of people who tried and turned back, or didn't make it at all. I kept nodding, asking questions, listening.

That was the first time I properly saw it . . . it was clear that they *wanted in*. Maybe, just maybe, it could be our journey, not just mine.

'You know you're going remote,' Guy said. 'Like . . . *really* remote. If something go wrong out there, no one is coming to finding you.'

'You shouldn't be going alone, it's too dangerous,' Eggy said.

'Oh, I'm not going alone,' I said, 'I'm meeting someone . . .

what was his name ... Aaron. Aaron from Sand Creek Village.' They exchanged puzzled looks.

'Aaron?' Guy said. 'You mean Chiny?'

'Chiny?' I repeated, confused. I didn't know a Chiny. Was that a nickname? I'd never heard it before.

'Yeah! Chiny man!' Eggy laughed, slapping his thighs as he leaned back, amused.

The nickname initially struck me as potentially offensive. Was Aaron of Chinese descent? All Ian had told me was that Aaron was a good bushman.

In Guyana, as in many indigenous communities globally, traditional skills and languages are fading, replaced by the modern allure of smartphones and social media. It's a significant cultural shift, one that's slowly eroding the rich heritage of Amerindian life.

Bushmen are hard to come by now with the traditional lifestyles slipping away. This isn't just about losing the ability to hunt or gather. It's about a whole way of life.

When the British took control, they replaced Dutch with English as the official language; this was clearly to cement their influence over the region, and was part of a broader strategy to dominate and reshape local cultures ... so as to align with British values and governance. Charming.

As part of this controlling colonial agenda, the British introduced churches to Guyana. These churches were more often than not strategically placed at the edges of forests, pulling Amerindian communities away from their traditional homes, which were deep within the jungle. As well as learning English, the promise of education and other benefits – like healthcare – was a powerful lure. Amerindians were not only physically relocated but they also found their cultural practices and languages shifting because of the church and the colonial government, which planted English as the primary language and introduced a lasting change in the cultural landscape of Guyana. Guyana gained independence in 1966.

The elders might still chat in their native tongue and some may not speak English at all, but the younger generations are taught English in schools and only hold on to their tribal language if they have a relative to converse with at home.

And it's not just the languages that are endangered. Skills like making and using a bow and arrow are disappearing too. These days, young people are more likely to be found slumped over, scrolling through their phone than learning traditional skills from their elders.

I wasn't sure if Guy and Eggy were true bushmen, but they certainly could talk. And it was obvious they'd thought deeply about this adventure. It made me wonder, if they had dreamed of this journey so much, why hadn't they undertaken it themselves? They lived on the north side, so what had stopped them from simply leaving Nappi and walking straight for the mountains and heading south? Then it hit me. The logistics, the navigation challenges, and, importantly, the cost of returning to their village if they succeeded, were daunting barriers and out of reach. Plus, it was a very dangerous thing to do.

I felt I could relate to them on some level and after a few hours of talking, I sensed I could trust them too. They seemed laid-back and had shown a good sense of humour once they had warmed up to me.

'OK, guys,' I said, 'I'd love for you to join me on this expedition, but on one condition . . .' Their eager nods told me everything I needed to know. They were in. I continued '. . . You need to go back to your families, your wives, pack your bags, and tell them that the adventure you've dreamed of your entire lives is happening, and we leave tomorrow.'

'Of course,' Guy interjected. His quick response told me that this is what he'd hoped for in coming here. 'But we have one condition for you too, Lucy.'

'Yes, anything.'

'Our mates come too.'

9. Two Become Six

THE ONCE TWO-PERSON TEAM had turned into six. We now had Guy, Eggy and their mates, Joe and Bento. We were to meet Aaron in Sand Creek. (Although they call him Chiny, I'll stick with Aaron.)

Joe was dubbed 'the map man' by Guy and Eggy, and he certainly looked the part – he had a compass strung around his neck when we first met. I had high hopes for his navigational skills.

Bento was a tall man who qualified as an elder, spoke very little English and was the only one who showed up armed with a bow and arrow. Now *he* was a bushman.

We piled the bags into the back of the 4x4 I had already prearranged to take me to Sand Creek. It was only meant to fit me and the driver in it originally, but now with my extra team mates, it meant that Bento and Joe would ride on the roof.

The journey took a whole day. We drove across the savannah, around the western Kanuku Mountains, handrailing the jungle, all on uneven, sandy dirt-track roads. Traffic was the least of our concerns . . . although the occasional cattle blockade or a giant anteater crossing did slow us down.

We finally arrived in Sand Creek. Within minutes, word

had spread and we were summoned by the village chief, known locally as the Toshao, into a small, low-built structure with a tin roof and bright-blue walls inside, the paint slightly peeling in places. It felt like the village's meeting place, plastic chairs lined up at the side, simple but official, and a visitor book open on the table.

Every Amerindian village has a Toshao. The Toshao is elected to coordinate with the village council, and oversees the community's affairs. If an outsider/non-Amerindian, like me, is to go through village-owned land, one must get permission from the community and this is signed off by the Toshao..

Amerindian land ownership is structured around communal rights. Although so much of the jungle in this area is unexplored, it is still 'owned' by different Amerindian communities. Essentially, the land is collectively managed by an entire tribe or village, rather than being held by individuals. This means that most of the time, the community, with the leadership from the Toshao, decides how their land is used and managed. The government recognizes this and has procedures for Amerindian groups to apply for legal title deeds to their lands. This in theory protects their territory from outside pressures like mining or logging, but it can be overruled by government and businesses, so it isn't as secure as it sounds.

I had been assured by Ian that he had contacted the Toshao and we had the necessary permissions, but that didn't stop this Toshao wanting more. He was an elderly, small and angry-looking man. He had a strip of facial hair on his upper lip, and was wearing a short-sleeved checked shirt, shorts and was barefoot. He refused to make eye contact with me, probably because I was a girl. Instead, he grunted and directed his questions to Guy: 'Who bring y'all here? Who she?'

Guy stood relaxed, hands by his sides. 'She bring us. This

Lucy. She leading expedition across Kanuku. We just passing through, my friend, headin' north.'

The Toshao narrowed his eyes. 'She not got permission? Me ain't see no paper.' This man still wouldn't look at me and so I stayed silent.

Guy went on. 'You know Ian, right? Ian Craddock. She say he say he talk to y'all already.'

'Hmph.' The Toshao scratched under his chin. 'What she doing?' The Toshao finally glanced at me, albeit briefly. Then looked back to Guy.

Guy chuckled. 'Hey, man, she wanna go across Kanuku! We're all going!'

'The Kanukus? Across to the north? Y'all get hurt, who gonna help? Y'all come back draggin' body?'

'No,' Guy said. 'She's strong, Ian rates her.'

The Toshao squinted. 'Hmph. Plan don't stop jaguar . . .' He paused and then added flatly, 'If y'all wan' pass, me need see something. Permission don't come free.'

Oh, I got it now. This man wanted cash. I bet he knew about me coming all along – Ian wouldn't have failed to have contact him. He was seeing what he could get.

'I know how these things work. I was Toshao for Nappi,' Guy said to me.

'Toshao Fredricks,' Eggy commented.

This surprised me as Guy didn't portray a serious, political manner. During the 4x4 journey, I'd realized that he had somewhat of a crude and dark humour, and wasn't afraid to make outlandish comments . . . Saying that though, perhaps that made him the perfect candidate for a politician.

I passed on a few notes to the Toshao and he finally softened. 'Sign de village visitor book. All of you. Put name, date, where y'all goin'.' He distanced himself as he pointed to the book, face crumpled up. 'If you don't come back, we know at least roughly when you disappeared.'

I smile. 'Thank you, sir.'

With that settled, it was now time to locate Aaron.

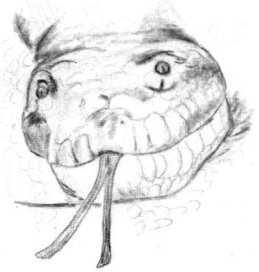

10. Water Dog

We ventured deeper into Sand Creek village, and in doing so we could feel we were getting closer to where the jungle met the savannah. The air got thicker, more humid, the birds got louder and insects began to fill the air. As we walked, we asked anyone we passed if they knew where Aaron was. Each time we asked, the response came with a burst of laughter: 'You're looking for Chiny man?' It was hard to tell if the laughter was out of affection . . . or were they were poking fun at him?

Eventually, someone pointed us towards the tuck shop, a small straw hut selling plantain chips and biscuits. As we approached, a man crouched by the shop stood up so quickly he nearly tripped over. He was dressed in oversized jungle boots and shorts, his red cap askew on his head, with a dark-green T-shirt bearing the words JUNGLE SHARP SHOOTER and a silhouette of an archer; below it read SNAKE EYES. A machete dangled from a rope tied loosely around his waist, and behind him rested his bow and arrows and a large camouflaged rucksack. I knew immediately that most of his kit had been supplied by Ian, including his T-shirt. This must be Aaron.

With a big but somewhat shy smile, Aaron called out, 'Lucy? Lucy?' and came over to shake my hand.

He was definitely off balance. His eyes were glazed over and his breath smelled a little of alcohol. I quickly explained how our team was more than just the two of us now.

'Hey, man. Heyyy, man,' he said as he went to greet the others.

'You had a big night, boy?' Eggy said. 'You OK, boy? You be wobbling all over the place, man.'

'No, man; no, man. Yeah, man; yeah, man,' Aaron answered. He was repeating every sentence. He turned to me. 'We going to have a big adventure through these Kanuku Mountains! These big Kanuku Mountains from Sand Creek all the way to Nappi!' He gestured dramatically.

This guy? This was the guy Ian had paired me with? I was suddenly very grateful that I had the likes of Guy and Eggy with me.

There wasn't time to dwell, it was time to move. Time for all of us to begin what we'd come here for. We swung our bags over our backs and headed north.

Before we could begin in the jungle, we had to move through long, dry grass, on the outskirts of the village. This open area was intensely hot from the afternoon sun.

As we walked, Aaron would repeatedly ask, 'You OK, Lucy?' At first, I thought it was kind of sweet, but then it got a tad annoying. I was beginning to think that his boozy antics from the night before were effecting him and his memory seemed to be that of a fish . . . Actually, scrap that, that's a lazy comparison. I have never liked the assumption that fish have bad memories, or three-second memories; surely that is not true, otherwise they wouldn't survive. Aaron just had a terrible short-term memory at this point. 'You OK, Lucy?' he'd say. Then a few seconds later, 'You OK, Lucy?' Deciding to roll with it, I hoped it was just a mix of hangover nerves and social awkwardness.

I also now understood why the other men were calling him 'Chiny man'. It wasn't because he was Chinese. He wasn't. He was Amerindian, but his eyes looked slightly Chinese to them. It felt uncomfortable to hear, a casual racism that no one seemed to question out here. Yes, Aaron was an interesting character, but his name was Aaron, not Chiny.

Reaching the edge of the jungle by the Rupununi River, we set up camp in the last slice of open space before the trees swallowed the sky. It hosted a sand bank and a convenient collection of rocks to bathe from. The river flowed gently beside us, glinting magically under the late-afternoon sun.

We each moved instinctively, which was a good sign for us as a team. Bento pulled out his machete and began clearing the closest patch of land from vines and thorns, while Guy sorted the fire pit. I unbuckled my pack, letting it drop to the ground with a satisfying thud. It was already dusty, and saturated with the sweat of the day.

Everyone claimed their hammock spot, close together like a real team – safety in numbers. The smell of the earth was warm and insect noise filled the air.

While the rest of the team and I bathed in the river, I realized that I hadn't seen where Aaron was. Then, spotting him in the distance, I watched as he swam out far. 'Water dog is Chiny,' Eggy chuckled.

Then as Aaron swam closer, he began to swim underwater next to a large boulder. He came up for air and yelled, 'Anaconda! Anaconda right here!'

Anacondas often take over the imagination when people think of jungle snakes. They are shrouded in myths and exaggerated tales. Many picture monstrous twenty-foot-long beasts that can swallow a human whole, but not before crushing them in a deadly embrace. While it's true that anacondas can grow impressively large, the stories of them hunting humans are more fiction than fact. These myths have painted anacondas as fearsome predators lurking in the underbrush, waiting for an unsuspecting victim to wander by, but the reality is far less dramatic. Anacondas mostly feed on fish or birds, and, occasionally, larger mammals. Human encounters of a deadly nature are exceedingly rare but, I suppose, not non-existent. You wouldn't want to get bitten by their powerful jaws, but their bite is not venomous.

This anaconda was underneath the water, sheltered inside a small cave within the boulder. With one hand steadying himself on the rock, Aaron called out, 'I'll get it for you, Lucy.'

I'm sorry, what? He was going to get the anaconda for me? He took one deep breath and then disappeared under the murky water.

I was confused. I would have been concerned if a sober man were to get an anaconda from its cave, let alone one that appeared to still be under the influence.

He'd been under a few seconds and I nudged Joe to pay attention with me. When should we go into action mode?

Aaron resurfaced. 'I've got it but it just won't budge.'

Then we should probably just leave it be, I thought to myself, but before I got a chance to make my thoughts known, Aaron was back under. He was six-feet down, essentially wrestling with the huge snake.

Thankfully, he surfaced and admitted defeat. We all applauded him back to the side. Bento and Eggy were in stitches. As Aaron was swimming back to us he called, 'Throw me the arrow.' Bento, without hesitation, tossed Aaron the arrow, just a metre to his side. Aaron retrieved it and went under for two seconds – then he was up with a fish spearheaded on the tip of the arrow. 'Dinner, Lucy!' he said with glee. OK, I was impressed. He was coming into his own.

'Water dog that Wapishana man!' Eggy laughed.

In that moment, I began to see why Ian had recommended Aaron. I could put to bed any concerns that his hangover and nervous energy had caused.

Wapishana is the tribe that Aaron is from. Guyana is made up of a tapestry of lots of different tribes, nine to be exact. Each tribe has their own language, traditions and history. Guy, Eggy, Bento and Joe are all from the Macushi tribe, making Aaron the only Wapishana of our group.

Historically, there were many wars between the different tribes and one of the most feared tribal communities were the Caribs, who were said to be warrior-like and made violent migrations around Guyana.

Bento, of the Macushi tribe, primarily only spoke Macushi.

I liked Bento, despite our language limitations. He had a humble smile and I expected he'd be very skilful once we got into the interior. I was looking forward to seeing him shine and now that Aaron was revealing his talents, I thought the two of them would be a great duo.

That night was spent meticulously studying my large A2 maps of the Kanuku mountain area. Securing these maps hadn't been straightforward; to get them, I'd had to acquire digital copies from official sources. While they appeared detailed by showcasing contours, heights of peaks and rivers, they were not entirely reliable. These maps were created fifty years ago by a Canadian pilot who photographed the landscape from above and then used those images to draw the terrain. In densely forested areas, this method has its limitations. Minor creeks and tributaries, hidden ravines and cliffs often go unseen. There's also the issue that these maps can't convey the forest's density, making it impossible to accurately predict the time it will take to weave through and navigate from one point to another. Despite all this, they did provide something to work with. I knew where we were and where we wanted to get to. This was going to be a case of following bearings as carefully as I could and, besides, Joe the map man was there on hand . . .

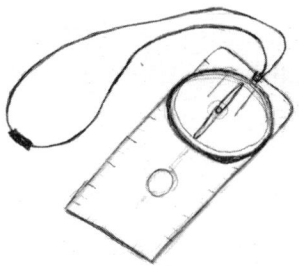

11. The Whistle

THE FIRST DAY OF THE SOUTH-TO-NORTH expedition with Guy, Eggy, Bento, Joe and Aaron was chaotic. Initially, I had decided to let Joe and Bento lead the way, as they were particularly keen to do so. I wanted to let them do their thing, somewhat assess them. After all, I was an outsider; for all I knew they were top-class orienteers! Pretty quickly, little alarms started ringing in my head. The slope of the land was wrong, we kept descending when I knew from the maps we should have been gradually climbing. I kept one eye on my compass, and also where the slight glimmer of sun rays were coming from through the canopy. Every few minutes, I'd check again, hoping I was wrong, but the unease in my gut grew heavier. After three hours of silently questioning our direction, going by my own instinct and my own navigational experience, I spoke up.

'We've gone completely in the wrong direction,' I said. That was my cue to take the navigational reins. The compass around Joe's neck was purely decorative. We'd strayed completely off course.

As the days unfolded, we tackled numerous tree-covered mountain climbs. Navigating was tricky but I was beginning to grasp what the Canadian pilot had meant when he'd sketched these maps. I really tried to get inside his head and it was a case of taking each day as it came.

Rations became a concern quickly, of course not helped by the rushed last-minute additions to our team, which stretched the food supply thin. Guy declared himself 'the chef', but I soon realized that I needed to monitor him. He had a heavy hand with the portions, often using too much too soon, which risked depleting our stocks prematurely. I'd squirm as he poured way too much farine into the pot every night and it wasn't long before I said something. Farine is a local food, granules that look a little like couscous, but made from cassava root. It packs a tonne of energy and is Amerindians' staple food. Unlike couscous, it can be eaten in many ways: dry, with cold or hot water, or even powdered milk. It can be eaten with salt or sugar, or fried. Really it's great to add to anything to bulk it up, making it the perfect field food, plus it doesn't go off and is lightweight. It powered us all on.

The terrain was steep and atmospherics were off, that's the only way I can describe it. It wasn't something I could see or hear, but I could *feel* it. Like the air had thickened slightly. It's like there was an unspoken tension all around us and between the trees. It was a gut-level unease, the type I've had when mountaineering before an avalanche sweeps past. It was like the jungle itself was watching, but not in a friendly way. I didn't feel like I could ever relax. Each night, we'd be sitting around the fire and Guy would spin tales of the jungle spirits that haunted the Kanuku Mountains; it was fascinating to hear about the Bush Dai Dai and Little Red Man. Both mythical creatures had a sense of being guardians of the forest and encouraged anyone who entered into the interior to do so with the upmost respect to the living beings within. I liked it, and felt these creatures were a metaphor and a guidebook to moving through the jungle safely.

However, the rest of my team were adamant these were not myths, that these were real creatures that lived in the forest and were to be feared.

Midway through our journey, where the jungle was at its thickest, my only connection to the outside world failed to work. I was carrying a backup safety device and tracker, called a Garmin inReach. It meant that I had the ability to send small Twitter-like word-count messages but it wasn't instantaneous. It would take multiple hours before it could send messages or coordinates and would take even longer to receive. This was because of the thick tree cover. Despite this, it still felt like a lifeline. But when this inReach stopped being able to send or receive messages for over twenty-four hours, we were even more isolated.

Of course, that's when things began to turn upside down.

The team had alerted me to the fact that every day we needed to start looking for a campsite early. This wasn't just a precaution – as Guy had told me, it was necessary because the wildlife, particularly snakes and big cats, become more active from 3 p.m. You might think this sounds like an old myth or some Amerindian folklore that I shouldn't be so quick to believe. However, this day would prove just how real and crucial this 'rule of the jungle' was.

It had been a long day, and we were descending a particularly steep mountain as the clock neared 3 p.m. The terrain was rugged, and the dense vegetation slowed us down. I kept glancing at my watch, anxious because we hadn't yet found a suitable spot to set up camp. The trees on the hillside, with their shallow roots, were useless for supporting a hammock, so we needed to find flat ground, and fast.

As we pushed forward, a massive fallen tree blocked our path. Its branches and vines created a near-impassable barrier. The atmosphere felt eerie, intensified by the tree blocking any remaining sunlight, but there was also a strange, lingering sense that we weren't alone.

Below our feet, a small stream ran, its gentle sound briefly soothing until Bento, who was leading, suddenly stopped us with a raised hand. He got out his arrow and aligned it in his bow. 'Jaguar,' Joe whispered from just behind Bento. 'He thinks there's one nearby.' My heart skipped a beat. The jaguar might not be visible to us, but it would certainly be aware of our presence.

Aaron nodded, 'Yes, big cat. I smell it.'

My skin prickled. I could hear nothing. No growl, no snap of a twig. I suppose that's the thing, isn't it? If a jaguar *is* there, you – well, I at least – would be the last to know. It would have seen us long before we saw it. Memories of my first jungle experience flooded back.

We all stood still. No one moved. The jungle felt suddenly smaller, like it was caving in on us.

Then Bento crouched down near the roots of the fallen tree and gestured. 'Ahh,' he said, pointing.

I went over to him and leaned down to see a pile of scat. The worrying observation from this? It was still warm and even pungent. It was pretty large and dense, and was packed with bone fragments and hair: peccary hair.

Aaron took a look. 'Jaguar,' he confirmed. 'Not puma. Too big.' He glanced at the log nearby. 'And there, you see? Scratches.' There was a smear of scat, a swipe mark. The jaguar had been marking its territory.

I swallowed. The signs were clear. We were in its space.

Gripping my machete tighter, I checked the time again – 3 p.m. on the dot. My senses heightened as we navigated through the cluttered forest debris, my eyes darting across every inch of the undergrowth in anticipation of a possible encounter. I was readying myself to be in fight-or-flight mode.

THE WHISTLE

As Bento worked to clear the path, a high-pitched whistling sound pierced the air. Initially, I didn't really pay attention to it, but then I noticed that the entire team had stopped in their tracks. The colour had drained from their faces, replaced by looks of pure fear. The whistle was a prolonged note, but then changed pitch, ending in a haunting tone.

'What is it?' I asked, my voice shaking.

'Bushmaster,' Guy replied.

My stomach churned. 'Oh, shit.' My face paled to match theirs.

Bushmaster snakes are huge, growing to twelve feet, and as their name suggests, they are masters of the bush. They ambush their prey easily because they are so incredibly camouflaged, making them very hard to see. They are the exact shade of brown as the jungle floor, and have a black, diamond pattern across their back. Their venomous bite is deadly.

'Move!' Aaron commanded, snapping us into action. There wasn't time for questions. I had no idea what the connection between the whistle and the bushmaster snake was, but it was time to follow orders and get out of the area as quickly as possible. We scrambled to find an alternative route. My heart pounded and my mouth was dry. Here we were, fleeing from the threat of a venomous snake, potentially heading straight towards a lurking jaguar.

The whistles continued, and then it sounded like there were more ahead. We kept descending and eventually reached a flat area. We could have continued to push on and escape the area, but now whistles were ahead of us too. We were surrounded. We had no choice but to make camp.

The drama didn't stop there. We were clearing the undergrowth for camp when I saw Bento stiffen, drop what he was holding and grip his wrist.

He didn't say anything, just a little shake of his head and a mutter of something low in his tribal Macushi language. His face didn't flinch, not even a crease of pain, but I knew.

'Bullet ant?' I asked.

He gave a short nod, eyes scanning the forest floor again. He was as calm as anything.

'Shit,' Guy declared behind me. I turned and he was already hopping backwards from where he'd been gathering wood. 'No! No, no, no. Argh, one got me too!'

I looked at his hand. The sting mark was there, angry and red, already swelling.

'It's going to burn,' Guy said. I think in a way he was a bit proud of the injury. 'Like fire. For twenty-four bloody hours. I hate these bastards! Oh well, I will keep going.'

He shook his hand dramatically, then held his wrist twice to restrict the blood flow. 'Worse than a wasp, worse than a scorpion.'

Bullet ants are no ordinary ants. They're big, about an inch long, and have a fearsome reputation. Their sting is ranked the most painful and notorious sting in the world, and their name suits them for this very reason – it feels like being shot. It's not just a quick pain; it's a deep, pulsating agony that feels like the area where you were stung is on fire and can cause sickness that lasts for over twenty-four hours. Some tribes in Central and South America have even used gloves filled with bullet ants to be worn as part of initiation tests.

Bento and Guy had both been stung by bullet ants before and so had a higher tolerance to their sting, which allowed them not to be completely bedbound.

It was just another incident to add to our day of dramas.

As we ate dinner with whistles all around us, it gave me a

THE WHISTLE

chance to question this whistle and learn more about the infamous bushmaster snake.

'Bushmasters travel in pairs, so if you spot one, there's another nearby,' Guy told me. Whether this had been scientifically proven, I wasn't sure, but I wasn't here to question.

Eggy intercepted, 'They track down humans and have been known to curl up underneath hammocks at night, and either strike when you least expect it or end up striking after an unsuspecting victim stands on it as they come out of their hammock.'

We couldn't risk getting near to these snakes.

Amerindians also believe that the bushmaster snakes in this area specifically, the Kanuku Mountains, are capable of emitting a two-tone whistling sound.

Their whistle has been long argued by scientists, who in recent years claim to have debunked the myth of the whistling bushmaster snake, saying that snakes cannot whistle and so put it down to a frog . . . but I couldn't help but listen to what my team mates had to say about this. They categorically swore that it was the bushmaster and claimed that whenever they heard this specific whistle, they always spotted a bushmaster soon after. Their ancestors had lived and breathed in the jungle for generations, and their knowledge went well beyond modern wisdom. Perhaps a practical way of looking at it would be, if Amerindian communities associate this particular whistling sound with the presence of bushmasters, then this belief could indeed serve as a protective function. Even if the whistle is not actually produced by the snake, using it as a warning signal helps increase vigilance and caution in areas where these dangerous snakes might be present.

That night, I made sure to light an extra fire to keep the animals at bay and we took it in turns to feed the fire over the course of the night.

That day marked a turning point for us as a team. Sometimes, it's through adversity that the strongest bonds are formed, and from then on, we really found our rhythm together.

After twelve intense days, we emerged at the northernmost point of the Kanuku Mountains, out of the jungle and on to a small plot of land growing cassava – Guy and Eggy called it a farm, but to me it looked too small. From there, I charmed the farmer to allow us to hitch a ride in his ox cart, which then carried us through the savannah and back to Lethem.

This journey not only showcased the magic of the region but also hinted at the vast mysteries yet to be explored in this untouched corner of the world. I felt an overwhelming connection to the area, and a deep feeling that we had barely begun to scratch the surface and uncover its secrets.

12. The Great Idea

I WAS A SIGHT FOR SORE EYES.

I had bug bites everywhere, including my bum, and I wasn't sure that they'd ever heal entirely. I was now thinking there was a high possibility that I'd have a permanently spotty bottom from here on out. Not exactly the look I was going for.

It was 11 p.m. and I was in the lobby of quite a cosmopolitan hotel in Georgetown, Guyana. Well, as cosmopolitan as you could get here. There was an element of shabby chic to the decor and even a bar selling suspicious frosty rum cocktails with pink umbrellas, one of which was in my hand.

The fan above me worked hard as it whipped up the hot city air. Guests came and went through the automatic doors next to me. Every time the doors opened, I was reminded where I was. The horns beeped and the boomboxes interrupted the rhythmic sound of crickets.

I was wearing my favourite black dress. I always take this dress travelling with me, no matter what I'm doing. You never know when you might need a little black dress. It's knee-length, has three-quarter lace sleeves and gives me a feeling of sophistication – but it didn't hide the open sores on my bare legs.

My brutalized skin was making sitting uncomfortable. I

shifted my weight back and forth, my skin protesting against the bar stool. My body was wrecked but my head was spinning, and that wasn't just from the rum. I'd only been out of the jungle for twenty-four hours. Weeks of hauling ourselves through the Kanuku Mountains, south to north, on foot with Bento, Guy, Eggy and Joe. We had made it.

I should have felt done. I should have wanted a proper hot bath, to be back home, some silence and safety. But this time, I didn't. Not really. There was already a flicker within, a restlessness deep inside me.

I was sitting opposite Ian Craddock. Ian had just finished a few days filming with Gordon Ramsay where he took Gordon into the jungle and threw him out of a helicopter (using ropes, of course). Gordon had eaten and cooked all kinds of weird and wonderful cuisines for his Nat Geo show.

I was so happy to see Ian . . .

As I sat here late at night, I was almost burned out. I'd just completed my biggest expedition to date.

Even here, at the end of my greatest triumph, I couldn't help but think, *What's next?* Perhaps the frosted rum had gone to my head, but I felt the same enthusiasm now as when my journey had just begun.

My thought must have been rather loud, because there was a brief pause as Ian confidently sat back on the sofa, put one leg on top of the other and shrugged his arms as if the answer was a no-brainer.

'Well you're just going to have to cross the whole thing now, aren't you.'

I looked at him in disbelief with a nervous smile. I always smile when I'm nervous.

He was suggesting that I cross the entire range of the Kanuku Mountains from east to west.

THE GREAT IDEA

'How far is that?' I asked.

'The whole range . . . almost the entire width of the country. You'd likely end up passing over 250 miles of jungle. You could start from the Essequibo River to avoid any argument of when they actually begin. You'd just have to start there and end at the most westerly point of the mountains at the savannah.'

'Is that even possible?' Asking that question made me excited. 'You've done this . . .'

What I'd just done was a fraction of what Ian was suggesting. Did I have it in me? Where would I get the funding? Would we be able to get permission to do it? There would need to be re-supplies, as there are no villages in the mountains. It sounded like a logistical nightmare, let alone a physical and mental one.

It was surreal having just finished the jungle expedition of a lifetime, and immediately finding myself contemplating something on this monumental scale. Some might call it an obsession.

That notion set off a chain of a million and one things in my head. Lightbulbs were firing on and off, as the butterflies in my stomach took flight.

I managed to regain clarity for a moment and looked up at Ian.

'Sounds like a great idea,' I said.

13. Summer Shock

FIVE MONTHS HAD PASSED. The sunlight streamed in through the blinds on that warm summer's morning in Suffolk. The birdsong had woken me, a welcome change to the city racket outside my London apartment.

I stared up at the beamed ceiling of my childhood bedroom. The room hadn't changed in over a decade. It still had one pale purple wall; you know, the kind of purple paint that was 'in' back when I was a teenager. Not that I had ever been particularly 'in' back then.

This room had been the place where so many of my adventures were born and it was easy to see why – the bookshelves were filled top to tail with adventure books that had mostly been gifted to me at different stages of my childhood. There was *Amazon* by Bruce Parry, *Arctic Dreams* by Barry Lopez, *Into Thin Air* by Jon Krakauer, *The Swiss Family Robinson* by Johann David Wyss, *Swallows and Amazons* by Arthur Ransome, and, above me, there was even a coloured drawing of Tarzan, who, embarrassingly, had played a key role in the fondness I now have for jungle environments.

Opposite my bed and taking centre stage was a large, brightly coloured world map covered in pins. There was one colour pin for all the places I had been to and another colour for all the places I still wanted to go to. As a child, I had admired the different countries and mountain ranges, and had imagined what it might be like to explore endlessly. That idea did, and still does, fill me with such hope and joy for the future. What an incredible floating ball of rock we live on. A whole world filled with so many experiences to be had. A map to me was where the start of any adventure truly lay.

Tim lay next to me and our dog, Sami, a miniature caramel-coloured Jack Russell, spooned my knees. Although the pandemic loomed over us and the daily news brought doom and gloom, I felt lucky to have my loved ones around me and to have access to the outdoors. I was even fortunate enough to have a goal to work towards as I planned my biggest expedition to date, one so ambitious that I referred to it as 'the Big One' – crossing the Kanukus from east to west. I had committed to it right there and then while with Ian in Georgetown, and was now in full preparation and training mode. Despite the odds, everything was good.

I rolled over and picked up my phone. I was always checking my phone first thing in the morning. It was a habit I knew I needed to get out of. Tim hated it, so I tried to conceal the glaring light with the duvet.

I squinted my eyes and looked at the screen.

My phone had one message: *Have you heard about Ian?*

What about Ian? I thought. I instinctively opened Google and typed into the search bar: Ian Craddock.

I read the first search result and there it was. Right there in black and white.

I was instantly awake and before I knew what to think, I was shaking Tim to wake him up.

'Ian is dead.' I'm surprised that I managed to even get those words out if I'm honest.

Tim's eyes began to stir.

'Ian is dead!' I said it louder and clearer this time. I could tell that I was about to be overcome by emotion.

Tim fully opened his eyes. Now I felt as though I could let go and my head sank into his shoulder as my tears began to stream. It didn't feel real.

I'd never had someone who I knew that well die so suddenly and I really didn't know how to respond but crying.

Ian Craddock found dead in Lethem, Guyana, after he collapsed while jogging. One of my first thoughts was that it wasn't true. They must have got it wrong. The media and journalists often get things wrong and this had happened on the other side of the world, so surely there was a possibility that it was incorrect.

But it wasn't. Ian was dead and I'd never see him again.

In the months leading up to this moment, we had begun to work out essential logistics for the Big One and we were both aware of what a mammoth undertaking this journey was. Ian had been just as passionate about it as I was. After all, it had been his idea and although he'd trusted me to take it on, he really held the key for enabling it to happen. He had all the contacts, the knowledge and the wealth of experience we needed to even conceivably have a shot of getting this off the ground, let alone finish it successfully – because his death also meant the fall of his company, Bushmasters.

You see, Ian had this invincible persona, and believed nothing could or would touch him. That might sound arrogant or ridiculous but it never once felt like that because, really, he had the right to have a Superman-like title from his years of working and playing hard. Always the last at the party but the first up at dawn for a run. He appeared unstoppable and everyone around him believed it too. It was admirable and contagious, and so, even with all of the dangerous stunts he'd spent his life doing, he had never written a will.

As a result, with no one named to take on the business, Bushmasters disappeared as quickly as Ian did. The country would lose out in the adventure tourism that the company brought in, because Bushmasters was a major contributor to Guyana's economy, and the Amerindian communities would also suffer as there would be far less employment now that Bushmasters was no more. It was clear right there and then that his death would be a terrible blow to not only the individuals who knew and worked with him but also for the whole country.

My expedition now seemed even more impossible without Ian's help because, now that he was gone, what chance did I have to see this through? Doubts flooded my mind.

What would have been a perfect morning turned into a tragic one. Tim held me as my tear-stained cheeks soaked his shoulder. I began to grasp the other loss that I now faced. I hadn't just lost a friend, I was also mourning for the loss of dreams not yet realized.

14. Carrying the Flame

How on earth was I going to pull off this expedition? On the very day of Ian's passing, 20 July, a delivery arrived for me: a Hennessy Hammock and a DD Tarpaulin, or tarp for short. I had ordered them a few weeks earlier in preparation for the Big One. Previously, I'd borrowed Ian's spare, but for an expedition of this magnitude... and with the real possibility that I might not make it back... I felt it was time to have my own.

If you're not familiar with the different types of hammocks and jungle setups, let me explain why this setup is superior. I'll try not to geek out.

Typically, when we think of hammocks, we envision a cloth or netting strung between two palm trees on a beach. A perfect setting for relaxation. But in the jungle, that just won't suffice. This hammock features a double-layered bottom made of tightly woven nylon, making it 100% mosquito-proof. Mosquitos or any bitey insect in the jungle are determined little critters; they can bite through anything given half the chance so the double layer is a must. It also includes a permanently attached insect mesh that you can access via a zipper.

You rig it up between trees using paracord at each end. Above the hammock, you rig a tarp; an extra-large tarp means you can have a whole area around your hammock that stays dry. I customize this by tying additional paracord to all corners, giving me more flexibility in positioning during setup. Directly above the hammock line, in the middle of the tarp, you rig another very tightly tied paracord. This serves a dual purpose: it acts as both a washing line/hanger (nothing can be left on the floor in the jungle or you face things calling it home or eating it) and an impact protector in case a branch falls. Dead fall is one of the most common causes for death in the jungle. There are just so many trees, so much competition, and dead branches falling naturally or as a result of monkeys or storms are common. The idea is that this super-strong paracord might – and I must stress, it's only a might – save your life. This 3x3-metre setup becomes home – a safety net from the unknown that lies beyond.

Buying the hammock had marked my first true commitment to this expedition. It's a ritual I've always followed: making a purchase (it could be anything) that declares, 'This is happening.' However, after Ian's sudden passing, the expedition's feasibility definitely wasn't a given. Ian had been the guy to make this happen and I wasn't sure it was possible without him, or even if it was possible to get to the start point. Was it foolish to attempt it without him there on the other end of the satphone in case shit hit the fan? Scrolling on my phone, I looked back on our recent emails to one another. We had only just begun to scratch the surface of our planning, but before his death, Ian and I had agreed on a few critical details that would guide the next stage of planning . . . if I were to consider continuing at all. One key decision was our starting point: the King William IV Falls. These rapids on the Essequibo River are significant not just in their challenge but also in their extent. Given their scale, it made sense to begin the expedition there after travelling upstream by boat for one to two days, rather than attempting to portage the boat around them for miles. We had also dismissed the idea of plane drops for resupplies. In reality, they would likely end up stuck in trees, so we needed to devise an alternative method, something we hadn't yet figured out. We also didn't even know if I'd get the permission from the government, the Amerindian affairs, the Amerindian villages or the Protected Areas Commission. Getting to the start was going to be an expedition in itself.

I decided to sleep in the hammock the same night it was delivered, right in my parents' garden. With the pandemic still having limitations on travel, venturing to the wilds of Scotland or Wales was out of the question, so this garden sleepover would have to do. I strung the hammock between two trees in front of the house and spent the night surrounded by the soothing sounds of the English countryside. It wasn't the jungle, but it was its own kind of paradise.

As I lay there, the serene night sounds surrounding me, Ian's sudden passing weighed heavy on my mind. I was reliving the moment I had picked up and read that message: *Have you heard about Ian?* over and over in my head. It was such a shock that he was gone. It just felt so unfair. I didn't know how long it would take to process it. Life really is unpredictable and you never know when your time is up. We don't know if we have tomorrow, or even this afternoon.

I tossed and turned and couldn't get my doubts about the expedition out of my head. What gave me the right to think I could achieve this? It felt ludicrous to even consider that without Ian's guidance I could do it. Expeditions on foot in the jungle are no joke.

When you ask the Special Forces which environment they

think is the hardest to operate in, they will, without a doubt, say the jungle. I remember his exact words: '*The jungle will chew you up and spit you out.*' Navigation is a nightmare and moving through the dense vegetation is unforgiving. The high humidity and relentless moisture is brutal on the body. Everything is wet, and I mean all of the time. Being soaked by rain and sweat isn't just uncomfortable, it wreaks havoc on the skin. It causes it to soften, leading it to become more susceptible to cuts and infections. Fungal infections just get worse and worse, not helped by the mud you have to constantly wade through. Bacteria love the jungle but it's not just bodies that suffer – equipment rots, too. It's a battle on the gear, the body and the mind.

Despite all of this, my mind was wondering: *what if?* Something deep inside of me was telling me that I could do this and that I had to trust myself.

I reflected on my times with Ian and how he would have encouraged me to plough ahead, to take matters into my own hands. I thought about how Ian might approach this and heard his voice in my head: *Lucy, you choose what to do with your life. If you are happy and in control of your own life, then you can make a difference to the wider world.*

The region we had discussed that I would try to cross was largely unprotected. This expedition could highlight and showcase its wonders. We had an opportunity to do something special here. We could show what was in this unexplored and lost world, and prove why it was important to preserve, potentially influencing the government to extend its protection. Now that would be something worth fighting for.

Fuelled by determination, I realized I had the will, the necessary contacts in Guyana and even a few potential team members in mind. *I'm going to do this for Ian*, I thought. *Well . . . I'm at least going to try.* How could I know if it was possible unless

I tried? It was time to get to work. As I closed my eyes, my grief began to transform into a burning desire to do Ian proud.

I made the decision right there and then, under the stars: the expedition had to happen.

15. Anders

I PLUNGED INTO THE PLANNING of the expedition, thinking back to my last Amazon journey. Even though it had been just us out there in that inhospitable jungle, I'd had the comforting knowledge that Ian was somewhere in the country. If something had gone horribly wrong, I knew he could kick into gear. He knew how to pull the right strings, had the contacts, the reputation, and he would always figure out a shortcut. He just made things happen.

Now, that safety net was gone.

Who could step in for Ian? No one really, but I needed to start somewhere. The first step was gathering as much information as I could. I thought about who might understand my ambitions and who knew the type of terrain I was looking at, the challenges that lay ahead. One name came to mind: Guy.

I reconnected with him via Facebook. Guy lives in Nappi, a small Amerindian village just north of the Kanukus. It's made up of thatched-roof huts and dusty yards where goats and dogs roam freely. It's often completely cut off during the floods, but somehow still gets a stronger Wi-Fi signal than most B&Bs in Suffolk. Facebook is king out there.

I sent him a message, explaining the vague bones of what I had in mind.

I'm planning an east-to-west Kanukus journey. Starting from the Essequibo River.

The typing dots appeared instantly.

You mean the whole range?

Then:

That's a long way.

Then came the warnings. I could hear his dry and serious tone through the screen.

Those rivers you'd be crossing have vampire fish in them. Proper nasty. They bite off your fingers. And the black caiman, you stay in that water too long, they'll come. You'll need to build rafts, you can't just swim it.

I stared at the messages, already feeling the familiar flutter of nerves and excitement rising up that I get when I plan expeditions. This one was different though – neither Ian nor I knew if this was possible. Right now, I had a strange combination of butterflies, exhilaration and utter disbelief that I was even considering this.

Vampire fish – or payara as they're called in the Amazon – are these wild-looking fish; they can grow up to three feet in length and have sabre-like teeth that stick out from their lower jaw, even when their mouths are shut. I suppose they're like the underwater version of a vampire, thanks to those massive fangs that they use to skewer their prey. These fish are super aggressive and love chasing down smaller fish for a quick snack but also won't hesitate to take off a few human fingers. They're a pretty big deal among fishermen too – catching one is a real test of skill as they're fast and fierce, and they really put up a fight.

And then let me tell you about the caimans: South America's answer to alligators. Most people, if they've heard of caimans at all, are probably thinking of the small ones – dwarf caiman – the kind you see in wildlife programmes that are being plucked out of the water by hand. But the ones out in Guyana? They're a different beast. A full-grown black caiman can be over five metres long and weigh as much as a small car! They move with an eerie silence, watching from the shadows with their ancient, unblinking eyes. They are, quite literally, living relics from the prehistoric era. They adapted so well to their environment so early on that they've barely needed to evolve. Their dark, rugged scales camouflage perfectly with the murky rivers and swamps where they live, and if you ever find yourself in the water, the key is not to splash. Splashing around can attract them because they think it's prey flailing about. That's usually enough for a caiman to check things out, which is the last thing you want.

Their powerful jaws and sheer enormous size make them a real threat to humans and I've met many Amerindians who tell me the tales of villagers who have either lost limbs to them, or their lives.

Guy's advice about building a raft was worth taking note of but it was a small piece of the puzzle to consider.

I was playing out the different scenarios in my head. One thing that I kept coming back to was that I still didn't know how to organize the much-needed resupplies. These would contain food, medical supplies and camera batteries. I thought we'd need three of them but, truthfully, I was unsure. No one knew how long this journey would take.

Then it hit me: Anders! I had met Anders back on my first trip to Guyana, the same time I met Ian. We both went on Ian's Bushmaster survival course.

What can I say about Anders?

Anders is Danish, smokes like a chimney and can drink like a fish, and like Ian, has a robust work ethic and no-nonsense type of attitude. You want him on your side. I have always liked and respected him enormously from the sidelines. He's the kind of guy who gets things done, no bullshit, again just like Ian, making him ideal to help plan this expedition and act as my right-hand man. However, at that point I had no clue what he was up to.

Anders has an interesting backstory. He hasn't always been the wild, bow-and-arrow armed man that he is now. He was previously in the corporate IT world, well groomed in a smart suit with a desk, a life as an account manager. He met and fell in love with a Danish girl, Sophia, who declared she was leaving Denmark to go to South America and he followed her. They met Ian and he offered them some work, which later led to them setting up their own tour company in Guyana. Even when I met Anders, when he'd only been in Guyana for a few weeks, he seemed like he was born to do this. He'd quickly left his smart, clean-shaven office look behind and let his natural Viking side emerge; with a huge beard and wide, wild eyes, he was catching animals left, right and centre. I couldn't imagine him as the neat, number-crunching office worker he used to be.

Sadly, after a few years Anders and Sophia's relationship ended. Anders then moved back to Denmark. Still, I wanted to check in on him after the news of Ian's death and shoot him the question that I had in mind. It seemed like a call worth making.

I sent him a message and, faster than expected, we had one scheduled.

The video call with Anders came through. I propped my phone against a water bottle and answered. His familiar wild-eyed, bearded face filled the screen. He looked like he hadn't left the jungle at all, not like someone who now lived in Copenhagen.

'Lucy!' he boomed, before I could even get a word in. 'I heard what you're planning. You crazy?'

I laughed. 'Possibly. But you're going to love it.'

He squinted at me, grinning, and in his Scandi accent said, 'So, you want to cross the entire Kanuku range, east to west?'

I nodded. 'The whole thing.'

Anders rubbed his face with both hands. 'Shit. This is so cool, Lucy. But you know that's a long way, right? That's not just an expedition. That's the moon landing of jungle expeditions.'

He wasn't saying it like he thought I *shouldn't* do it. More like he knew exactly what kind of beast it was. I could tell he wanted in.

I filled him in on the idea. The scope. Ian's input so far. How things had changed.

'I don't have Ian,' I said, 'but I need someone like him.'

He raised an eyebrow. 'And you're calling me?'

I shrugged, but gave a half-smile. 'You're the only other person mad enough.'

Anders let out a long breath, then sat back. 'Lucy, you know I would really like to take this on with you and help you get there.'

That was it. No hesitations. He didn't even let me ask him officially.

We started bouncing ideas back and forth like no time had passed. We went through how we might handle resupplies, the permissions, the paperwork.

'What about food drops?' I said. 'I was thinking three?'

Anders grimaced. 'Maybe four. You don't know how slow this jungle will be. And camera gear? You'll be sweating batteries.'

He pulled out a pad and pen. Of course he already had a checklist. He was way ahead of me. 'We'll need to get the permits in quick. Are you filming this one?'

Anders knew my filming background and my ambitions for the future.

'Yes. I will be filming it.' I had already decided that I was going to film the whole expedition with the plan to get it broadcasted and, all being well, it would be the type of adventure documentary I grew up inspired by. Getting it on national television meant that even further permits and paperwork would need to be obtained. The whole telly thing requires so many official things. This also added the issue of extra weight and less space for food in our bags. Camera kit is not lightweight. But despite all this, we both knew the importance of filming it. Yes, it would be cool to have it on TV, but telling the story was more than that. We felt we owed it to Ian.

Anders continued, 'Right, this means permits from PAC, Ministry of Amerindian Affairs and more. You'll want to go in dry season, hopefully travel will have opened up again. I think if we plan for September next year, that will be possible.'

I hesitated. 'One thing. I don't have the sponsorship yet.'

He just waved a hand. 'I'll come out. No fee.'

I blinked. 'Seriously?'

'Ian would've wanted this to happen,' he said. 'We're not letting this die with him.'

I could feel the lump in my throat before I could stop it. He must've seen it too, because he quickly changed the subject.

'Right. Who are you having as your merry men?'

We had slipped straight into the thick of things. I loved how contagious our energy was towards one another.

Over the next few weeks we had a number of calls.

We bounced ideas on who would be good team members and also agreed that Anders would need to get to Guyana a few weeks earlier to make sure things were in order. As this was coming together, it also meant we were able to construct an accurate budget, which would include camera kit, for me to then go and seek out the sponsorship required. I tallied up that this expedition, including all the things we had to pay for beforehand, like medical training courses, kit, Anders' recces, would be £30,000. Boy, that was a lot of money. I'd never raised anything near to that in my life. Over the years I'd been doing these expeditions the cost had never come close to this.

The majority of my expeditions had been between £1,500 to £2,500. To get this money in the past, I'd applied for young people's grants, won awards from young filmmaker competitions, which had financial rewards that would contribute, and I had saved everything I could from my work at ITN. I'd cycled to work to avoid paying for the Tube, brought in my lunches and didn't spend anything unless it had a reason to propel me forward into the adventure world. But this was never going to get me to £30,000.

It was an eye-watering amount but I knew that this was still significantly less than Everest expeditions, and don't get me started on the cost to ski to the North or South Poles. I'd heard that these expeditions could be hundreds of thousands, if not millions of pounds.

But if other people could raise that sort of money, why couldn't I raise this? This was real exploration, which is so hard to find nowadays.

I threw myself into the world of 'pitching' and sent emails and made calls daily in a hope to edge that bit closer to finding a backer.

In more recent years I've been able to get funding from brand partnerships and some of my expeditions qualified for society funding because they included citizen science. This is like science for dummies. I'm not a scientist and I don't create the right environment during my expeditions for full-blown scientific experiments, but citizen science allows me to find out how I can be of use to researchers and scientists with the limitations I have. On the last jungle expedition, I teamed up with a scientist who was doing her PhD. I collected river water and sediment samples at different locations to test for microplastics – spoiler: they were there.

Anders was throwing himself back into the bush life, and his excitement was on the same level as mine. I could tell he was looking forward to this as much as I was, even though he wasn't going to be on the actual expedition – instead, he was going to be in his element: the sorter. With our strategy set, I felt a solid plan was finally taking shape. Now it was time to pull everything together and somehow find the £30,000 needed.

We were going to find a way to do this.

16. Planning

THE MONTHS FOLLOWING MY INITIAL conversations with Anders became a whirlwind. We decided on a departure for next September, so had a little over a year to prepare. I knuckled down on training for the expedition. I had to improve my endurance so I ran regularly – eight to twelve miles, four times a week – and trekked with my seventy-five-litre rucksack packed full. I did all of this in a fasted state, without water, even in the sweltering summer months. I had to prepare my body for the high probability it would need to function with very little food and water. Functional strength and mobility training was also important.

All of this was done at my home in London – when I could get back – or at my parents' in Suffolk. The ever-present risk of Covid kept showing its face and periodically there'd be a threat of another lockdown. I tried to spend lockdowns in Suffolk where I was fortunate to have access to an outside area and it made training that bit easier, and I also managed to make some trips to Wales when it was OK to travel.

I wasn't alone on those training trips as my Jack Russell, Sami, was always by my side. Normally, Tim would have been there too, but since June, everything had changed. He'd fallen seriously ill after what we thought was a routine medical decision. A cascade of symptoms began. It was strange and worrying – it didn't all make sense but here it was happening: nerve problems, extreme fatigue, alarming weight loss, and ultimately a blood clot in his lung. He was hospitalized multiple times, and spent large periods of time bedbound. Watching someone as fit and full of energy as Tim lose so much muscle and become a shell of himself was deeply unsettling. He would become vacant and seem to go somewhere else. It was made harder because doctors couldn't seem to agree on what was going on.

There was no diagnosis that made total sense. We were left with fragments of answers and a list of treatments that didn't quite help. It wasn't until much later that he started to realize his symptoms mirrored those reported by some people after having the Covid vaccine. We have no way of knowing if it was linked, but it was a pattern that caught our attention.

While his dad stepped in and took the lead in supporting him, I still found it incredibly difficult to walk out the door and head to the mountains, knowing Tim was barely able to move. There was guilt in that, of course. But I also knew I had to keep preparing and training. The expedition was bigger than me and I had to keep moving forward. Tim was supportive and knew the importance of training for the expedition. Sami became my constant training partner, small and mighty. Perhaps without knowing it, she helped me carry the emotional load of that strange and uncertain time.

When I got Sami on 15 May 2020, she instantly became my everything. She was smaller than a guinea pig. She was handed to me as soon as I arrived to collect her and she was so chilled, didn't wriggle one bit. Her mum and dad came over to me and I crouched down to let them lick her goodbye – it felt like they were saying that. It was the sight of her mum, a lilac mini Jack

Russell, that made me choose Sami in the first place. I love that dog so much.

Tim and I speak to her like a person and because of it she understands so much. Her emotional intelligence is out of this world and she surprises us all the time. I bet all dog owners say that, but I really mean it. I can have long conversations with her and she even understands future time references. We've got her to understand the words 'later' and 'tomorrow' – we repeatedly say 'not now, tomorrow' if we're talking about something exciting that's coming up. You can genuinely see the cogs going in her brain as she contains her excitement for the future event. But it goes even further: if we've told her the previous day that something exciting is going to happen 'tomorrow' – like she's going to be seeing Tim's dad's dogs, Alfie and Bertie – then she will wake up the next day knowing that today she's allowed to be excited. It's incredible! And don't even get me started on the amount of names she knows. She even has different reactions to them. With my childhood best friend Harry, she lets out a specific tone of bark; with Mum and Dad's cat, Chris, she leaps up and down, tail and bum in the air.

Already the idea of leaving her for multiple months while I suffered it out in the jungle was weighing on my mind. She had become a symbol of what home was for me. But I knew I'd have to remove her from my mind completely as soon as I stepped foot on the plane to South America.

Anders was working from Denmark and making good progress piecing together what we'd need in order to legally do the expedition. Meanwhile, I still wasn't having much luck with sponsorship. More often than not, companies just wouldn't answer. I'd obviously have preferred to go in person, knocking on doors, but Covid stopped this, so I had to put my trust in emails and phone calls.

Things all changed when one day I received news that the director of an investment company named Napkin Group had heard about the expedition and wanted to fund the majority of it. I couldn't believe it! They had even volunteered and I was ecstatic.

The morning following that news didn't feel real. I could have sworn I'd dreamed it, but no. The vast majority of the sponsorship had been secured and led to the remaining being funded by the Scientific Exploration Society on the terms I'd bring about more awareness to the society, which in turn led to the expedition becoming officially endorsed by the society, giving a little kudos and much-needed credibility to it.

With funding sorted, I put my attention on how best to film the journey. I reached out to my contacts in the television industry, both UK and US.

My conversations with my US contacts resulted in some very positive steps, although I was the one to retreat when one well-known US broadcaster said they'd love to get behind this expedition, but said they'd want to send a male co-host to go with me and a large crew . . . I roll my eyes just thinking about this now. Firstly, a male co-host?! This wasn't the first time I'd heard this. I can't count on one hand how many times heads of channels have suggested I bring a man along. Then the crew – the idea of bringing multiple people would not just screw up the authenticity of the adventure but also put the lives of those working at risk. They clearly didn't understand what I was trying to do, which was to create a real adventure show for adventure's sake. It was going to be up to me to film this and sell it afterwards. I was OK with that. I had faith that with every hurdle and new direction taken, the story was getting stronger and stronger. This expedition wasn't just another project; it was a pivotal leap towards a full-time career in adventure, a declaration of my commitment to exploring and documenting the world on my terms.

The Big One

17. Make Good Decisions

I T IS 24 SEPTEMBER, CLOSE TO MIDNIGHT. I'm sitting on the plane looking down at the city lights as we descend into Georgetown.

My dad came up from Suffolk to drive me to the airport and Tim had gathered enough energy to join, too. He's been beginning to show signs of slowly getting better, mainly his strong mindset and grit to recover, but it's going to be a long road ahead.

The goodbye felt significant.

Dad and Tim hovered in the airport while I checked in my three bags. I hugged my dad first.

'Thank you for the lift. See you soon, Dad.' I always say this. It's a way of saying, *Don't worry, I'll be back before you know it.*

'Don't do anything I wouldn't do!' he said, with a humorous tone.

'I think we're a little past that,' I replied, grinning.

'But seriously, be very careful.' His smile faded, and he shifted his weight from one foot to the other, glancing down before meeting my eyes with a worried look.

'I will, Dad. Love you lots.' I gave him one last hug and then turned to where Tim was standing. We embraced tightly, ear to ear.

He held me close and I tried to bank this memory for when I'd need it in the jungle. His arms wrapped around my shoulders with that familiar warmth. His face rested against mine. There was no tension between us, just a quiet sadness at saying goodbye, but we'd done this before. I breathed him in, holding on to this last moment of home before everything changed again.

'Make good decisions. Be safe and look after the team,' he whispered. His words landed.

'I will. I love you. I hope you begin to feel better.'

'Me too,' he said. 'I love you and I can't wait to see you when you get back. Lots of fun things to do together when that happens. Now go out there and get it done. You've trained, you can do it. Ian would be so proud. I'm proud of you for even getting this far.'

We shared a kiss and then hugged again, aware my dad was waiting. One last squeeze and then I forced myself to separate and peel off from them, waving, miming 'I love you'.

I had a momentary thought that this could possibly be the last time I'd ever see them, but I was quick to remove that from my mind. I could not let any level of doubt corrode my outlook, especially not now. I had done all I could to prepare. I'd gone through every scenario; I'd taken courses, refreshed my medical skills – I'd made sure I was as ready as I could be.

And with that, it was time for me to go. I couldn't wait to get on the other side of security. It wasn't because I wanted to leave Tim and Dad, it was because I felt this huge sense of calling to start this adventure. I waved to them as I went out of sight and with that, it had begun.

Descending into Georgetown feels familiar – the hum of the Caribbean Airlines plane, the sight of the coastal lights below, but what lies beneath has changed beyond recognition from my first time here in 2014. As I look out at the illuminated city, I'm reminded of the complexity of Guyana.

It seems to be a country of contrasts, from its untamed wilderness to its developing vibrant urban city. Georgetown, like the rest of the country, is a blend of the old and the new, the traditional and the modern. The capital has seen incredible change in recent years. The significant discovery of offshore oil, just one year after my first visit to the country in 2015, would change the path of Guyana forever. American company ExxonMobil jumped on the opportunity and rapid development began soon after. Who could blame them? A country that is one of the poorest in South America being suddenly presented with an opportunity that presented the chance to go from rags to riches.

Fancy skyscrapers were built to house the new American visitors and display wealth. These glitzy buildings stand alongside old stilted houses and shacks, while the markets that are filled with Caribbean flavours line the streets amid littered alleys.

Georgetown was built below sea level and sits on a flood plain, meaning it has a constant threat of rising sea levels. Before becoming British, Georgetown was under Dutch control and the Dutch influence is evident throughout the city. There are sea walls and canals that attempt to mitigate flooding issues and now there is even a broader plan to create a new city – 'Silica City' – which is well underway and located further inland. This will help counter the risks associated with living in low-lying Georgetown and is situated in a hillier region. It represents a strategic shift and rather admirable action from the government to the frightening and inevitable climate changes.

Culturally, Georgetown is a melting pot – from African to Caribbean, Indian to Chinese – but what it seems to be missing is indigenous Amerindian influence. This is found upon leaving Georgetown, when you head south towards the pristine jungles.

After getting my three duffle bags of kit to balance on the trolley, I go through customs and present my carnet for all the camera kit I'm bringing into the country. All goes well and then, I am out and faced with the familiar but foreign buzz of Georgetown airport at 1 a.m. The hot tropical air is intense and sticky, a world away from London.

Georgetown is anything but quiet when a plane lands, even during the early hours. Every taxi driver in the neighbourhood turns up to barter the fresh blood and it's certainly a culture shock. Everyone cries for my attention, desperate for me to pick them to take me to my location. I don't need their help. I've prearranged Mr Singh, a friend of Anders. I scan the crowds of people, held back by a metal gate. Men repeatedly try to take my bags and lure me to their taxi, but I hold strong until I spot Mr Singh. We greet one another and I feel quietly smug as I shut the door of his taxi, knowing I've overcome the first hurdle to adjust back into this way of life.

I should be exhausted by now, but adrenaline fills my veins and as we drive away, I can't help but feel a rush of anticipation. This is no longer just a dream; I'm back in Guyana, surrounded by locals who understand the daunting reality of their jungles. The grand adventure I've been craving is truly about to begin.

I check into my hotel, the same hotel where Ian presented me with the idea of this expedition eighteen months ago. I take a minute to stare at the exact location where we sat and had the conversation about the Big One – a conversation that changed everything. It's like Ian is etched in my mind, sat on that same chair where he leaned back and said, 'Well you're going to have to cross the whole thing now, aren't you?' The confidence in his words and his belief in me flood my body. I need to hold on to

MAKE GOOD DECISIONS

this feeling. I can feel his presence and already have a sense that he will be alongside me throughout this adventure.

The next few days are jam-packed. Anders has scheduled my diary so we have something booked every hour of the day, from government meetings to shopping for essentials. Anders is so matter-of-fact and he has such a charm that it's hard not to say yes to him.

I don't really have a moment to stop and think, I'm just enjoying the process of ticking all the last-minute jobs off. I love working with Anders and making things happen; it's satisfying. My feet hardly touch the ground.

We manage to squeeze in a visit to the Botanical Gardens to meet Vivian Smith. Vivian is one of the team members that Anders put forward as a strong candidate originally, and I was happy to take his recommendation and commit to Vivian being on the team without meeting him beforehand. All I know about him is he's mid-thirties, kind, strong and excellent in the forest.

Meeting Vivian, I'm confronted with a short man, but then I remind myself that Amerindians are short by nature. It'll be me who's the odd one out when the full team assembles.

'Vivian?' I call out.

He turns and smiles, walking over with a quiet and polite confidence. 'Miss Lucy,' he says, reaching out a hand. 'Is nice to meet you. I glad to be a part of this adventure.'

'No need for the "miss",' I say, shaking his hand firmly. 'Just Lucy.'

Vivian chuckles softly. 'All right then, Lucy.'

There is a warmth in the way he says it. No nerves, no awkwardness. Just a shared sense that we both know what we're getting into. He's dressed smartly in jeans and a long shirt with a small rucksack high on his back.

'Thanks for being here,' I say. 'I've heard great things.'

'Me too,' he nods, then grins. 'And I am very excited. This journey, it feels big. I knew immediately that I wanted to be in your team.'

We wander a little through the gardens, talking about the expedition and what is going on in our lives. I make a point not to dominate the conversation. I want Vivian to see me not as the outsider who's brought a camera, but as someone who is all in. Not the leader, but part of the team. Not just colleagues, but future friends. Turns out Vivian has just finished a government course on solar panel repair . . . something I didn't expect.

'Is good,' he says, adjusting his rucksack. 'Now I can go back to the village and fix what nobody can fix. You know, most panels don't work after one year. Now I fix them.'

'That's amazing,' I say. He must be smart. 'It's so important and so useful! You might want to start your own business.'

Vivian shrugs modestly, but I can tell he is proud.

The government has been distributing solar panels to Amerindian villages for a number of years, paid for in a credit agreement by the Indian Government, but with these comes the necessity of training people in the trade so they can be installed, maintained and serviced. Vivian has volunteered in Georgetown to take up this training and has an obvious interest to understand it. I'm fascinated that he has this other string to his bow.

At one point, when we're sitting under a tree going over the route, I pull out my notebook and show him some of the river crossing waypoints I've been working on. 'Anything look off to you?' I ask. 'You know the rivers better than I ever will.' Although no one knows the interior, the rivers have been well travelled.

He leans in and studies the map, then points. 'This area here, fast rapids, Lucy. We may need to search for a different crossing.'

'Good call,' I nod, and make a note.

It feels like we're building something solid. Something based on shared goals and respect. That is all I want. Just to begin this thing, properly, as team mates.

Vivian glances at the folded map in my hand, then back at me with a small, genuine smile.

'I feel proud to be part of your expedition,' he says.

I shake my head immediately. 'No . . . it's *ours*, Vivian. Our expedition! We've got a big adventure ahead of us!'

He nods slowly.

'We're only going to make it through if we're in it for the right reasons and together,' I add. 'That means every step we are in this, as a team.'

Vivian lets the words settle, then grins.

'OK. *Our* expedition.'

We've broken the ice. I see Vivian's confidence rise and his guard come down.

He tilts his head and asks, 'You want to see something special?'

'Go on.'

'Come, I'll show you.' I was thinking he meant in the jungle, but it looks like he means right now.

He leads me through a shaded path towards the far edge of the Botanical Gardens. The sunlight plays across the water, or at least it would, if not for the floating plastic bags and empty bottles muddling the surface. Georgetown has a serious litter problem.

Vivian doesn't comment on the rubbish. Instead, he picks up a few long blades of grass. I watch as he crouches by the bank and starts swishing them in the water with a flicking motion.

Three seconds, maybe less, and a smooth grey head breaks the surface. Big. Wrinkled. Gentle. A manatee. I've never seen anything like it!

'They like the grass,' he says, without looking at me.

Another manatee rises, and then another. I count seven in total. They all appear through the water like ghostly giants.

I crouch down beside him, grab some grass and try the same flicking motion, and sure enough, one glides right over. Its mouth hoovers it up like a slow vacuum cleaner or conveyor belt, taking the grass straight from my hand and munching it politely with its multiple rows of teeth.

'They're like river elephants,' I say, watching it chew. Its tough skin is so similar to that of an elephant.

Vivian chuckles. 'I never seen elephant. But these are peaceful. I like them.'

Sharing this moment, in the silent company of these unlikely gentle giants, softens something between us. We're both smiling now not out of politeness, but from the joy of being in the present moment in each other's company.

This might be the start of a great friendship.

We say our goodbyes. I'll meet Vivian again with the rest of the team with me, next week at his home in Rewa village, before we begin our journey deeper into the wild.

18. Assemble

Although Georgetown has that vibrant energy, I am ready to get going after our week here, and leaving is like a breath of fresh air. Anders and I board the small propeller plane and before we know it, we are soaring over an endless sea of green. It's a complete blanket of trees and you'd be forgiven if you didn't think that there was a deforestation problem. But as you look closer, a disturbing patchwork emerges near to the waterways. Areas of barren land where forests once stood, cleared away in the ruthless hunt for gold. These gaping wounds are usually near rivers, and the fallout is severe: mercury pollution that ravages the waterways, contaminating everything downstream, especially impacting the indigenous communities who rely on these rivers for their livelihood. Once away from any rivers, it's unlikely you'll see any evidence of human activity, which is what makes our expedition such a mammoth undertaking. There are no records of anyone making the journey and there are large stretches where even the Amerindians believe that no human has been before. The main reason for this is that there isn't a logical reason to go there. Historically, just like now, the best way of getting around the jungle was by river. It's faster, safer and means you have access to food. Only the insane would choose to walk for large distances . . . What does that say about me? I'm glued to the window, eager to get my first glimpse of part of my route. I feel like a kid in a candy shop – the opportunities of adventures down there are endless! We'll be smaller than a needle in a haystack.

The plane begins its descent towards Lethem, our destination. As we near, the landscape below shifts dramatically as the flat expanses give way to the imposing jungle-covered Kanuku Mountains. They rise starkly from the earth, high into the sky and there are a lot of them – a rugged barrier slicing through the savannah and with flat jungle either side. From the air, they look even more formidable than I remember, their peaks casting long shadows over Lethem like ancient guardians of the land.

Lethem itself is known as a frontier town; a gateway to the vast expanses of the Rupununi Savannah and the dense jungle beyond. It's built up a lot since my first visit here. It's got a Wild West feel to it which is hard to come by nowadays. It shows no sign of wealth like the odd skyscraper in Georgetown; in fact, quite the opposite. It's a place where the roads are so dusty and sandy that that everything they touch is stained a deep red. Small homes that fit a whole family with roofs made from corrugated metal and toilet shacks outside are common. This small town serves as a hub for the surrounding Amerindian villages, a place where the wilderness meets a semblance of urbanity.

As the plane touches the ground, I notice a guy crouched down against the wired fence, filming our landing. 'That must be Luke,' I say to Anders.

He looks out the window. 'Oh good, he made it.'

Luke is in his early twenties and lives in Lethem. He's British and came here a few years ago, met a local girl and ended up staying . . . a tale as old as time!

I'd told Anders that I wanted someone in Lethem to film our arrival, but finding someone here with a camera is slim pickings. Luckily, Luke had one and was a keen videographer.

Stepping off the plane I am blasted by that hit of tropical savannah air. I look out into the distance to get eyes on the Kanukus again. It creates a strange sensation in my stomach – a mixture of butterflies ranging from nervousness to excitement. The unforgiving dense jungles cover mountain after mountain, off into the distance, and I realize that I'm not even looking at a third of my journey. What I'm looking at is probably the last ten days or so . . . Would we even get that far?

I snap out of the 'what if' mindset and go to greet Luke.

'Hey, you must be Luke,' I say, shaking his hand. 'Thank you so much for coming out to film today, and for the next couple of days too. It means a lot.'

'No worries at all. It's great to be a small part of it,' he smiles. 'Happy to help.'

Now it's time to do just that: meet the team. I'm really excited about seeing the familiar faces of Lionel and Aaron again.

Anders, Luke and I are dropped off at our guest house, just a few hundred metres from the airport. The sunshine and palm trees make it feel almost holiday-like, but neither it nor Lethem is that kind of place. No pool. Just overpowering warm, humid air and faded concrete. Caribbean music blares from the speakers outside, next to the outdoor bar; it feels like a Guyanese sort of welcome.

Waiting in the shade, I see a silhouette. Aaron. He grins and gives me a one-armed, slightly awkward hug. His cap is still tilted sideways and his clothes are two sizes too big. It is the same old Aaron. Still shy, still endearing, and I can tell he is glad to be here. He seems a bit more sober this time; I'll see if he can stay that way.

I look around for Lionel.

It has been seven years since I last saw him . . . in fact, not since the jaguar incident. Back then, I was young, naive and pretty incompetent in the jungle, to be honest. But him, he was calm, capable and oh-so-knowledgeable. Ian had trusted him completely. He wouldn't have paired me up with him if he hadn't. It was common knowledge that Lionel had been his right-hand man, his go-to; as Lionel put it, Ian was his Boss Man. I couldn't imagine Ian without Lionel nearby.

I spot him leaning against the wall with his arms crossed, watching everything with that wise and steady gaze. Our eyes meet, he gives me a nod and walks over.

'Long time,' he says.

'Too long,' I reply, and we hug. It's the type of hug that's brief, but says a lot.

'You good?' I ask.

He nods. 'Yeah . . . just missing Boss Man.'

I pause. There it was and said so simply. The effects of his passing are so hugely felt.

'I know,' I say. 'Me too.'

He nods again, then looks out at the sun, and to Aaron and Anders, who are waiting at the sidelines. 'He would've liked this trip.'

'I think so,' I agree. 'I think he'd be proud that we've made it out here, going on this together.'

Lionel doesn't say anything to that, but his jaw clenches slightly, and that is enough.

I am glad he is here. Really glad. Having him on the team means more than I can explain, not just for what he can do, but for who he is, and what he carries forward with him. It is a full-circle moment, not just for Lionel, Anders or Ian, but for me as well.

ASSEMBLE

This isn't just my expedition. It is a continuation of something Ian started. And Lionel? He is part of that through and through.

We make a trip to the supermarket to get supplies, everyone filling their baskets with additional bits and bobs. Everything from extra soap, toothbrushes to bug spray. Then, we are pretty much ready to begin distributing it between us.

We take over the hotel benab: a roofed structure that you can place hammocks under or lay out kit.

We carefully pack up our rations. Seventeen days' worth for the first leg, topped up by whatever we can hunt or catch. Tins of sardines, bags of farine, toilet paper and packets of noodles are placed in the middle. Then there's the team kit – rope, medical kit, camera kit, sat phone... The real challenge is making it all fit. There are also a couple of small bottles of rum, which I've hidden from sight.

My bag comes in at 35 kg, and that's not including water. It's brutal, but I'm able to just about get it over and on to my back, with a little help.

It took some time for Anders and me to put together this team. Now, watching them for the first time together, moving around the benab as we prep our packs and ration bags, I feel a sense land that this is us, minus Vivian, who we collect tomorrow.

Lionel sits on a low stool, already offering unsolicited advice about how Aaron is packing his bag and that 'he'll regret that knot come nightfall'. I clock the way the others nod without question. He's the oldest and he carries himself like he's seen it all... which to be fair he probably has. But I do get the feeling that this expedition will throw up some surprises for him. There's wisdom in Lionel and an experience that I know we'll need. However, I also know that when it comes to the tough calls, I'll need to watch him. He might think he knows best, but on an expedition of this size, it's about more than authority: it's about having the bigger picture. Although Lionel has spent the most time moving through the jungle at once, twelve days, it's a fraction of what we expect to take . . . which is closer to the forties. Things need to be done with that in mind.

Aaron is nearby, humming to himself, talking a bit of gibberish, the way I remember he did last time I was with him. He's repacking his bag for the third time, dramatically sighing every few minutes; it's not *quite* right. I've seen Aaron when he's in his element, when he's deep in the bush and something inside him clicks and he becomes the person I know he is. That happened back in 2020, when we crossed the Kanukus from south to north. I got a glimpse of that version of Aaron, confident, sharp, assured . . . I want him to find that again on this journey. I think he can.

Then there's Mikey, the youngest of us all. He's taking things seriously, and is the only one who hasn't yet spoken over anyone else. I can tell he's got a cheeky side. He's a ranger with the Protected Areas Commission (PAC). It's because of the PAC partnership that this expedition is officially allowed to happen. Just because he's been allocated to be on the team, doesn't mean he's an outsider though. He's Amerindian too, passionate about the forest. He actively volunteered to be part of this team. Mikey's smart, seems worldly and asks the right questions. He's sharp, tech-savvy, and has already taken an interest in my camera in a way that makes me think he might play a bigger role here than expected. He's got a sort of quiet curiosity. He hasn't let his guard fully down. I get the sense that he's observing, especially me. I'm a woman and that's odd for him; I'm excited to widen his perspective. He's taking us all in, figuring out where he fits. I like that.

ASSEMBLE

Looking at them, Lionel, Aaron and Mikey, and thinking about Vivian, I feel a deep and strange kind of pride. We're all wildly different. Different ages, backgrounds, personalities. But here, we're united: we've said yes to something big. Something ambitious and, frankly, a little mad.

I call everyone over for a safety and medical briefing. We're sitting on the edge of the benab, our packed bags lined up behind us. I unroll the team med kit in the centre, hoping to create intrigue. It does the job and everyone goes quiet and leans in.

'All right,' I say, lifting out the two tourniquets. 'Let's start with these. If there's one thing I'm worried about, it's cutting arteries with our cutlasses. So if someone takes a deep one to the leg or arm, you get this on, above the wound.' I proceed to put it on Aaron's thigh. 'Get it on tight. Don't hesitate.'

Mikey nods. Aaron watches closely at his own leg. I pass it to Lionel. 'You try.'

He examines it, and gets the gist quickly. I watch as he straps it on to his own thigh, testing the twist.

'Snakebite,' I continue. 'Let's not pretend we can do much. If it's a bushmaster . . .' The tone shifts. I've mentioned the one creature I know everyone is afraid of. 'It's about staying calm, demobilizing and hoping we can get you out.' The team each give sombre looks.

'I've got ibuprofen, antihistamines and antibiotics; I'll put Lionel in charge of looking after the med kit with the tablets in.' I trust him with these medicines, because of his years working with Ian. He's used to looking after these.

I hold up the Garmin inReach next. 'This is our lifeline. You all need to know how to use it, not just Mikey.' I call out Mikey because I know he's the most tech-savvy.

I show them how to open the SOS flap, how to hold it steady and patient until it pings. 'It won't work well under thick canopy, might take hours or even days, we can't rely on it solely. We'd probably need to get to a clearing if it was a real emergency. Same goes for the sat phone. If we have to call for help, someone's clearing bush and making space.'

'And helicopter?' Mikey asks.

'If there's one in country. It's not guaranteed. Nothing is here. We can't count on it.'

They're quiet now and really listening.

'There's a tree bark for bites,' Lionel says, eventually. 'Boil it, drink it slow.'

'And tree sap for tummy bugs,' Aaron adds.

I nod. 'Yes, we'll gather as we go. Anything you think would be sensible to collect, do it. I've seen it work. But you also tell me how you are feeling . . . always. This is not about being super strong, so no hiding fevers, no pretending it's nothing. Understood?'

They nod again. Aaron raises his hand like a schoolboy and jokingly says, 'What if we just get grumpy . . . because no rum?' They all burst out laughing. His question was predictable and classic Aaron. He's already defining himself as the joker of the team, which is fine for now; I trust we'll all see him flourish.

'Then we'll find a rum tree!'

They laugh again. But this time, there's trust under the humour. Little do they know that that rum tree lives in my bag!

We spend the rest of the day looking at the multiple maps. I spread them all out to show our proposed route. Everyone is focused, intensely following the contours, imagining our journey ahead that lies within these maps. I know I have got everyone excited about this big adventure.

19. Go Time

FOUR A.M. AND THE ALARM GOES OFF, but I'm already wide awake. It's unsurprisingly a disturbed sleep. I feel this immense pressure to enjoy the comfort I'm surrounded by, but so much so that I can't relax. The bed, the safety of these solid four walls, the comfortable temperature and the flushing toilet within stumbling distance from where I sleep. I don't feel like anything is watching me nor am I fearful of branches falling above my head. This morning marks goodbye to all of these luxuries that we take for granted in our modern world. Leaving these behind gives me a real understanding of just how lucky I am. I mean, how lucky are we if we're able to go to bed, not concerned for our safety? There are so many less fortunate, in war-torn areas, environmental disaster zones, or those who are forced to sleep on the streets with uncertain and unsettled nights as the norm.

I change into my jungle gear, which, like my last expedition here, is a simple fast-drying pair of dark-grey trousers, a fast-drying green shirt and a hefty belt with my machete attached to it. All of this is accessorized with my black Altberg jungle boots. Jungle boots are sturdy leather boots above ankle but what makes them different from regular hiking boots is that they have the ability to let out water. Mine have mesh in the middle. Waterproof boots are no use in the jungle. It's inevitable that you'll be in water, wading in creeks and rivers – there's no point resisting the fact that you'll get wet. Instead, you let the water flood in, but then when you come out of the water, your footsteps plunge it back out of the mesh. Obviously this means that your feet, socks and boots get soaked and remain wet, but they are not swimming in water held in by waterproof boots. Simple but effective.

I use this last opportunity, while I'm waiting for the rest of the team to emerge, to use the Wi-Fi and FaceTime my parents. Thankfully they answer. I can tell Mum is worried by her cracked voice. I don't blame her. 'Be careful, darling,' she says. 'Don't take any unnecessary risks.' It's something she always says, I don't know if she realizes she does it every time.

'I'll try not to,' I answer. I can't outright say no as I have no idea what's ahead. 'I'll be OK, don't worry. Take good care of Sami.'

Mum and Dad are looking after Sami because Tim is still unwell. I know she will be fine there. She'll definitely miss me but she'll be busy with my parents' dogs and cat.

I'm going to have to actively stop myself from thinking about my Sami girl during the expedition and won't give myself the treat of thinking about her, or the likes of warm showers, until the end is within throwing distance; otherwise, it'll be torture.

I tell my mum and dad I love them and say goodbye. I glance at my Casio watch: I have just a few minutes left before we leave. I must call Tim. It rings twice before his face appears on the screen. He looks tired but he manages a smile.

'Hey, you,' he says, his voice low but warm. He is the sound of home.

'Hey. You awake?'

'Of course, I hoped you'd call.'

There's a pause. I can tell he's trying to muster energy, sit a little taller. The strong ex-Royal Marine part of him flickers to the surface.

'You've done the work,' he says, looking right at me. 'Keep your head. Trust your gut. Don't be afraid to voice your thoughts.'

I nod. I feel my eyes glaze with water and a lump rising in my throat. I swallow it down.

'I will, I promise.'

'And look after the team,' he adds. 'You've got good people with you. You're a great team.'

His words are calm and grounded; it's the Tim I've always relied on. Even now, when his body's fragile, he can activate his mind. 'You've got this, Luce. I'm proud of you,' he says.

That's the bit that gets me. I nod again but am unable to say much more.

'I'll try to message if I can get inReach connection,' I say quickly, trying to shake out of the emotion. I need to stay sharp, especially today.

'I'll be here,' he says. That's the thing: I know he means it. He's watching, waiting, cheering me on from a distance, plus, he *gets* it. This is his world too.

'I love you,' I say, my voice barely above a whisper.

'I love you too. Now go be brilliant.'

I hang up, staring at the black screen for a second before slipping the phone into my pocket. My heart is full. I feel steadier now. Grounded. I'm lucky to have such a strong support network back home.

As I'm waiting outside the hotel, in the darkness of the early hours, Anders joins me. 'I just went to get Chiny up,' he says. 'I knocked, then opened the door and he leapt out of bed, fully clothed and sleeping with his cutlass. He jumped up, cutlass still in hand: "I'm ready, Anders!" He's wasted.'

Oh gosh. He must have gone out last night. Although Lethem is a small town, it may as well be Las Vegas if compared to Sand Creek village, where Aaron is from. He's hit the bars, and when I say bars I mean shacks selling suspicious 'alcohol' and probably with a cookout (barbecue) smoking next to it.

It's going to be a repeat of the first expedition with Aaron. That's OK though, I've seen what happens once the booze eventually leaves his system. That's the man I'm holding out for. Until then, I suspect I'm going to have to put up with a lot of silliness from him and repeated phrases. Let's see.

Aaron comes out and Anders is spot on, he's wasted. As he exits the hotel lights into the dark air he's swirling his hips left to right, and pumping the air with his cutlass. 'We're going to cross the Kanukus, Lucy!' he shouts.

'Shhhhh, yes we sure are, but keep it down, other people are still sleeping!'

Aaron smirks. He comes closer to me. 'We are gonna make it, Lucy. Yes, Lucy, oh my we are going to make it!' It's like he's convincing himself that it's all going to be all right. He might seem confident, but this isn't Aaron confident. This is his auto-reaction, his crutch. I mean, I'm all for fake it till you make it, but not to your own detriment.

He keeps repeating the phrase and needing reassurance. I ask him if he happened to be out drinking last night; he simply puts up his hand and gestures with his fingers together, 'Yes, Lucy, a little, Lucy.'

Lionel is staring on from a distance. He and Aaron haven't spent time together before and although they're almost exactly the same age, there's a glaringly obvious difference between the two men. Lionel's close relationship with Ian, and Lionel's nature in general, means that he comes from a professional mindset. I can tell he's approaching this so far as just another course, like the dozens, maybe hundreds he led with Ian, but this is very different. I need him to know this is a team venture. I know he won't have all the answers and I know he will find it challenging (as we all will) in parts. I plan on being the lead navigator, but I've decided to let Lionel do his thing to begin with. I can get the lie of the land and then gradually lead more and more. I'll begin leading from the back with suggestions on how to operate but once it's clear that what I've been proposing might work, then I'll feel like I have a little more authority to better establish my role.

Our journey begins with a rugged ride in a convoy of two 4x4s. We drive across the savannah in the early hours and are rewarded with one of the most beautiful sunrises I've ever seen. We can't help but all stop the cars and get out in awe of the red sun's glow as it lights up the flat savannah around us. The light is blindingly beautiful and comforting.

After a day of driving, it's time to move to the river. Two aluminium boats wait for us and we make our way through miles of river, surrounded by dense greenery. Eventually, we get to Rewa village. It's mid-afternoon and upon arrival, the village presents itself modestly with wooden structures scattered along the riverbank. Children run to greet us and another rows past in a small dugout canoe, chasing a caiman in front.

After unloading the boat, Vivian comes to greet us. He looks different than when we met in Georgetown and were feeding the manatees. He's in full jungle mode, trousers tucked into boots, cutlass on his hip, and looks way more comfortable in his skin than he did in that oversized shirt in the city.

He gives a small nod, a quiet smile and then goes to shake hands with everyone. The team is together!

Rewa village, Vivian's home, is a remote Amerindian settlement deep in Guyana, characterized by its simplicity and close-knit community life. Rewa really is a tranquil paradise that instantly reminds you you're far from the city's glamour. It's the simple life. Of course living here is not without its challenges, but it comes with a feeling of freedom and peace that I think we all crave.

It's home to a successful eco lodge, where they have visitors mainly from other parts of Guyana but also a few Westerners, who visit for a glimpse of jungle life and to take part in activities such as fishing. The homes here are built on stilts with thatched roofs and are partly open at the sides, allowing the jungle's sounds (and bugs) to fill the air night and day.

I lay out the maps on the floor for scale and study them again, this time for Vivian's benefit. It can't just be me who has the route visualized. I try to gauge everyone's interpretation of them, and see who can really read them and who is just saying they can. At this point, I get the impression that Mikey at least has a basic grasp. I'm pretty sure he knows how to mark waypoints on the GPS, which is a good start.

Lionel has been saying a lot of words whenever I bring out the maps and points to ridges on the mountains, calling them 'bumps', but I am not too confident that he is as clear in his head with them as he makes out to be. Aaron is definitely not a map reader, but what he will be great at – and I include Vivian and Lionel in this bracket, too – is route finding once we are on the ground in the interior. This is something I am more than aware that I am not good at from previous experience . . . Actually I suck at it. It's so hard to be able to pierce your eyes through the thick vegetation, trying to spot which route makes sense and is the most energy-efficient while under the shadow of the canopy. But that's OK, that's why you bring in different people with different skills.

Vivian's map-reading ability I haven't quite figured out yet, but I'm hoping to encourage him to learn from me on that. He is certainly keen to get going and seems to have an open mind, so I am excited to explore this.

I can feel that there is a sense of team camaraderie developing as we look at the maps, and as I glance around, I see everyone smiling and laughing with a little hint of nervous energy in the humid air. I can't help but smile myself. I am finally here. Anders and I have made this happen, and we've brought these people together to do what others have told us is impossible. Actually, it isn't us: Ian is the one responsible for bringing this group of incredibly diverse, kind, talented people together.

The night comes quickly in the jungle. It is time for bed.

I pack up the maps and turn to the team.

'All right, goodnight, everyone,' I say, stretching my arms. As Aaron stands to leave, I give him a look. 'Aaron . . . promise me you're not going off to find any of that local brew tonight, yeah?'

He gives me a sheepish grin. 'No, no, Lucy. I promise. Straight to bed.'

'Good,' I say, smiling. 'We need you in tip-top shape. Sleep well.'

The glistening stars light up the sky. Rewa village marks the end of any civilization for the next however many months. I stop to take in the never-ending darkness. It's so clear that I can even make out the Milky Way. It's so unique to be on this Earth and it makes me sad that in so many places there's a disconnect with the planet and the stars because, well, we just can't see them. There's something so magical about looking up into the sky and feeling a part of something so big.

Anders has the cabin next to mine and as I walk by I wish

him goodnight. It's not lost on me that this is the last night for a long time where I'll be going to sleep with four walls around me.

The hut has a dim light that is due to cut off soon. I get out my head torch and make sure it's accessible during the night. I climb into bed, pull the mosquito netting all around the mattress and close my eyes.

As I lie in my bed, the jungle's wild chorus takes over. Howler monkeys fill the dark with their calls, as do little scurries in the undergrowth outside my hut.

I'm woken by a frantic fluttering and the sharp whirr of wings slicing through the darkness. Half-asleep, I lay there listening to it swoop and dive, the noise echoing off the thin, wooden walls of my hut. Something small and fast is darting around above me, and then . . . THUD. It smacks straight into my mosquito net. I jolt upright, heart pounding, trying to focus my bleary eyes. It takes a second to realize what it is: a bat, trapped inside the hut, flinging itself from one corner to the other. Instantly, my mind goes to those stories I heard about vampire bats and unsuspecting sleepers.

I met an Amerindian ranger a few days prior who had just come out of the jungle after a few weeks' work, and had been bitten unknowingly by one. He'd been woken up in his hammock by the feeling of warm liquid seeping down his back. He'd then gone back to sleep, and woke up in the morning only to realize that the liquid was his very own blood! He couldn't see any holes in his hammock, no sign of anything getting in, but came to the conclusion it must have been a vampire bat. It had perched on his hammock and inserted a numbing agent. Because of this, he hadn't felt its fangs as they pierced through his skin and sucked his blood through the hammock. It left no trace in the hammock because its fangs were so tiny! He'd continued bleeding because even after the bat had enjoyed enough of his blood, the bat's saliva prevented the blood from clotting so it kept flowing.

With that thought, I make sure I'm not touching the netting of the mosquito net, out of reach as potential bat food . . . at least for one more night. I settle down again, hoping the bat will find its own way out.

Our alarms are set for the ungodly hour of 3 a.m. because it's the only time the village Wi-Fi flickers to life. I roll out of bed with my phone in hand. As I walk to the hut with the internet, I expect to be the only one to sacrifice sleep for a little connection . . . but oh, how wrong was I! As I step into the internet hut, I find a whole crowd already there, all crouched over their phones, their faces glowing in the darkness, completely mesmerized. It seems that the entire village felt the pull of this digital lifeline, a surreal contrast to the remote setting. There, under the dim glow of a single bulb in the village barn, we connect briefly with the outside world. I manage to send off a drone compliance document – last minute, I know – and a requested image of me in the full jungle kit to my PR, Rachel, (the *Mirror* had shown interest in running the story) before bidding another virtual farewell, this time only by messages on WhatsApp, to my family. *Now it's focus time*, I think to myself as I switch my phone to airplane mode.

We have one last job to do that links us with the outside world before our reclusive adventure can begin, and that's Covid tests . . . Yes, I know. It's part of an insurance agreement – to ensure that none of us, or the boat crew dropping us off, have Covid. I guess it makes sense: if one of us did find that we had it in a few days and got really sick, once we were on our own in the jungle, it would lead to a whole bunch of problems.

Anders and I hover around the used Covid tests, waiting patiently for the results. 'Oh that's very good,' Anders says. 'All clear. Well, they can't say we didn't take precautions now, can they?'

I nod. 'Let's get a picture for evidence,' I say, and both Anders and I snap a shot of the tests, each matched up with all of our names.

I can hear roaring engines echoing in the distance. They sound like they're coming from downstream. Four in the morning. The sun hasn't risen yet. The roars can only mean one thing. Our boats have arrived.

It is time to leave the comfort of our Rewa lodge and continue our journey further into the jungle, towards our insertion point. I grab a spoonful of scrambled eggs and a couple of 'bakes' (which are like a fried bread roll), the remainder of what's left from our team breakfast, and shovel them into my mouth. It's basic rations from now on. Basic rations signifies that I'm on an adventure . . . and I couldn't be more excited about that!

Anders gets everyone's attention. 'We've got a long way to go today. Let's get the bags together and ready at the landing site.' He puts a cigarette into his mouth, lights it and takes a big breath before saying, 'Make sure you have every-single-thing. This is your last opportunity. Let's go, guys.' The cigarette flops up and down as he speaks, and I can see the cogs in his brain turning as he goes through every thing we need to check.

I look at my bursting rucksack with slight dread at how it might feel to sling over my shoulder. I've got the tallest bag, which is probably going to hinder me when we're moving in the bush. I'm already the tallest team member, which is not exactly surprising, given that Amerindians are known for their petite height.

To be short is, of course, an advantage where we're going. It means that everyone else can dash through the jungle, under vines, through passageways that would otherwise prove demanding. Me on the other hand, well, I'm going to have to work twice as hard to crouch and crawl when they don't need to. Although it does mean climbing over fallen trees and other obstacles will be to my advantage. I've got to think on the bright side! I'm desperately trying to see the positive in everything at this point.

We weighed our bags yesterday and mine came in at 34 kg once I'd added a day's water. It's a weight that would grind anyone down after a while and I think how important it will be to have frequent water breaks, not just to hydrate but to give our backs the chance to flex out.

As I look at my bag, I tell myself that this first leg will be the hardest and longest and therefore we are carrying the most rations for this part of the journey. All of this means there's no way the bag will weigh more than this 34 kg after the first day. Every day that goes by, it'll get lighter.

I take the arm straps, one in each hand, and in one swift movement I lift the bag on to my knee; then, using some help from my knee and momentum, I swerve it on to my back. It's a solid weight. I clip the waist and chest straps. Mikey looks at me.

'Lucy, do these bags have a chest strap too?' He's looking for one on the bag he's wearing.

'It doesn't look like it but maybe we can come up with something.'

'OK, OK, it's fine for now. Thanks, thanks, Lucy.'

Mikey leaves the light of the lodge and walks off. I sigh at the sight of his flimsy trainers. He's insisted on wearing them instead of the Altberg jungle boots that I bought. He says he's walked miles and miles in them, and that they're 'comfy and sturdy', but I'm concerned that they will cause us a headache down the line. He hobbles towards the river. I know for certain that he's carrying too much food. He's a fairly big guy for his size but he must be fetching (the Amerindian way of saying carrying) more than four times the food weight I have. He's not alone. All the guys are clearly carrying too much food, except for Lionel, who I suspect has too little.

I am a bit concerned for Aaron though.

As I follow Mikey, I watch Aaron approach the boat with his bag still on. He already looks worried. I saw him earlier, while we were rationing food, packing more than 10 kg of farine into his bag. I wanted to say something, but until I've properly earned a bit of respect and proved myself, it doesn't feel like my place to challenge them on things like that. I might be wrong too. In a way, it's better if they figure out for themselves how much they can handle.

We all form a chain and begin to pass the rucksacks from person to person and then into the boat.

I catch Anders in the corner of my eye. He's talking with the boat captain, Neville.

I listen in. I want to hear how long the boat trip is going to take and what we can expect. Was it worth getting up so early in the morning?

'Thank you for being on time, man. You guys are great,' says Anders, cigarette still hanging out of his mouth. Anders will be with these guys for a few days as he drops us off and returns back here to Rewa, so he needs to create a relationship with them and, just like me with my team, earn respect. 'How far do you think we can get today?' he asks.

Neville isn't making eye contact. 'Maybe halfway. River is high.'

'That means we can get there quicker?'

'Maybe.'

'And these boat engines. You're sure fifteen is enough?'

I glance at the engines. Fifteen horsepower. I have no idea about engines.

Neville scratches his head. 'It will do.'

Anders is clearly thinking hard as he takes a long drag of his cigarette. 'What do you mean, it will do?' He is getting closer to Neville.

'We will get there.' Neville doesn't seem bothered by Anders' concern.

'The lodge told me fifteen would be enough. We were meant to have the larger engine but it didn't show. Are the rapids big out there?'

Neville shrugs. 'I don't know, no one's been down there all year.'

'Ah. The lodge told me you'd been out there last month. Fine. But I don't want us taking chances, OK? I'm trusting you, man.'

Neville just nods and goes to help secure the bags.

All the rucksacks are together in the middle of one boat. Neville and Jenson, the bow boy, take a large silver tarp and put it over all the bags. They tuck it underneath at the edges. They then secure it with cord but I'm pretty sure the cord isn't actually attached to the boat in any way. At least they will be covered from downpours . . . Not that we really need them to be; they won't be protected once we're in the jungle!

I look at my watch: 4.30 a.m. It's time to leave. I clamber into the second boat, the one without the bags. I rock the boat from side to side; it splashes dangerously close to either side as I find my balance and take a seat on the hard wood. Anders and Mikey follow into the same one and sit behind me. Everyone else finds a way to perch in the other boat, alongside the rucksacks.

The boats are basic but clearly cared for by Neville. These are his breadwinners and I expect they've been with the captain for many decades. The boats are long and made from aluminium.

They're clearly workhorses, covered in dents and scratches, showing their age. I presume the dents are where they've hit rocks and other debris in their many voyages along this river. Although, it sounds like they haven't been where we're going.

Our destination is King William IV Falls. German-born explorer Sir Robert Schomburgk – who carried out geographical, ethnological and botanical studies in South America and the West Indies for Great Britain – named them in honour of the then British monarch and first patron of the Royal Geographical Society. Schomburgk also has a mountain at the edge of the savannah: Schomburgk's Peak. This peak shoulders Lethem and is at the end of the Kanuku range. If we make it that far, it will almost mark the end of our expedition.

The King William IV Falls are ferocious. The boat won't be able to go any further than this but they fall in exactly the middle of the range, as the crow flies, and so our expedition on foot will begin here.

Our boat is pushed from the landing and Neville pulls the engine cord. After the third try, the engine roars and disrupts the morning birdsong.

We're off. The sky is pastel pink, but the sun is still nowhere to be seen. The boat splits the calm and reflective water and it's not long before we reach the mouth of the Essequibo River. Frequently named the mighty Essequibo, it's the largest river in Guyana. It's also home to many rapids, although it's hard to imagine that right now as we cut through its calm and placid waters.

Pelicans fly low and macaws in pairs above us.

I look over at the jungle canopy on either side of the riverbank. It's dense and dark – a completely different story than the calm and open experience we're having right now.

Looking into those trees fills me with fear and anxiety. There's a reason most jungle expeditions are done by taking advantage of rivers and not under the canopy. There's also a reason why historically people didn't live far from the river, even thousands of years ago. We've always needed rivers to move efficiently and would not normally choose to travel by foot through the thick vegetation. But that's what makes this expedition special. *Think positive, think positive. This is why you're here*, I tell myself. I swallow. It looks so treacherous out there.

I turn again to face where we're heading. Jenson's in front. As a bow boy, his job is to point out anything that might be a threat in the water but it's so peaceful right now, I wouldn't be too surprised if he's sat there with his eyes closed.

As the sun rises higher in the sky, we all begin to feel the scorching heat. The tops of my thighs burn, even though they're covered with trousers. Every so often I scoop up water and pour it on to them.

The heat and rhythm of the boat eventually rocks me to sleep. I find myself drifting in and out of consciousness, but every time my head tilts back, my cap gets caught by the wind and in one quick reaction I'm awake, catching the cap in mid-air.

After eleven hours, we are all beginning to get fidgety, have sore backsides and really need to stretch our legs.

We stop at the first landing we see. A landing is essentially just where the riverbank isn't sheer and has ground, preferably sand, that the boat can dock at.

I stand up and sway with the rock of the boat as I walk towards the bow to step off.

'We must be almost done for today?' I ask Neville.

'We can camp just a few more kilometres upstream,' he says.

I'm eager to get to our camp today and get as much real rest as possible because the start of the hard work is so scarily close now.

I look down at my feet and notice there are hundreds, maybe thousands, of what I think are wasps on the ground. I immediately scan for a nest but can't see one. I peer a little closer and notice that they're acting in a peculiar way.

They are digging the sand. I mean, actual digging, like a dog digs to hide a bone. They're good at it too; sand is literally flying as they dig!

It dawns on me that perhaps there's a weird, interconnected wasp network beneath our feet.

I point at them and ask Lionel, 'Are these wasps dangerous? Why are they burrowing?'

He comes over, head tilted. 'Actually, they won't harm you if you are calm and don't bother them.'

I swear whenever someone tells me to be calm, my heart rate speeds up a little.

Lionel points to one of the wasps that are actively digging.

'They dig to either find another insect to inject their eggs into or take an insect down with them so that they can lay their eggs on it.'

'So they use the insect as a host for their own eggs. No wonder they're doing it in such a rush. They look like they've just committed a crime and are hiding the evidence.' I stare at them, suddenly feeling a mix of fascination and unease for all the weird and wonderful things that lay ahead. The jungle doesn't mess about. 'There's always a survival reason for any organism here to act the way they do!' I say. 'Everything in the jungle has some way of getting by.'

I look at Lionel and he smiles.

It's exciting to have learned something new about the wildlife already. I want to learn everything and ask as many questions as I can, and I think that the guys will enjoy telling me too.

I look up and see Anders finish his cigarette. He makes eye

contact with me and nods. I nod back in agreement to what he's about to say.

'Right, guys, let's make a move, everybody have a good stretch of the legs.'

I step into the boat, and it once again rocks and puts me off balance. I try to anticipate it this time and not let it move me in one direction. I'm trying to be slick. There's a lot to prove in this first week and I don't want to be labelled by my team as being weak in any way. They need to trust me, and the slight stumble might make them doubt my capabilities.

I sit back down. Anders sits behind me with Mikey behind him. We are all in the middle to balance out the weight.

Neville points to the life jackets. I take that as a hint that we soon might be in some rougher water. We strap on the blue jackets, securing each clip.

After a few goes from Neville, the engine is whirring once again.

Our boat leads the way and the other follows.

I've been filming the journey and I take this, being static in the boat, as an opportunity to get more footage. I film ahead, I film the other boat, I film the toucans, macaws and swallows above, and the water rushing past, splashing the boat. I'm careful not to let any hit the camera.

I zoom in on everyone's anticipating faces as they look out at the wall of forest. I film Anders, knowing this will be used to introduce him and then ask him to film me as I do a piece to camera explaining what we are about to do.

This camera is my baby, and it needs to last as long as this expedition does.

I see a little white water ahead. My stomach tightens. I put the camera into a dry bag. I've got two dry bags at my feet: one with the camera and the other with some food, safety equipment, the drone and microphones. The rest of my gear is with the other boat.

The white water is coming fast now. I can see the ripples build, churning into frothy waves. My heart starts thumping. Rapids mean things are about to get rough. I glance at the others around me. Mikey has a focused look, crouched low, gripping both the sides with his knees bent. Anders looks nervous; his smile has gone.

The boat tips forward into the first rapid and suddenly we're in it. The water claps the bottom of the boat, a tinny smack that vibrates right up through my feet and into my chest.

We bounce up, the boat lifting off the surface. We're airborne for just a moment. We crash back down with a slap that jars my spine. My grip tightens on the boat, knuckles white. I try to even out my weight, and move with it as it bucks and jumps beneath me.

These aren't big rapids by any stretch but every thump from below is a reminder of how thin this aluminium hull is. We are so vulnerable on this river. One wrong angle or a submerged rock... and we're flipped.

I continue to brace myself and I feel every slam as the boat comes down. Water sprays over us. It's cool against my skin. I hear Neville, the boat captain, behind me, shouting something I can't make out over the roar of water and engine.

Then, almost as quickly as it began, the chaos calms. The froth evens out into dark, swirling water again. I release my death grip on the sides, my arms trembling from the tension. I glance back at the others. Mikey gives a small nod. Relief washes through me.

But as we float onwards, my mind is already racing with the risks still ahead.

These rapids have made me more nervous about further rapids upstream. It's not like we're taking them on aggressively; in fact, the river almost feels like it's going faster than us in some places. If this is what the baby rapids feel like, I know we'll be in trouble the further we travel . . .

You see, as the wide river narrows and goes into separate smaller streams, it gets more dangerous. These smaller streams are often shallower, and littered with rocks or trees that cause further obstruction and turbulence. It's the same force of water but squeezed into a much smaller space, which causes it to become more violent.

From my memory of looking at the map, it's about here that the Essequibo begins to separate into multiple smaller rivers and it's a matter of picking which is the best route to take. That's the boat captain's expertise and his decision to make.

20. The Capsize

THE ESSEQUIBO RIVER STRETCHES WIDE and calm, but it's deceiving. Somewhere ahead, I hear an unmistakable roar. Anders catches my eye, half-grinning for the camera, and says, 'Don't try this at home.' There's a flicker of nerves in his voice, but it doesn't feel like a warning... more like a promise of adventure. I smile back, gripping the boat a little tighter. Adventure is why we're here.

I can see crashing white rapids fifty metres in front. I look back at Anders; he's also spotted them. I get out my phone to film. A little action will be great for the start of the film, I think.

I knew this was coming; the rapids mark progress. They mean we're inching closer to the insertion point, where the real expedition begins. But first, we've got to navigate through what the mighty Essequibo River offers us.

Neville slows the boat. His voice carries over the river's rumble as he calls Jenson back to the engine. Jenson is young, barely more than a teenager, and while I admire his enthusiasm, I'd rather not have a rookie steering us into an unknown, churning cauldron of water. My rational brain refrains from judgement yet. Perhaps this means that these rapids won't be that bad, and Neville sees this as a training opportunity.

Jenson follows Neville's order, stepping past me to take the motor.

We slow down as the engine changes hands. I'm smiling, getting myself ready for an adrenaline rush. I think I've always smiled when I'm nervous to enjoy the scarier aspects of adventure. Maybe it's a form of protection and so that others aren't concerned for me. If I smile, it's harder to let fear take hold.

The boat lurches forward again. My phone is in one hand, recording the approach, while my other hand clenches so hard on the side of the boat it might as well be glued. The water looks angrier the closer we get, crashing over rocks the size of cars and swirling into a vicious whirlpool just left of centre. Beyond it, the river narrows into a chute of foam and thunder. I shift uneasily but take peace in the fact that these guys are used to these sorts of conditions. I look back at Neville and Jenson.

Neville has done this a hundred times, maybe more, but even he seems tense. Jenson's nostrils flare as his eyes flicker down at the water's edge. He's calm, or at least he's forcing himself to look it. The boat hums with effort as the little fifteen-horsepower engine fights to hold its own against the force of water.

I can feel every vibration through the aluminium hull. Then, a sputter. Silence.

The engine cuts out.

'What the hell?' Anders mutters, and I turn to give him a look. The boat drifts, caught now in the current's grip. Neville yells something, and the engine sputters back to life. Relief washes over me, only to be immediately swept away. We're still going too slow as we approach the white water ahead.

Thirty metres. Twenty metres. Ten.

The boat slams into the first wave. We bounce up, airborne, and come crashing down, half-submerged, with water spilling over the sides. 'Come on!' I shout, trying to will the boat forward.

But we're stuck. The nose has cleared the rapid, but the rest of the boat is pinned by the current, refusing to budge.

Behind us, the whirlpool looms, a dark and hungry abyss. I glance at Neville, hoping for some sign that this is all under control. Instead, he and Jenson are shouting over each other, scrambling to move weight to the front of the boat. Mikey joins them, rocking the boat from side to side in a desperate attempt to free us. It's not working.

We start slipping. We can't afford for the angle of the boat to change, but slowly, the current pulls us backwards. The boat creaks ominously as it twists in the water . . . we're losing alignment. If the bow turns any further, we'll flip for sure. Something in my gut tells me to stop filming and shove my phone into my zipped pocket. I take hold of the dry bag that's holding my camera. I'd made sure not to squeeze out all of the air, so it feels like it could be buoyant. I need both my hands for what I can feel is coming.

Then, it happens.

In a sudden action, the water catches us and the boat tips. It happens so fast there's no time to shout or even take a deep breath. One moment I'm gripping the side, and the next I'm catapulted out and underwater. The outside world goes silent before the thunder of water pounding above me overwhelms my senses. I can't see the boat, I can't see anyone, just white, thrashing chaos. My lungs scream for air, but I try to force myself to stay calm. Breathe when you can, not when you want.

Somehow, I surface, gasping. I'm clinging on to my camera bag as the current takes me rapidly downstream. The overturned boat is nearby, and I claw for its edge. My hands slip on the slick metal as I try but then, a hand grabs mine. It's Jenson's. Together we steady ourselves against the current. I've never been so relieved. I grip his hand as tightly as I can.

THE CAPSIZE

The rapids spit us out into calmer waters. I look around, dazed, and spot the second boat coming to our rescue. Anders clings to the overturned hull, his face white as a ghost. Neville and Mikey are already retrieving floating dry bags out of the water. The engine – our poor, pathetic engine – bobs nearby and miraculously, it's still in one piece.

We scramble on to a large rock to regroup. Everyone's soaked but safe. Aaron, who had been watching from the other boat from behind, looks the most shaken. 'The first time I ever seen that happen,' he says, with fear in his eyes. I can literally sense it.

Out of everyone, Aaron has the right to feel the fear. Before he left, many of his villagers warned him that if he was to attempt to cross these mountains, he would never come back, none of us would. However, when he recounted this back to us, he said it with pride. He was doing this regardless of what others said and that's what made this a real adventure, just like his elders would have done. But now, this idea is presenting real worry in him. I can see he is questioning whether his villagers were right. He hints that it may have been a test from the jungle spirits, to warn us off from our journey.

'It's a good job everyone's safe,' I say.

'That could've gone so bad,' he mutters, his voice low. I don't answer – he's not wrong.

We really are at the mercy of the jungle now. Maybe it's a good reminder for us all to realize that we are very much on our own and we only have one another to rely on. I look at the men around me. Just a few days ago two of these men (Vivian and Mikey) were strangers to me. Now we are united in the face of nature's ferocity. This is no walk in the park, this is life or death.

We watch on as the other boat finishes getting all the things they can find before then coming over to us. We clamber in and make it to the other side of the riverbank. We've still got another day's boating to go. I think back to just ten minutes ago, before we hit those rapids, where we were going to stop and find camp in this area. We should have stopped then and there, I think.

But I can't dwell on this. We are all OK, after all.

That's the thing about mistakes, or failures if you like. They are a part of life. There's that famous saying: *Fail fast, fail often*. Failures propel us forward by teaching us to do things differently. If any of us were scared of failure, we wouldn't be here. The chance of failing this expedition, whatever that looks like, is huge, but there's something pulling us all to try anyway. Instead of asking what if we can't do it, ask: well, what if we do it? The one per cent. Isn't that what hope is?

Once on land, our salvaged gear is piled in a soggy mess around us. Somehow, we haven't lost much, just a few food items, my cap and the water filter. I'll just have to hope my stomach holds up. I've gone without water filters before when they clog up with all the grit, so this is no different. In fact, we are so remote, technically it should be very fresh!

The Ortlieb dry bags have done their job. I reach for my green dry bag, the one I had clung on to when we went into the water, and unclip the strap and roll out the bag. I put my hand inside and woah, a sigh of relief. My camera is safe! It's dry as a bone! My iPhone has also survived; I'd put it in my only zip pocket in my trousers and so it had thankfully stayed put . . . A testament to Apple too – iPhones are indeed rapid waterproof!

Anders is going through his wet kit and I see him laying out the release forms on a horizontal vine in the sun. We've got release forms from everyone so we have no trouble filming and Anders' act shows just what a professional he is – saving the paperwork. Maybe that's his past accounting life sneaking in. They are soaked, but salvageable.

'Well, Lucy,' Anders says, 'at least it's going to make a good start to the film!' I laugh and can't pretend I hadn't thought this already. Whether I manage to get this made into a film or TV, this will be a great cliffhanger. 'You wanted real adventure, oh well, Guyana will definitely give you that!'

I can't help thinking that this whole thing is a blessing in disguise. The jungle doesn't give second chances. Better to learn these lessons now and sharpen up while we're still close to the river.

'Ian is looking down, testing us. Making sure we're ready to begin,' I say. I can honestly say that it sure does feel like that.

I feel the relief wash over me as I start pulling out bits of kit to set up camp. Adrenaline still fizzes inside of me. I'm happy to be on land, smelling the earthy jungle smells. We are getting deeper into the jungle.

I'm tying my hammock to a tree, trying to focus on the simple rhythm of camp setup, when I feel a tickling sensation on my wrist.

Out of nowhere, red ants begin to invade my hammock strings, all marching in a line. I can't spot where they're coming from and then see Lionel is having the same problem. More fall as branches move above me, landing on my hair and going down my shirt, stinging my back and neck. I try to swat them away as I slather Vaseline on the hammock strings to stop them from marching all over the hammock and causing chaos. This Vaseline trick works beautifully by stopping the ants from coming any further. They avoid it. It's too thick and sludgy for them. It's the only reason I bring it out here. A capsize and fire ants. Welcome to the jungle.

21. Insertion Point

WE'VE FINALLY MADE IT to the start – King William IV Falls. It's an impressive array of white water, crashing into rocks that spans a few hundred metres. After yesterday's close calls, there was a real chance this expedition might never happen and that it was destined for failure, but here we are.

The night in the hammock was as lively as ever. From midnight to 1 a.m. I lay awake, tuning into the jungle's symphony. I don't mind as I listen to the splashing of fish leaping from the water, peculiar scents drifting by, leaves crunching under the weight of unseen creatures. My imaginative brain is going wild and I have to actively stop it from entertaining the idea that everything I hear is a jaguar about to pounce.

By sunrise, the guys, including the boat crew and Anders, are already fishing. It's comforting to be part of such a large group, especially with a boat nearby. It feels safe, familiar; we have an exit strategy. Plus, we know exactly where we are on the map. This warm and fuzzy feeling is all about to change tomorrow morning when we say goodbye.

Aaron, whom everyone here is still calling Chiny, despite my best efforts to formalize his name, catches two sizeable catfish.

He needs that boost, not just because we managed to lose a couple of days' rations in the capsize, but also because his confidence has noticeably been shaken from watching our capsize unfold.

Embarking the boat feels a bit daunting this morning. Our lives and our trust are in the hands of the boat captain and bow boy, and their underpowered fifteen-horsepower engine once again. We now know for certain that the fifteen horsepower is far less capable than the forty horsepower needed for these waters. When going through all the possible scenarios during this expedition, I didn't anticipate worrying about this part of the journey so much but really, I should have. Water is a quick killer and should be treated with so much caution and respect. I guess I thought that my role wouldn't really come into play until the expedition started, but now I think of it, this expedition started a long time ago.

Today we take a different approach and decide to scout alternative routes whenever we hit any rapids.

Throughout the day, we lighten the boat at various points along the route to ease its passage through the tricky rapids. We unload the kit and carry it along the river's edge while the boat crew attempts to navigate the churning water. But at one particularly sketchy section, it isn't enough to just lighten the load; the water is too violent and unpredictable to risk steering from inside alone.

Instead, we all get into the river to guide it through by hand. Some of us hold on to ropes tied to the boat, using our weight and strength to keep it from drifting off course. Others grip the sides directly, bracing our feet against submerged rocks to keep our balance as the current crashes around our legs. Aaron takes the lead, as always comfortable in the water, wading deep ahead of the bow to pull it forward against the torrent. I remember how at ease he was in the water during the last expedition: 'the Water Dog'.

As we drift back on to the calm flat water, Anders and I exchange looks of mutual understanding. Yesterday's ordeals have left us both very wary of rapids and rivers in general.

We've set up camp on the eastern bank of King William IV Falls and tomorrow morning we will cross over to officially begin our trek.

The campsite is idyllic. The sandy shore, warmed by the sun, gives it a beach-like feel. I've settled my camp a little further back against a hillside but we are all nicely close together. Strength in numbers.

We've dubbed our starting location the 'insertion point', a term Anders and Lionel prefer, likely due to their time working on Discovery Channel shows like *Naked and Afraid* and also from working with Ian – he would definitely have used that phrase.

Insertion point. Sounds quite military, doesn't it? Much of my life seems to echo a military theme, whether it be mentors from military backgrounds . . . or boyfriends!

We stand on the bank of a small tributary with our rucksacks next to us, and wave goodbye to Anders and the boat crew. They reverse their boat, waving as they go, and suddenly, they are out of sight. We are on our own. On one side of me I have four men, all looking at me for the first instruction – a wave of responsibility comes over me. It's up to me to keep us all safe. Yes, they may have a lifetime of experience in the jungle and hold skills I could only dream of learning, but as the expedition leader, it's up to me to call the shots. Anything happens to them and it's my fault, as it should be.

On the other side of me is a wall of dense and unknown

forest. It's daunting, knowing only one thing for sure: that what stands between us now and us completing this is miles and miles of jungle. I can only imagine the stories we will have to tell if we make it through to the other side. This thought is enough for me to snap into action.

'OK, guys, this is it. Vivian, as discussed, you're in front today cutting line.' Cutting line means cutting a way through the undergrowth. It's not like you're making a 'path' but chopping fast-growing vines and roots out of the way in order to get through. 'Vivian, you're also first snake eyes. Lionel, you're second snake eyes. Me, I'll be navigating and instructing directions – Mikey, if you could assist me on this when I ask. And, Aaron, you're at the back acting as cat eyes.'

Snake eyes and cat eyes are important roles in jungle travel – keeping a watch for predators ahead or sneaking up on us.

Jaguars and pumas and any other big cats are not normally a real threat to humans moving through the jungle, as most of the time they're likely to get out of the way. But in an area where no humans are, and possibly have never ever been before, at least not in the past hundred years, they may be curious. I of course have my own close-encounter story with the jaguar during that long night on my first jungle expedition. I'll never quite forget that feeling of knowing it was moving around me. The memory still haunts me a little. Plus, both Lionel and Aaron have multiple stories to tell about the times when they have been attacked by jaguars.

We can't take any chances, especially as we'll be largely moving silently through the jungle and could startle unassuming cats at any time.

Vivian is the first to load up his rucksack on to his back.

'Phoar, that's a big pack, Vivian!' He smiles at me. I say it with an almost complimentary tone. I know that everyone is going to suffer with the weight of these bags, so my thought is – if I can show respect and admiration, and basically give everyone a bit of a pat on the back for being so strong, then it might help morale and set the tone that this isn't going to be a walk in the park. I need to manage expectations and make everyone feel that we are all in this together, through the inevitable suffering that is to come.

We all follow Vivian and put on our packs. I point in the direction of travel for Vivian to see and he begins. 'Into the jungle we go!' I say, as we leave the few sun rays hitting us at the riverbank and go into the undergrowth, our fate now with the jungle. Butterflies fill my stomach as I take the first steps of what will be millions, and I'm transported back to being a child again.

Adventures always do this for me. I think they have the ability to transport me into a time capsule. I am the same Lucy, so confident with my identity when I am on these adventures. I am not shaped by the complexities of modern life, nor do I care how I come across or how I look. I am the truest form of me that there is and that's a beautiful thing about stripping everything back. There's nowhere to hide and I know that although some of us here are almost strangers to one another, it won't be long before we are sharing our deepest and darkest secrets, our hopes, our dreams and our fears.

It's what, in my opinion, life is about. Real, raw relationships and living for the now, which is a really hard thing to do with our busy and stressful lives. This version of myself can really shine out here and I'm happy to be with her again. My smile beams from my face.

Fifty minutes in and I call for a break. 'That's fifty minutes done, ten minutes to hydrate, have a snack and do whatever you need to do.' I find that this fifty minutes on, ten minutes off works well and means if you have some sort of personal admin to sort out, it can wait until then instead of a stop-start situation which can get very frustrating.

We sit on our rucksacks and Lionel looks at me. 'That was only fifty minutes? Oh my my.' Everyone joins his concern and nervous laughter fills the air. 'Lunch time already?' Lionel asks me, only half joking.

'No, not yet, we've still got a way to go before a longer break. Come on, everyone, be happy!' I say this in the hope there's some positive energy to peer through to conquer the nervousness. 'Aaron, are you happy?'

'Yes yes, Lucy!' he replies in his usual jolly tone. I can't say that I one hundred per cent believe him; he's telling me what I want to hear right now and hasn't yet broken down his barrier to be real with me, or the team. Plus, knowing Aaron, he might still have alcohol in his system, clouding his judgement.

I have brought a few small bottles of El Dorado rum with me, but I'm carrying all of them. I don't want a repeat of the last expedition, where I bought the team a litre bottle of the stuff and by the first night everyone was hammered. To be honest, I didn't even want to bring these four bottles, but I have to get brownie points sometime and it is good to know I can bring some smiles to the team when I feel they need it most. At least I have some say in how much is drunk as no one else knows how much I have on me and once it's gone, it's gone.

Ten minutes goes in a flash and before I know it, it's time to start the fifty-minute timer again. I take the straps of my bag and with Mikey's assistance, I get the mighty beast on to my back again. I better get used to this.

Our morning of moving feels very disjointed. It will take us time to get a rhythm within the team and even longer before we work as a well-oiled machine. Lionel keeps directing Vivian to avoid obstacles, such as fallen trees, but by doing it too often, it's easy to come off the compass bearing I've set. They spot a riverbed that on the surface seems like a good idea to follow; it's tempting to just keep on it because it's clear and we can walk without cutting line. But riverbeds are not straight lines and so the pull to follow the nice flat and open path draws Vivian and Lionel in too much. I can tell something is off and we're going off course.

I've decided to do a little experiment these first few days and so don't put my leadership input forth with too much conviction. I want to see the navigational capabilities of the team and observe a little, getting an idea of how best to lead with such different individuals. I figure I can't just go in with all guns blazing, dictating to these four jungle experts which way is best. I have my ideas and they have theirs, so let's see where theirs take us initially and hopefully I'll be able to match up my thought process with theirs.

As we rest on our bags for lunch, I break open a packet of biscuits and peanuts. The jungle fills the silence with a chorus of birdsong. I can't distinguish what it is . . . yet. I watch Lionel gazing out into the trees. Something about the quiet moment makes me want to speak up about why we're really here.

'You know,' I say, breaking the silence, 'one of the reasons I want to do this journey and why filming it feels so important, is because I want to show people just how beautiful and special it is here.'

Lionel looks over at me, chewing thoughtfully. 'Hmm.'

'If people see it, maybe they'll care more,' I continue. 'Maybe the Protected Areas Commission, hey, even the Guyanese Government might see why this whole region needs protecting, not just the bit that's already protected.'

Lionel nods, his face serious. 'You know, Lucy . . . I think like this too. Even in my village, people are forgetting. They just want city life now. They don't appreciate the forest like before.'

I frown. 'Really? Even in the Amerindian villages?'

'Yes,' he says, 'even there. You know, Lucy, just the other day, some people asked me why it was bad to kill harpy eagles. I told them, people from other places come to see these birds, these animals. If we kill them, they won't come. But they don't see why it matters.'

I feel a heaviness in my chest. It's sad that this disconnect from nature is getting everywhere.

'Well,' I say, looking between Lionel and Aaron, who is nodding along, 'maybe with this film, with the stories we bring back, we can inspire people to care again. To see that we're part of it all, not separate.'

Lionel gives a small smile. 'Yeah . . . there's power in stories.'

'Exactly. That's why we're here.' I pause. 'Have you heard of David Attenborough?' I look around at my team. They are stumped. 'The nature documentary maker?' Still nothing.

'Oh yes,' Vivian calls out. Phew, I was beginning to get worried that none of my team had heard of the legendary David Attenborough!

'We once showed one of his documentaries in Rewa village,' Vivian recalls.

'Well, his documentaries have led to huge behaviour change and inspired whole new generations to care more about the planet! It is possible if it's done in the right way,' I say.

Mikey is intrigued. 'You will have to get us copies of these documentaries for us to show our villages.'

'Ah yes, and in the schools!' Aaron calls out.

Vivian looks at my watch. 'Is it time now?'

I check my wrist. 'Yes, time to see what the rest of the day brings!'

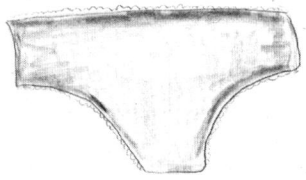

22. Going Commando

BY THREE IN THE AFTERNOON WE'VE MADE CAMP. I'm relieved that everyone is in agreement that we try as best we can to stick with the 3 p.m. rule – 3 p.m. is when the wildlife comes out.

It helps that I have Aaron here to back me up so that I don't sound like a hysterical outsider. Since we all met as a team, he's been relaying our stories from our last expedition together, and our encounters with the whistling bushmaster snake. He tells the story well, and with real fear across his face, which makes everyone sit up and listen. He is not a fan of bushmaster snakes, none of my team are, which I can understand. They all have friends who have been bitten by deadly snakes and the bushmaster is the one to be the most wary of here, according to Amerindians. They are mystical, beautiful snakes, but from a distance. I doubt they'd go in search of us, despite what Aaron tells me, but the problem would be if we stumble across one or worse, unexpectedly stand on one. If it strikes, for us out here there is no rescue coming in time to save us.

I've been asked on a number of occasions if we'll be carrying anti-venom, but it's just not possible for two reasons. One, anti-venom needs to be kept refrigerated and, although we are carrying such big rucksacks, a powered refrigerator is too much for even this strong team. And two, anti-venom can be more dangerous than a bite. You need to administer the correct anti-venom for the correct snake bite, which means you need to be able to accurately identify the snake and give the correct dose. This can be really hard because it could disappear into the undergrowth before you know it. Get it wrong and it could prove fatal.

We all manage to fit in a dinner of noodles and a wash (as best we can) in the 30 cm shallow creek, before getting into our dry night clothes. The light fades quickly in the jungle. We're now all ready for bed . . . at six in the evening.

Then, as if the jungle is teasing us, a high-pitched whistle brings everyone to attention. Aaron is the first to say what we're all thinking: 'Bushmaster!'

Great, already the sound of a bushmaster and we're on day one. It just goes to show how far away we are from civilization, or any human activity. And as I said before, if it's not the snake making that whistle, it nonetheless usually means there's a snake not far away, from the team's experience.

From the shelter of my hammock, I light up the map with my head torch and balance the GPS on my thighs. The GPS isn't showing anything in the form of detail, but I am able to put in our waypoint of camp and compare that with where our insertion point was. From what I can tell, we've only covered a distance of 1.5 km today, as the crow flies. Crikes, that isn't going to cut it. It'll take over a year if we keep this pace up. I'll put it down to first-day niggles – there are plenty of kinks to iron out. I'm positive and think back to the previous expedition, actually, any expedition. The first day is where you figure out the problems and that applies more than ever when the maps are renowned for being unreliable.

*

The next morning, I find myself being woken up by Aaron and Lionel. One word in particular breaks me from my slumber – bushmaster. Lionel spotted the bushmaster after I'd gone to bed and Aaron also went to investigate. It shook its tail as a warning before Aaron was able to get closer, almost like a rattlesnake. I'm glad they didn't wake me up in the middle of the night to tell me.

Breakfast feels a little like we're gearing up for battle. We huddle around the cracking fire. Smoke fills the air and creates an atmospheric scene as it moves through the sun rays. We all sit there, silently spooning in oats and farine. The bushmaster sighting, along with yesterday's slow progress, has only intensified the team's thoughts of *what the hell are we doing here* and the nervous energy is palpable.

I slide into my soaking-wet day clothes, socks and boots, pack away my hammock, and notice I'm only joined by Vivian in readiness. We all agreed on a 9 a.m. departure, but neither Mikey, Aaron nor Lionel are showing any sign of urgency. I then realize that Vivian and I are the only ones with watches. Ah. This could prove to be a problem. Being punctual is something I take for granted back home. We're surrounded by the constant presence of time in our modern lives from all our devices . . . We live our lives by the clock, which can prove to be a burden, but at least it is the common denominator. Amerindian time can be a little more, well, casual.

'Guys, it's five past nine, let's pack up and go,' I urge, in the hope to spur on a little more action. I make a mental note to verbally count down the time each morning so everyone gets sharper with their packing-up drills and we're all in sync. We need to be moving as a team on the same timeframe.

Over the course of the next few days, the team's time strategy improves; we're leaving at eight in the morning, and keeping our promise to finish at three in the afternoon. I'm still fine-tuning my navigational skills and getting more confident as every day goes by. One thing that's really apparent is that everyone here, and everyone full stop, has a dominant leg. What I mean by this is that we all think we can walk in a straight line, but over a long distance, one leg is dominant, usually the right one, meaning we turn left without realizing. To overrule this, I'm there, number three in line with my compass focused on staying on the bearing I've set by looking at the two people in front of me, calling, 'Right a little bit, not that much, yes that's it!' Vivian must be sick of hearing me shout this at him but if I don't, we'll end up going around in circles!

Physically, the journey is already taking its toll. I've noticed Mikey's pace slows over the course of the day, but when I ask him if there's anything wrong, all I get is, 'I'm OK, Lucy. I feel good, Lucy.' I don't blame anyone who's feeling a bit of pain. My body is going through it and I'm covered in bruises from I don't know where. Insect bites, bloody slices on my hands and arms from razor grass, and one small persistent cut on my thigh.

The cut gets worse each day. I think it started because of the knickers I wore on day one, which I swapped out pretty quickly after I realized, but the damage was done. Every day, in wet clothes and crawling through undergrowth or doing the splits over fallen trees, the cut just keeps ripping open. It never has time to heal. Nothing does here. At night my body and the scab tries its best, but the jungle isn't exactly sterile. By the next morning, five minutes into the day, it's raw and dirty again. I've started taking antibiotics, but so far, no luck.

One night around the fire, I mention it to Vivian. He's stirring the pot of farine when I tell him it's driving me mad and is a concern, this stupid thigh cut that won't heal.

He listens and nods. 'Hmm. I've had that before,' he says thoughtfully. 'You know what I did, Lucy?'

I shake my head, slightly worried.

'No underwear,' he says simply, then glances at me quickly. 'It helps.'

I laugh, not expecting that. 'Really? Makes sense I guess . . . Less rubbing. More air.'

He nods, dead serious. 'Try it. I never wear underwear now.'

'Well then,' I say, 'I guess I'm going commando from now on. Jungle rules.'

Vivian chuckles and goes back to stirring. I like talking to him. He has such a gentle nature and a calm demeanour. Even when the topic is a bit awkward, we have a laugh.

Earlier that evening, he told me about his family and how proud he is to be here representing them. He wants to show his two children that traditional Amerindian skills still matter. 'They don't think it's cool,' he says, 'but this is the knowledge we should be holding on to.'

This, his cheerfulness and attitude towards my stubborn cut, it's something I need to hear. It gives me a lift. Especially when contrasted with Lionel, who intentionally or not seems hell-bent on bringing the mood down lately.

We're not even a week in and Lionel is leading the charge with the pessimistic attitude. I know why: it's because he's struggling and doesn't want to be alone, but his negativity is infectious. He's been muttering things like, 'We're moving too slow, we'll never make it like this,' or, 'This bush is too thick, we better turn back before someone gets hurt.' Even in moments when we're making good progress, he'll undercut it with something like, 'Still a long, long way to go though . . .' – just loud enough for everyone to hear. He's saying it with a slight humorous twang, so that he isn't seen to be giving up, but words matter. I see Aaron taking in everything he says like gospel. Without fail, Aaron will nod to what Lionel says and with Lionel's worry, it is infectious to Aaron. I see it in his face. The look of concern about what's ahead. It's the last thing he needs.

Aaron is fragile at this early stage and I know he needs time to regain his bushman confidence again, but Lionel's constant doubts and throwaway comments don't help.

At least with Vivian I feel a sense of camaraderie. We've yet to make a distance past 3.5 km in a single day in the dense forest, but even so, at the end of every day we exchange a knowing look, an unspoken agreement to push a bit further the next day. It's usually followed by a comment like 'Not bad, let's make it a little more tomorrow.' Vivian's a glass-half-full kind of guy, just like me, and I appreciate it. I need this sort of energy to extend to the others.

23. Routines

TEN DAYS IN AND, I'LL BE HONEST, I've never felt less dignified in my life than I do right now. They don't tell you about this part of expeditions and, really, I don't think I've ever stooped this low before. When we think of what a jungle adventure would be, we think of Indiana Jones or Lara Croft, swinging from vine to vine in glorious lush forest. That's just not the case on expedition. Here I am crouched over a fire in twilight, wearing just a T-shirt soaked in sweat (my 'clean' night T-shirt), a pair of red Crocs that are sinking into the soggy mud and my pink knickers with my legs spread as I try to dry my infected thighs. Actually, I don't need to hide here: it's my infected groin, which in turn has spread to my thighs.

I've just bathed in the worst bathing pool yet. This one really was a muddy puddle. It was the best bath I could find in the immediate vicinity and I wasn't going to look any further, not because of snakes tonight but because everywhere is just one sinking bog.

We are essentially in a swamp right now. Bathing in the jungle can either be a thing of dreams – I'm talking waterfalls, deep rock pools and the cleanest water you've ever seen – or it can be the opposite. A muddy puddle where the only way to wash is to

ROUTINES

scoop up water to toss over yourself using your food bowl. It's actually pretty tricky. You have to be careful not to disturb any of the surrounding mud and sand that would get in there, and throw that over you. Repeat until you feel that the sweat, mud and bacteria on your body has been switched to the bacteria of that of the pool. It sounds silly that this is done so religiously, no matter what water resource you have, but you really have to wash every day. Go two days without doing this and you'll face big problems – any insect bite or tick might get infected and you might even find a mosquito has had enough time to bury a botfly egg under your skin.

I learned a long time ago the importance of consistent bathing in the jungle. During my first expedition with Lionel, I found it odd that every decent water pool we found, Lionel and Harold were jumping in; washing, wringing out their clothes. It didn't take me long to realize that they knew the art of jungle personal hygiene, but given their keep-to-themselves nature, they didn't think to tell me.

I learned the hard way, a few weeks in when I started to get a really itchy back. I'd developed a friendship with Lionel by that point so was able to ask him to check underneath my shirt. As I lifted my shirt up, it was clear from his concerned sounds that something was wrong.

I'd got heat rash all over my body.

Heat rash, or prickly heat rash, is when the sweat glands in your skin become blocked and so the sweat gets trapped in your pores, making it red and agonizingly itchy. I'd got it on my back where I was carrying the rucksack and clearly hadn't been scrubbing myself enough at the end of each day.

I remember Lionel tutting and saying it was very bad. In the end, I had to get him to lather cream all over the rash and continue doing so from that moment on. It could have been worse of course, but it was enough of a lesson to make sure I never go a day without washing, as long as I can help it.

The key to all of this is the soap you use. The best has to be antibacterial soap and you have to just go for it – scrub every crevice in your body as well as your day clothes. This is called the 'wet and dry routine' and is essentially the most important bit of admin advice I can give you if you ever find yourself in the jungle.

The idea is to only have two sets of clothes. Your day clothes are the ones that get soaked, and when I say soaked I don't just mean by the torrential tropical downpours, but also by sweat and constant river crossings. It's impossible to stay dry and the 100% humidity alone ensures this, so getting used to soggy clothes, socks and boots is a must.

Once at camp, you strip from these drenched clothes and wash and rinse them before changing into your dry night clothes. These inevitably get a little wet as there's no way to dry your bathed body, but they allow for you to be warm during the dark hours and feel delightful in comparison. Come morning there's the pretty soul-destroying chore of putting those wet day clothes back on, ready for the day ahead. All of this means you always have one set of dry and warm clothes, which in turn gives your body and sores a small chance to heal in a non-damp environment.

My thigh sore is causing me to worry now. It's yellow on the sides and red raw all around. What was once a small one-inch cut from chafing, just a few days ago, is now a sore the size of an open book. How foolish would I look if this was the reason for failure? I have to use my mind to override the pain I feel during every step I take in the day, but the doubt that keeps flooding my mind is what if it gets so infected that sepsis becomes a real problem? The commando trick in the day is a good one, but I think the cut was too far gone by the time I started it for it to have too much of an impact. Instead of changing into my dry nighttime trousers, I'm wearing these pink knickers and sometimes my sleeping bag liner as a sarong for a little decency, but I get a feeling I won't even bother with that soon. We're all friends here and there's nothing wrong with walking about in knickers . . . I've certainly caught other members of the team flashing without realizing and I've done the same to them too. The only form of privacy blockade is the hammock and that is not full body length when we're standing changing!

I am holding on to the hope that my body's resilience will come into play and I'll get over this. In the meantime, I focus on trying new ways to stop this sore from opening during the day. So far, I've tried wrapping the clingfilm we have in the medical kit (normally used for burns) around my whole upper leg, just to stop anything touching it. That was useless as it just rolled down from the moisture immediately. I've tried bandages – nope, they didn't work; plaster and tape – nope, the humidity is just too much. At least by keeping my mind occupied and taking action, it stops the overwhelming fear from setting in that this might cause me to stop.

At talks, I get called 'brave' or 'fearless' regularly. I'm asked, 'Are you afraid of anything? Do you ever get scared?' And the truth is, yes. I'm probably scared more than the average person and reminded of my fears constantly. The fears here are pretty black and white, and there's a sense of immediacy to the risks we are facing, but metaphorically, we *all* have our own jungle. There are snakes lurking in dark corners in all aspects of life.

With my injured thigh, I'm faced with the fear of failure, as well as the fear of injury. It's terrifying. All I can do is control what I can, keep it clean in the night and hope my body's immune system kicks in, and quick.

24. Sufferfest

Over the next few days, I'm able to click a switch in my brain to not think about the pain I feel while I move through the jungle. It feels a little like a superpower and to do it I actively think of clicking that switch at the start of the day.

I throw myself into leadership and have been holding two map briefings a day for the team to stay in sync with where we are, and so they can see the progress we make.

In the evening, I show everyone on the map where we've travelled and where we are and every night, I plan for the following day's movements. I have been coming up with three possible options for camp spots: A, B and C. It's a bit of a lottery each time to choose camp options that have a water source good enough to bathe in and get water from, as the maps don't show small creeks. I have to look at the contours on the map and estimate where the most likely place is for water to trickle down from the mountains. It's practically only small creeks here as there are no major rivers for miles, not on the map anyway. I have the three options because I also don't know how far we're going to get each day – it depends on how thick the vegetation is. In the morning, I share my plan with the group so they are able to visualize the day ahead. It's much better if the whole team have context on what we're doing. Otherwise we just blindly follow directions.

For the two weeks we've been moving, we've been inching our way west, closer to the first resupply. We're averaging just three kilometres a day, which might not seem like much, but my god, every metre is hard-earned. The forest is so dense. Vines wrap around your legs like tripwires and there are fallen trees blocking our bearing every ten steps.

We always have to crawl under, climb over or hack through just to make a few metres of ground. It's pretty soul-destroying if I give too much thought to how slowly we move across the map.

I focus on what's in front – ducking under razor-sharp palm fronds, balancing on slippery logs and wading through cloudy brown creeks and swamps.

On 12 October I write in my diary:

Fuck me this is brutal.

My thighs are getting worse. Redness is spreading. I'm taking antibiotics, cleaning it when I can. My gosh it's painful.

I'm not the only one suffering. Everyone's feet are agony. This is not easy.

That's the truth of it. I get it. Three kilometres a day might sound laughable from the outside, but in here? It's our reality . . . It's unforgiving!

Mikey's decision to wear his trusty walking trainers for the whole expedition and not switch to proper jungle boots was honestly bonkers. We're submerged in water for most of the day, wading through swamps in this lowland section and his feet must be paying the price.

The jungle is just wet. Even when we're not in direct water, we're not exactly moving on dry land. It is a living organism and is in a constant state of decay. Life and death flows through the forest and the floor of the jungle is like walking in a compost bin. It's warm, wet and spongey with all the decaying vegetation. The ants and termites do their best to clean up but not enough to prevent suction with every footstep.

Mikey is still saying it's all fine, putting on a brave face. I'm continuing to notice him slowing down later in the day but he brushes off my check-ins with, 'Oh I'm good, I'm good, Lucy,' and, 'All well here.'

But today, something in his walk looked off. I noticed a slight limp. Once at camp, hammocks set up, I go over to him.

'Mikey, seriously. Show me your feet.'

He shrugs. 'Ah, it's nothing. Just wet.'

'Mikey,' I say, firmer, but with what I hope is also a warm and concerned friendly tone. 'Let me see.'

'OK, if you *really* want to see my feet.' He gives in and goes to sit on a fallen log. Slowly, he takes off his trainers then peels off his soggy socks. They're soaked and cling to his skin. What is underneath makes my stomach turn. His foot is red raw, wrinkled like a prune but with patches of skin that look on the verge of breaking down.

'Jesus,' I mutter. 'It looks like you're getting the early signs of trench foot.'

He winces as the air hits his foot. 'It's all the sand getting into my shoe and then rubbing. It'll be OK. No fuss.'

Lionel is lying in his hammock listening and calls out, 'My feet are also no good.' Then he mutters, 'Actually, I think we won't make it past the first resupply. Oh boy, no we won't.'

'Hey, Lionel!' I respond. 'Let me come to your feet next, but don't worry, no negativity here. We will take it one step at a time.'

My focus is back on Mikey. I crouch beside him. 'Mikey, this is not good. This is the kind of thing that needs fuss – you've been walking on those! Ouch! That must be so painful. I wish I'd looked sooner. We can't afford for this to get worse.' He nods and is clearly frustrated with himself. I can see it: he's been hiding it to be tough, hoping it'll get better. It's classic young-man, the need to keep up and prove himself, which in a way I admire, but gosh it must really hurt! I catch myself thinking maybe I should've insisted he wear jungle boots, but I didn't really know him then and he was adamant that his trainers were up for the job. It would have been on me if he'd had any problems with his feet if he'd worn boots. At least with this problem, he made the call and has to own it. Only thing is, now I have to fix it. I think I can, just. Then at least in the long run it helps build trust – I respected his autonomy.

We get some antiseptic on the worst parts and air his feet. I dose Mikey up with fungal foot powder and suggest he shows them to me daily from now on. Hopefully we've caught it in time.

Mikey then rubs the side of his armpits and when I look to see what the problem is, he is bruised all over. 'It's the bag, it doesn't have a chest strap.' The weight of his bag has dug into his arms and armpits so much that it's created sores. He hasn't complained at all; I can't imagine the pain he's in. I give him paracetamol and managing to cushion the bag.

Mikey's not one for fuss, so I need to make a fuss of him. He's been showing a real interest in the filming side of things. Now that I'm getting my jungle legs, I'm filming a lot more. There have been a few occasions where I've asked Mikey to film with the second camera, the iPhone, and when looking back on the footage, it's clear that he has a real eye for film and photography. I'm impressed. Framing a shot does not come naturally to most people, but Mikey instinctively knows the rule of thirds and how to take a good portrait. I've been giving advice here and there, especially when it comes to filming, and he's eagerly taken it on board. Like Aaron, Mikey's easily influenced by Lionel's flippant negative comments and will join in just to get some laughs. But I see something more in Mikey and don't want him sucked into Lionel's pessimistic ways. I think by giving Mikey an added purpose – filming – it will focus him on our mission and stop his mind from wandering too much, hopefully deterring him from one: thinking about his feet, and two: getting homesick. Having finished with Mikey, I now go to check Lionel over too, but his feet look more like mine. Wet and wrinkled, but not red raw. I tell both Mikey and Lionel that if they show signs of becoming infected, we can start an antibiotics course. I point over to the medical bag under Lionel's tarp.

Mikey pipes up, 'We could just take one now and see how it goes?'

I look over at him. 'If you're taking antibiotics, you need to take the full course, otherwise it leads to a whole list of problems.' I shouldn't be too surprised that the team don't know how to take antibiotics, but it does catch me a little off guard. 'Let's give it a few days and see how your feet go. Keep powdering them, day and night.'

Powdering our feet might sound like a losing battle. Every morning, before putting on my wet socks, I religiously cover my feet with the stuff, and even fill my socks and boots before popping them on. It's all very well until about twenty metres into the hike when we're inevitably stepping in another creek. It might seem like the powder isn't doing anything because within minutes it's washed away, but I think it's got to be doing something and really it's the discipline of keeping standards high that counts the most, and will count over the long run. I try to convey this to Mikey and Lionel so that they can follow my lead, and use action as the remedy for pain.

As this is going on, Vivian is moving quietly around camp, pouring hot water, checking we have what we need. He doesn't make a show of it, just helps. His sort of attitude is gold out here. I clock it . . . I'm grateful. In the back of my mind, I know if this all gets harder – who am I kidding, *when* it gets harder – having Vivian in my corner is going to make all the difference. It crosses my mind that if everyone pulls out, I still have Vivian. Maybe there's a chance it's us two who finish this alone.

The next day, as we trudge through the jungle, I consciously make extra conversation with Mikey, so he can take his mind off his foot pain.

'You have a kid, right, Mikey?' I ask, briefly turning to him.

'I got a daughter, y'know,' he says casually, shifting his pack on his shoulders.

'Yeah? How old is she?'

'She's one, Lucy.'

'That's lovely,' I say, directing my voice behind me. 'You're with her mum?'

'Um, I suppose . . . kind of. She's my baby mother.'

I pause and turn to look at him. 'Your . . . what?'

'My baby mother,' he repeats, grinning wider at my confused expression. 'The mother of my child. That's what we say.'

'Right. Straight to the point then. Keeps it ordered!'

We laugh and the conversation keeps flowing. Mikey is sharp and curious about everything.

'Wait, so you brought how many batteries for the camera?' he asks, eyes wide with genuine interest.

'I've got enough to average two hours of filming per day.'

'And you said you film everything back home too?'

'Well I guess I capture a lot of normal home life. Make home movies for Tim or whatever. Memory keepsakes.'

'Ah right. That's very lovely, Lucy. Tim's your boyfriend, right?'

'Yeah,' I nod.

'He ever done jungle stuff too?'

'Not jungle but a lot of cold and high places . . . the opposite to here! But he's not been well. Maybe he will join us . . . if . . . big if . . . actually, no, *when* we get to the end for the celebrations.'

Mikey's face softens. 'Oh yes, I would like to meet Tim. He is a lucky man and sorry he is not his best. That's rough.'

'Thanks. Sami's looking after him. Probably cuddling him every night in bed under the duvet to be honest!'

'Sami?'

'Our dog. Mini Jack Russell.'

'You have a dog named Sami and she sleeps in the bed with you?' he says, shocked and eyebrows raised.

'Of course she does!'

He laughs again and shakes his head as he cuts a vine above him with his cutlass. 'You lot are wild over there!'

25. The Land of the Giants

GUYANA IS KNOWN AS THE LAND of the giants. It might as well be a page out of a *Jurassic Park* script with its unspoiled rainforests and enigmatic lost worlds. From the giant otters and anacondas in the rivers, to the termite mounds and anteaters roaming the savannahs, to the jaguars and tapirs that prowl deeper into the forest – even the ants here seem like they're on steroids.

This place is a playground for anyone with a curious mind, rewarding the observant with endless natural wonders. Just yesterday, I had my first snake encounter (not including the endless whistles we hear), a vine snake perched at eye level, living up to its name.

We were in a dense section where the light barely filters through. We'd paused for a water break and while I was stretching my legs I took a step towards one of the vines, looking for a place to take a good photo of the team, when I heard Mikey's calm voice. 'Oh, Lucy . . . Luce, there's a snake.'

I stopped instantly. 'Where?' I saw nothing. He pointed again and then, yep, there it was.

It was coiled neatly around one of the thinner vines, just inches from my eyeline, a vine snake. So perfectly blending in with its greenish-brown body, it looked like part of the vine. The only giveaway was its flickering tongue, tasting the air and sussing us out.

I backed away slowly, trying not to snag myself on any of the web of vines and branches behind me.

If it weren't for Mikey's keen eyes, I might have walked face-first into it. Luckily it's not deadly to humans but it wouldn't have been ideal to walk into. They still bite.

Today, we've ventured into what you could call 'spider territory'. You get used to the spiders quickly here; they're everywhere. While some can be deadly, they mostly keep to themselves, and I've gotten pretty good at brushing them off my gear without a second thought.

It's at night where you truly realize the extent of spider life because as you shine your torch into the undergrowth, you have hundreds, if not thousands, of beady eyes looking back at you, almost like stars lighting up the night sky or concert goers shining their phone lights in the air. It's easier to assume all of those eyes are spiders, or your mind goes wandering!

Being the land of the giants, it wouldn't be complete without having a gigantic spider too. The biggest spider in the world in fact!

Guyana is home to the Goliath birdeater. I know, what a name! It's the size of a dinner plate and got its name because occasionally it's been known to feed on birds, but day to day it mainly goes for an easier food source, like rodents. As they burrow holes, they leave a web as a trap and patiently wait until they are alerted to prey. I thought that it would be hard to see one but Vivian, who's something of a Goliath whisperer back home in Rewa village, has promised to show me one. As we climb a hill, he points out a burrow the size of a tennis ball. I marvel at the sheer force it must take for a spider to create such a home.

Vivian skilfully coaxes the spider out by taking a very thin stick and twirling it in a figure of eight around the hole, imitating an insect, much like he did when he was feeding the manatees in Georgetown. It's like a scene from a horror film as more and more of its long, hairy limbs emerge until finally, its massive body is fully visible. Though not lethal to humans, a bite from those enormous fangs would be excruciating.

Everything in the jungle might seem scary but really it just has to have some kind of a defence mechanism. There is so much life competing for space and resources, they need to have evolved in some way to stay alive.

The spider has another defensive trick up its sleeve: launching its irritating hairs into the air to deter predators.

'In my village, Rewa, we eat them a lot. They make a tasty snack.' Vivian chuckles, throwing his head back.

Aaron laughs and agrees, 'Oh yes. Nice roasted, Lucy.'

I'll take their word for it, for now. Our rations will suffice, though it's good to know that roasted Goliath birdeater could be on the menu if we need it!

There have been so many things that the team have told me are great snacks that, so far, I've said we don't need to go tasting. One of the more controversial ones was when we spotted a tortoise. Amerindians call tortoises different names, depending on where they are found. You have mountain bog or swamp bog. Don't ask me why, I haven't managed to get to the bottom of this yet, but I find the nicknames pretty adorable.

I think the bogs themselves are really sweet. They're no bigger than a melon, often covered in mud. We've been spotting a lot of swamp bogs, slowly going about their daily business. Aaron likes to pick them up and show me, but I admire them without touching. With a smile but also deadly serious, I tell him to put them down. The poor things are just going about their day;

the last thing they need is to magically be plucked from the earth and tipped upside down by a human.

It's quite incredible that they are surviving in this harsh environment with their homes on their backs. Here we are with our homes on our backs too – I can relate to them. Although, not all are so lucky. We passed the remains of one today, likely killed by a big cat as its shell was broken into and body eaten whole. I hope the same doesn't end up happening to us. I can't help thinking there's a cat nearby. Who knows, it could be watching us right now.

It's these moments where I have to remind myself just how lucky I am to be here. I love feeling a part of this ecosystem. There's a balance that is nothing short of magical and it makes me appreciate how wonderful it is to even exist.

Take the cicada bees for example, otherwise known as the electric bee. Every morning at 6.15 a.m. they sound our natural jungle alarm, which might be mistaken for an alarm clock. There's a rhythm to the jungle; everything works tirelessly. As I move through it, I can't help but think about the fragility of this world and how vulnerable everything I'm experiencing is to the warming global temperatures. I wish that world leaders would connect with the natural environment more, remember what we are all a part of. It's like what astronauts say when they see Earth from space: they get the overview effect. The feeling that this is our joint home and we must protect it with all we can. I get the same feeling when I'm immersed in these ancient landscapes on expedition. I feel connected to it and part of something much larger, with a duty and responsibility to look after this planet, in order to pass it on to the next generation in a better state than when we got it.

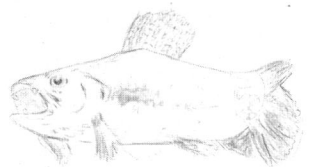

26. Wolf Fish

It's late afternoon and the jungle is a furnace. The air is heavy. We all have sweat pouring off us. Vivian's leading the way, Lionel just ahead of me. The ground squelches with each step, vines cling to our legs, and the heat presses in from all sides. My clothes are soaked through. Everyone's tired today.

Lionel raises his machete to slice through a thick vine and *whoosh* . . . it slips. It flies through the air, rotating *whoosh whoosh whoosh*.

It's so fast I don't register what's happening as I follow its direction. Then it lands . . . right on my foot.

There's a gasp. Vivian turns. Lionel freezes. I look down and see the machete blade, half-buried in the top of my boot.

I'm scared to move. The blade is buried in my boot, I must have lost my toes. I pull it out slowly, heart pounding, ready for the blood. The blade's gone clean through the leather. I brace . . . but miraculously, there's no blood. It's stopped just short of slicing my toes off. A few millimetres more and that would've been it.

The boot's OK, just one clean slice, and my foot is fine. These Altberg boots saved me.

We all stand still, wide-eyed, hearts racing. Lionel's face is pale.

'Woooah. That was close,' I mutter, my voice low but tight.

'I am so sorry, Lucy,' Lionel says, in shock.

'It's all good. I'll leave more space between me and the person in front from now on.'

Weaving through thick and demoralizing bush, I can't hide my frustration. It really is getting exhausting, trying to maintain a positive front when the team's spirits are so low. They're struggling more than I anticipated, and that surprises me. Perhaps my drive to push forward is just that much stronger?

Mikey's feet are beginning to improve with the powder, but Lionel keeps referring to his knee preventing him from leading in front. Last night when I asked Lionel to pass me the medical kit so that I could give him some ibuprofen, I noticed a problem. Half of the tablets were missing.

I sat beside Lionel, holding up the half-empty blister pack of ibuprofen that I'd just discovered.

'Hey, quick question,' I said, tilting my head, ready to confront and switch on my 'boss mode'. 'Have you been opening the medical kit?'

Lionel gave a sheepish smile. 'Yeah. Aaron's been sore, I've been aching . . . I thought it'd help.'

Aaron nodded just as sheepishly beside him.

I glanced at him, then back to Lionel before Aaron chipped in, grinning guiltily, 'He's been camp doctor.'

I raised an eyebrow. 'OK, Doctor Lionel. I appreciate the initiative, but the med kit isn't to be opened without me knowing. This is team kit that I need to keep track of and, plus, ibuprofen's not exactly jelly beans. Too much and your stomach's going to hate you. It will wreck your gut.'

Lionel looked genuinely surprised but I was also surprised. I had trusted Lionel with this kit.

'From now on, no one takes anything without checking with me first. We're running low and we need to be smart. Agreed?'

Aaron leaned over and whispered, 'So . . . no more jungle prescriptions?'

I can only hope that Anders includes more painkillers in our first resupply.

It's no wonder Lionel is struggling with his knee. Vines are everywhere, ensnaring our legs, forcing us to climb and step over endless obstacles. The air is filled with the incessant buzz of bush cow flies. These are like the jungle's version of horse flies and they have become a constant annoyance. They are maddening creatures that make it impossible to think. They are bigger than normal horseflies and hang around you, periodically landing, biting and sucking your blood. As we move, I try to lighten the mood by keeping conversation flowing and our minds busy.

By late afternoon, water still eludes us. We wander off our path slightly and finally stumble upon a swamp with a trickle of flowing water. It's not ideal, but it's something.

Nearby, bullet ants parade ominously along a tree next to Vivian. 'I hope the team's spirits lift soon,' I muse to myself. It feels like I'm forever playing the role of motivator, the 'boss lady' driven by my own vision.

Meanwhile, as I wade through a swamp to then make camp – and I mean literally in a swamp – I receive a message from Tim:

> *Hi lovely, how are you doing. Made it out today. First proper outing and event in months. Went to Maddox and consumed too much champagne . . . and it was fucking great!*

He means Maddox Gallery in London. I'm so happy to hear that he's left the house and is socializing. Maddox holds swanky events, and then here I am, in a swamp . . . The contrast couldn't be starker.

The next day proves challenging. We've been finding ourselves in unrelenting, thick, bamboo bush patches, but this time it seems never ending. Bamboo bush is vicious; it has lethal spikes at the joinings and grows so close together. It is really like being in one giant bush full of spears.

Vivian leads, hacking away inch by gruelling inch. The terrain is treacherous as crisscrossed bamboo forms precarious bridges over dips and rises in the forest floor, and we force ourselves through it, getting tied up at every possibility. The heat is intense and sweat pours down every bit of us. We're completely boxed in.

I drop my pack to the ground with a heavy *thud* and exhale sharply. 'Right,' I say, wiping the sweat from my forehead. 'Let's try to get the drone up. For all we know we might be handrailing beautiful open forest while stuck in bamboo prison.' It's possible we're following one long, thin section of bamboo yet there could be more open forest just ten metres away, but we wouldn't know. We can't see a metre in front of us.

We take the time to cut a whole area down and set up the drone. We're surrounded by bamboo but are able to figure out the best direction to go in order to escape it. After another three hours of hacking through, we make it.

At one point, I felt something heavy crawling on my shoulder and froze; I knew by the weight it wasn't a regular-sized insect. I was about to swat at it when Mikey got there first.

'Don't move,' he said quickly, and in one smooth motion, he swiped it off me before it could sink its jaws in. 'Bullet ant.'

However, just as you never know how the jungle is going to

treat you on any given day, our spirits are finally revived when we reach a sizeable creek by evening. About time!

The sight of clear, flowing water injects a new energy into the group. I feel ecstatic and can't contain my sense of relief. My spirits lift so much and I don't want it to go to waste, so I decide to find the strength to take on everyone's camp tasks, to give them all a rest. I put up their hammocks, chop the wood and light the fire, while they lay down, boots off, by the creek. It's good to go the extra mile when you can. I swear helping others in turn helps yourself. I gain energy from doing a little more for my team, plus I never know when I might be the one in need.

Tonight, bathing becomes a tactical operation. Lionel and I go together, keeping vigilant for anacondas or electric eels. You should never bathe in the exact same spot as someone else, to avoid unwanted surprises, so the team and I always keep a few metres between us. The wildlife is likely to be curious and come over, so the quicker you can be and not hang around the better. I carefully get into the creek, holding on to anything I can find as I slip around on the muddy bank in my red Crocs to join Lionel, who's already soaping his body up. As I submerge into the water and begin to wash, he shouts, 'Aimara! Aimara!' pointing at the water just behind me.

The aimara is a formidable wolf fish the team has been eager to catch all trip. In fact, it's all they talk about. I think Lionel was expecting to be at these sorts of picture-perfect creeks more often, but instead we've been in muddy water and swamps.

The aimara is a huge fish and takes some catching. Vivian and Aaron spring into action with their arrows while Mikey readies the fishing line. There's excitement and anticipation in the air – everyone is lively and full of joyful energy again! The sight of this aimara brings so much promise with it.

Vivian, readying his silencer as he's poised on a rock in his underwear, and Aaron in the water doing the same, it is fantastic to see them having fun – and also, hopefully we get to eat well tonight! It takes several attempts from Vivian but he never misses; every arrow hits it but this fish is tough and it takes time. Eventually they do it. 'Dinner is served!' I say.

As Aaron and Vivian haul the huge wolf fish from the water, it's obvious why it took so long to kill. It's more than a metre in length!

Vivian is keen to show me our dinner. He opens up the mouth, revealing a set of sharp teeth. 'That's why they call it a wolf fish, Lucy. This will give you a nasty bite!'

Amid our celebration, nature's drama unfolds beside us with the most bizarre sound.

CROWERAHHH! CROWERAHHH!

'What the hell is that?' I ask.

Lionel doesn't even look up. 'Frog,' he says casually . . . as if it's obvious.

'Doesn't sound like a frog.'

'Snake's got it,' he adds. So it's a frog emitting a distress call. Poor frog is stuck in the deadly grip of a snake. The jungle never ceases to remind me of its raw and untamed essence; I love it.

Before we've even begun preparing the aimara, Aaron calls, 'Come over here! Come over here!'

We all rush over; the drama is showing no sign of stopping tonight and I'm here for it!

Aaron's grinning and holding something above his head like a trophy.

'Look! Electric eel!' he beams.

It's dark grey, slimy and as long as me. 'Careful!' I shout, half-laughing. 'That thing might shock you!'

'No, man, it's fine if we don't touch it . . .' he starts to say, just as the eel brushes against a piece of wet wood he's still clutching.

ZAP

Aaron jolts back and drops the wet wood. 'Ah, it got me! It shocked me with the wet wood!'

He's clearly fine, and we all roar out in laughter. Mikey's nearly crying but managing to hold the phone to film, Vivian's doubled over, and Lionel just keeps saying, 'Oh you joker! You felt it good!' Aaron lets the eel go and soaks up the glory of being the centre of the laughter. He flexes his muscles and strikes a pose as if the shock has made him stronger. We keep laughing.

With bellies getting full and hearts lighter, we gather around the fire. Vivian, ever the jungle expert, doesn't throw anything unnecessary away and even savours the fish's intestines. He stuffs the intestines with blood and any organ he can find and it reminds me of what black pudding looks like. I'm happy with just the white meat and the odd fish eyeball that always seems to creep in.

The bonds that are building between us are palpable as we discuss everything from what the forest means to each of us to what we get out of having adventures. We all seem to be taking in every moment and suddenly, things don't seem so bad. I mean, look at this. I'm in the middle of unexplored jungle, with a great group of guys, eating fresh aimara around the fire, sharing stories. This is living!

The day's bamboo hardships completely dissolve into the night, marked by a communal contentment only a shared meal on an adventure can bring.

Despite the days, actually no, weeks of challenges, moments like these reassure me that every struggle is worth it. As long as we can stay sharp and don't get unlucky, this could work. We have such a long way to go but up until this evening, I wasn't sure if we were even in for a chance. Today we feel like we've reached a turning point. We are now a team, taking on problem after problem and solving them together. I'm now starting to realize that here in the heart of Guyana, every hardship is countered by moments of profound connection and stark, raw beauty. The good and the bad times come in waves.

27. The Invisible Danger

IT'S BEEN TWO DAYS SINCE OUR JOYOUS night at the creek and I'm starting to understand that if I don't appreciate every moment in this godforsaken place, there's a strong possibility that it might break me. I know I need to embrace each day with both arms and be a show-and-not-tell leader, and that I've got to bring the energy every single day – but my gosh is it brutal.

I always knew it would be like this, but I really didn't expect everyone to suffer as much, and as quickly, as they are right now. Morale is low. In the past forty-eight hours, we've been battered by relentless rain. The lack of any UV wreaks havoc with your mind. The rain has turned every slope into a mudslide, making every step that bit harder to take. Mikey's foot has got worse again after a short-lived improvement and Lionel's knee isn't letting up. He's quiet, which isn't like him – it's making the rest of us uneasy.

I think the question of 'what have we signed up for?' has prematurely entered everybody's minds. It's toxic when that happens. If I can't stop it, it'll be like a mental parasite that burrows deeper, becoming near impossible to get out. I've got to be the example of why this journey is an important one to complete. *Something has to change before it's too late. Tonight is the night that I'll turn it around,* I think.

I'm sat in my hammock with my farine and sardines. I take tiny portions with my spoon to make it last longer. It's only 4 p.m. and I'm getting used to having meals so early. I mean, the alternative of getting the fire alight in the pitch black with the risk of standing on a snake or being pounced on by a big cat while I crouch with the matches doesn't sound too appealing, so I'm pretty happy with the early meal time.

Vivian sits in his hammock opposite me with his legs hanging out and his bowl on his lap. I watch as he too treasures every bite of his food. He's got noodles *and* sardines tonight, an absolute feast, but he definitely deserves the 'substantial' meal. He has been a saint so far and is the only one cutting line at the front, which is a gruelling task. The others will need to step up because it can't continue like this. I definitely look to him for reassurance on my decision-making and can't imagine doing this without him.

He's so fatigued right now, I can tell. I'm scared that he might lose his enthusiasm because at the moment, it's just me and him who are dishing that out for the rest of the team to feed off and I'm not sure it'll work if it's just me keeping the positive energy up.

As I observe him eating, what I think is a breeze whips through camp.

'Rain,' mumbles Lionel. Lionel likes to be the first to call something out; I think he does it to remind us of his age and experience.

Vivian looks up and nods. 'Mmm hmm.' Which is Vivian's way of agreeing in the most efficient way.

I still find it confusing to differentiate between wind and rain. The leaves shaking on to one another with a breeze sounds just like raindrops falling on to the trees.

Lionel is indeed correct and it begins to rain. Big, slow

raindrops to begin with, followed by a torrential downpour. Then the thunder roars in the distance, which makes me jump, but when I look up at Vivian, he doesn't move an inch. He takes the last spoon of his sardines before stepping down and retrieving his socks and T-shirt, which are hanging outside of his tarp while the lightning illuminates the camp.

It's a reminder for me to do the same so I slide out of my hammock, into my Crocs, and take my damp, green jungle shirt off of the paracord it's draped from.

This is the cue for all of us to hibernate for the evening. Once everything is sheltered from getting soaked, we each go to our individual refuges. Thankfully, I have started to consider my hammock as a refuge, something that I was worried might not happen.

I previously thought that the nights would fill me with fear but, actually, it's the only opportunity to rest my wrecked body.

I zip up my hammock. Peace. I always find it incredible that being off the ground and having just a millimetre-thin piece of fabric beneath and a net around you creates a sense of safety. It is of course only a *sense* of safety, and is not entirely justified.

The rain is loud, and nothing else but the hammering of water on my tarp can be heard.

I look at my watch and realize it's Saturday. Yes! Saturday means music! When the expedition began, I promised myself that once a week on a Saturday, I'd allow myself to sacrifice a small amount of phone battery for ten minutes of music. I switch on my phone, pull out my headphones, plug them in and hit shuffle on a playlist. The music doesn't quite pierce through the noise of the rain but it makes it feel surreal, as if what is outside of my hammock is not actually happening to me.

I think back to what I promised myself: to enjoy and embrace each moment, even the hardships.

Up until now, I had only browsed at photos from home, especially of my wee dog, Sami. Maybe it's time to think what it might be like when this adventure is over and I'm back into mundane 'normal' life. These harsh times I currently face will be overrun by how special this is and was.

As the music plays in my ears and the lightning illuminates the forest floor, I scroll through photos I've taken of the expedition so far. I feel disconnected in a positive way, like I can appreciate what I've been doing for the past three weeks. I scroll and see smiles, adventure and camaraderie. *This is why I'm here*, I think. *This will be worth it, I can feel it.* My hammock swings with the wind and, for the first time since we were left at our insertion point, I regain a sense of mental control.

The thunder then shakes my hammock, which in turn shakes my core. The storm's intensity peaks around us. I briefly worry that a branch or tree might fall, but I trust my camp is set up properly and even catch myself smiling. 'I've got this,' I mutter.

I wake up to the screaming piha birds. This sound is most definitely the noise of the jungle and is my alarm clock every morning. I look over and Aaron is already awake and drying his damp socks over the fire. The screaming piha birds make a high-pitched *weewOH* call, which is a way louder sound than you'd think a bird of that tiny size would make, hence their name. When lots of them call frequently, it normally means that it's going to rain today and that they're cheering it on. Let's see if they're right.

The floor is sodden and our tarps are saturated, but it doesn't matter, I'm going to grab today with both hands just like I committed to last night.

I try to keep some lighthearted conversation flowing as we pack up camp.

THE INVISIBLE DANGER

Vivian comes over to me. 'This. This is why you always check your things.' He shows me the inside of his cap. 'I was about to put this on.'

He's waiting for me to react.

I look closer and see a black scorpion in the centre.

'Would have got me right on the head. We must always check.'

Here's me trying to be positive and take the reins but, already, this early on in the day we've received a curveball to remind us where we are and that we're constantly at the mercy of the jungle – it's never the other way around.

Once suited and booted, I make a throwaway comment that I've found myself coming back to. 'Let's see what today brings!' I want everyone to feel that same uplifting and grateful spirit that I'm desperately trying to master. Lionel looks at me and then at his knee. It's clearly bothering him to some degree, but I also think he's probably using his knee as an excuse to fall back on, or as something to blame if he does decide to leave the expedition at a resupply. I'm not certain, but it's what I suspect and is a technique I've seen others use on other expeditions.

The terrain is kind and progress is good. Vivian is in the lead, cutting line, with Lionel second and me in the middle. Mikey and Aaron are behind me.

I still need Lionel's frame of mind to lift. He's looked up to by the rest of the team and if I can get his eagerness for the challenge back, the eagerness I saw when we all met in Lethem, then the others will follow. It's become a bit of a personal mission for me to boost his attitude.

Lionel and I chit-chat as we walk along, and he begins to tell me about an Australian guy that he took through the jungle once.

'I always ask people if there's anything that they're really scared of before going into the jungle and I asked him the same thing. He said that he wasn't afraid of anything.'

I think back to if Lionel had ever asked me that same question when I first met him in 2014. I think I probably replied with 'jaguars', thinking that was a fair one to be afraid of. Now, after hearing Lionel's multiple close encounters with these giant cats, I think that my answer would have passed the test.

Lionel continues talking about the Australian man. 'Actually, we hadn't even got a hundred yards from our lodge when he screams spider! I thought there was something like a Goliath birdeater or that he'd been bitten, but there was just a tiny spider on a leaf next to him. He decided he wanted to go back there and then!'

We laugh, and as if by magic I see a spider on a leaf. 'A spider like this one?'

Lionel pauses and looks. 'Yes, a tiny one just like that.'

I acknowledge that it's a good job I'm not afraid of these, or, at least, I pretend not to be, which I think becomes the same thing.

We resume moving and it doesn't take us long to catch up with Vivian.

'Is there anything you're afraid of, Lionel?' As I ask that question I feel that I'm being thoughtful.

'Everyone always asks that question.'

Maybe not.

'Actually, I always answer the same way to everybody, whether it be my wife, my children, boss man or outsiders.' When they say outsiders they usually mean westerners. 'I say venomous snakes because they are invisible. They could be on a vine, a branch or the ground, and you just can't see them.'

Suddenly, Vivian throws his cutlass and silencer, and yells: 'Bushmaster snake!'

28. Bushmaster

'GET BACK FROM IT! ARE YOU HURT, VIVIAN?'
As I say this I'm backing up, undoing my rucksack and about to get the tourniquet out from the top zip of my rucksack. I have to presume the worst. I know this. I'm following what I've learned and there's no time to waste.

'I'm fine!' he mumbles, his voice shaking. Phew. I breathe a sigh of relief but remain vigilant. I still don't have eyes on the snake.

My eyes dart around to try to get a sighting. Mikey positions himself behind me, creating barriers between himself and the snake. 'Lucy, give me the camera.' I hand the iPhone to him.

Aaron, beside me, mutters worriedly, 'It's very dangerous, Lucy, oh my.' He is shaking his head.

The irony doesn't escape me; just as Lionel and I were discussing his fear of snakes, this happens. It's hard not to just put it down to coincidence and it would be lying to say I don't think there's a larger force at play.

Aaron helps me scan the undergrowth. I hold my breath, my eyes flicking from root to vine, trying to detect a snake pattern in the tangle of leaves and shadows. Nothing. Then – movement.

Just a subtle shift in the leaf litter is enough for me to spot it. My heart jolts. There it is. A thick, coiled body, dappled in perfect camouflage. It's barely distinguishable from the forest floor! Its tail twitches. I think it is angry. It's a slow, deliberate movement like a warning. The triangle head lifts and I know without doubt: bushmaster.

Everything in me tightens. We are too close. Far too close.

I look at Vivian; he's ready to run, but there's something missing... his bow and cutlass. Is the snake too close to these for us to retrieve them safely?

He paces a few steps away from where it all happened and is still breathing deeply. He shakes his head and uses his wrist to wipe the sweat from his brow.

'I went to cut this vine,' he says, his voice tight, pointing at the vine just ahead of us. 'I swung my cutlass like this, down, and then something made me look down.'

He pauses while glancing at the ground like he still can't quite believe it and is taking it in.

'It was right by my foot.' He holds two fingers up just a few inches apart. 'I don't know why I looked exactly there, but something made me... Thank god I did. If I hadn't...' He stops himself from going further, still rattled. I know what he is about to say but no one speaks. Mikey swallows. Aaron just keeps shaking his head, eyes fixed on the snake. We all knew it could happen, but seeing it nearly happen? That's different. This shit is real, and scary.

Vivian looks back at me; I sense anger behind his eyes. 'That was close. Even if I hadn't seen it... it would have been one of you to step on it...' he trails off.

Vivian's quick reflexes not only saved him, they saved all of us.

He saw it and without a second further, his reactions kicked in. I'm so glad Vivian is OK and I have him to thank that this encounter wasn't worse. I am immensely grateful to him and can't believe he was able to spot it.

I zoom in to film a shot of the bushmaster but am very careful not to get close – these snakes move fast. It's visibly angry and shaking its tail. I don't blame it but equally don't want to be the one it takes that anger out on. I step away.

'What now?' I'm presuming that we'll give it a wide berth and be on our way, but what about Vivian's tools?

'Kill it,' Vivian responds, with no emotion.

I'm taken aback. He must be joking. We can't kill it, not really.

But Aaron nods in agreement.

I blink. 'Wait, what? You're serious?'

Vivian doesn't even look at me. 'It's too dangerous to leave it. And I need my tools.'

Aaron chimes in, nodding, 'He's right. It could follow us. They do that sometimes.'

'Wait wait wait.' I hold up a hand. 'Can't we just, I don't know, move it on? Scare it away somehow?'

Lionel shakes his head. 'It's a *bushmaster*. You don't chase off a bushmaster. You leave it, it disappears, and next time you're walking by, someone steps on it.'

'But no one else *is* walking by,' I argue.

'It's better to deal with it now,' Vivian adds.

I look between them all, four men with decades of jungle experience between them and they're all looking at me like this is obvious. But to me, it's anything but. I feel this strange pull of sympathy for the snake and fear at what it could do to us.

'But it's not doing anything. It's not striking, it's not chasing us now. It's angry, sure, but it's just chilling,' I argue. 'There has to be another way.'

I feel the heat and passion to their argument, and would like to argue my case further, but their minds are clearly made up. 'This is what we must do,' Aaron tells me. This is the first time I've seen him be so forthright and he appears to be taking the lead.

Mikey, who's been quiet until now, glances at me. 'Lucy. These guys, they know what they're talking about.'

I exhale, heart pounding. He's right. They have the experience. The air between us feels thick. I hate this. Everything in me resists the idea. But I'm the only one who does.

I can tell that it is not my place to inflict my own personal beliefs or views.

I think about what it might look like. Five humans going into what is presumed to be unexplored territory and killing a snake. I know snakes haven't got the greatest reputation but they are often wrongly villainized. This is their home, after all, and we are just passing through.

I would hate to be accused of doing what Spielberg did to sharks with *Jaws* – terrifying everyone about sharks and possibly harming the conservation efforts. Bushmasters are not evil; they're not scary either. Scary is something us humans have made up. Scary is subjective, it means different things to everybody. Bushmasters are creatures who have adapted to their environment beautifully and are something to be admired from afar.

I feel terrible that we are deciding this snake's fate. At the same time, I'm not here to inflict my perhaps 'western' views in a way that interferes with my team, either.

Aaron is already preparing his bow. He rolls the string, tightening it, and bends the leopard-wood bow, named because of the beautiful ring markings the wood has on it, which turns the long piece of wood into a curved killing weapon. Aaron is focused as Lionel keeps his eyes firmly on the snake.

As this is going on, there's suddenly a whistle in the vicinity.

Vivian frowns. Aaron's not surprised by the nearby whistle as Lionel tells me that the snake's mate is around.

I'm watching Aaron with intrigue but also hesitation. I've not seen him like this, and can't hide my apprehension.

'Have you done this before?'

Aaron doesn't look at me. 'Yeah,' he replies, choosing an arrow.

What follows makes me feel deeply unsettled. It is the first time in these few weeks where I've felt out of my depth and overrun by the team. I must remember that if this is what they would normally do, then I must respect this.

I stand just behind Aaron, watching as the thick body of the bushmaster coils itself slowly around Vivian's machete, which is half-buried in the undergrowth. I catch a flash of its black eyes, unblinking, and the slow flicker of its tongue, tasting the air. Aaron pulls back the bowstring and releases the arrow. It's a precise shot. The snake wriggles in what I can only assume is agony, pinned to the forest floor. Lionel then hands Aaron a three-metre-long piece of wood which Aaron uses to mercifully end its suffering from a distance.

Aaron uses the end of his bow to hoist the snake into the air. The beautiful but now deceased creature is about nine feet in length. Vivian collects his tools.

The nearby whistle goes again. Our cue to get out of here. Before we do, I learn of another Amerindian ritual.

'You must now find a piece of dead wood to put on top of the snake,' Lionel tells me.

Mikey continues, 'It's so that if any other snakes pass by, it will see the dead snake and think that it was killed by fallen branches instead of humans so it will not look for revenge.'

Now this ritual might seem like one step too far, but as with everything in the jungle, you just never know – every precaution has its place. That's the magic of the jungle; there's so much we don't know! If that's what has been done for generation after generation, then who am I to break it?

I find a suitable piece of wood and, as we each pass by the deceased snake, we solemnly place our pieces on it.

Rain begins to fall hard and heavy. It feels fitting to accompany our departure from the snake and continue our journey into the unknown with the eerie whistles fading behind us.

The encounter has left Vivian rattled. I can feel a loss of enthusiasm in the air, which is a real blow. I really thought things were starting to improve after our aimara catch, but once again, it feels like just me fighting to keep this expedition alive. Not only that, food is once again scarce and snacks low. There's a sombre atmosphere and a sense of 'oh fuck' to the whole team – it's like everyone has it written on their foreheads.

This thick blanket of doom remains for the rest of the day. If I'm being honest, I feel it too, but I try to push any thought like this away and refocus on what we as a team can control in this untamed place. It's all I've got. That encounter was really scary and a reminder to always expect the unexpected. I know that I shouldn't be surprised as the jungle has not given me any reason to think otherwise.

We've been walking for hours and barely spoken for the past few. Even Aaron, usually humming or joking, has fallen silent. My back aches from the weight of my bag and my legs feel heavy from pushing through thick, unrelenting bush. Every step feels heavier than the last today.

Lionel is limping again. Mikey's eyes are vacant, glazed with exhaustion and hunger. My own vision keeps blurring with sweat and dehydration, and I know I wouldn't spot a bushmaster even if it was right in front of me.

For the last hour, we've been convinced we *must* be close to Rewa River and our resupply. Soon we must be there. The air is thick.

Then, a shift.

I point – there's a brighter patch of sky. I even feel it before I see it: a tiny bit of breeze on my cheeks. It feels different. This means open air; open air means river.

'Wait!' I say, stopping in my tracks and squinting further forward. 'Guys! Do you see that?'

Aaron lifts his head, follows my gaze. 'Light!' he cheers.

Suddenly, we're moving again. Faster now, my back no longer aches. I'm pulled by the promise of a horizon. The trees thin. The ground levels. The walls of green that have boxed us in for weeks start to fall away.

We all burst through the final trees by the riverbank as if we're breaking out of a trap. 'We've done it!' I declare.

Rewa River.

Wide and calm, the river glistens in the afternoon sun. The sky stretches open above it like a gift. For the first time in nearly three weeks, we see the full sky. I inhale deeply, really taking in the sound of water lapping gently at the bank. It's beautiful. My worries fall away.

No one says much. We just stand there. All beaming with smiles and pride, letting this wash over us.

Vivian takes a few steps down to the water's edge and reaches down. He scoops up a handful of water and splashes it on his face with a sigh. Aaron drops his pack, and just stares at the view while Lionel and Mikey chuckle with me.

We've made it. Leg one is done.

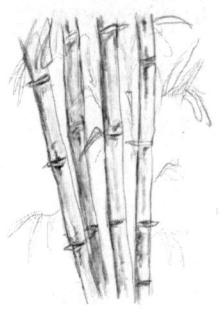

29. Bamboo

STEPPING OUT OF THE CANOPY AND INTO the open light after twenty-one days of battling through dense jungle feels like a milestone. Even though the heavens opened during the last hour of moving, it's like someone has flipped on the lights at the end of a long, dark tunnel. As the light hits my skin, I get an instant feeling of safety. We reach the Rewa riverbank, with Corona Falls not far from here and, with it, there's a real boost that makes us all stop to soak it in. This is leg one, a third of our journey, complete. If we can get this far, maybe we can just keep doing the same thing, day after day, and eventually, we'll get there.

Being able to see in front of us after days of darkness, dampness and gloom does wonders for everyone's mood. It's not just about getting a break from the shadows, it's like the few sun rays that are breaking through are charging us up, giving us a new lease on life right when we need it, for us all to truly believe that we can go into leg two of our journey with a chance of succeeding.

And then there's the resupply. My GPS kicks into action, able to work now we're not under thick canopy. I've marked the coordinate points that Anders sent through and very quickly, we find three blue barrels waiting for us.

We've only gone and fricking done it! This resupply means so much and I walk to it feeling lighter.

Mikey is first to dive straight in. There's this rush of energy among the team as we go through the snacks and find new additions to our diet; new biscuits are the big excitement.

This is more than just stocking up on essentials, these are literally our lifeline. Hunting and fishing in the jungle hasn't been nearly as fruitful as we imagined. Instead of fresh fruits, luxurious waterfalls and creeks, we've been faced with bamboo bush, bracken-like undergrowth and bushmaster snakes. That first glimpse of fresh food after weeks on our last scraps feels like Christmas morning and, because of our slower-than-expected progress, we went over our supplies by three days so are ravenous. I was even struggling to walk straight.

As we rummage through the barrels, we're reminded there's life outside the forest.

Standing at the expansive and raging Rewa River, there is a mix of relief and apprehension. During my nightly map reviews, I've been focused on this obstacle. Our planned route is to find a way to cross the river – probably by making a raft – and then handrail it north until the Mapari mountains open up. I've anticipated this will take about five days, if it turns out that the bank is home to bamboo bush.

Then it strikes me: why not extend our raft journey further north? If we're taking the time to build a raft, shouldn't we use it to go all the way until the Mapari mountains entrance? We could utilize the north downstream current to our advantage.

There are two reasons for building a raft. One is because the river is really wide, far too wide to swim across, and we also don't have a rope long enough to haul bags over. The second reason is because it has been a higher-than-average rainfall season. The water levels are still very high which means that there are still many caiman in the water. Usually, when the rainy season begins to drop off, the caiman go upstream to avoid getting stuck in shallow waters. Their presence means that any thrashing about in the water would likely attract unwanted attention from them.

The only problem is, I've never built a raft before. When I asked the group if they'd ever built something like this, it was only Lionel who raised his hand. Even so, the skill and intuition that these men have shown already means I don't doubt their capability to build something robust enough. It'll take a couple of days to construct, which means that this isn't a hard sell to the team. Not only will we be in one place for two days but we'll also cut our walking time by potentially five days if we get this raft right.

We set out to gather bamboo, which isn't hard to find. Now to get revenge on our . . . enemy. Finally it can be of use.

We all get to work. We'll need at least three layers of bamboo to keep us above water, but will also use the barrels that the resupply came in for added floatation. Once we finish with the raft, I'll ping Anders a message with where the barrels have been left so he can make the journey via boat to collect them.

For hours, we cut planks of bamboo. Luckily, this is Guyana, the land of the giants, so the bamboo reaches heights of one hundred feet into the air. Then we separate into groups. Vivian, Mikey and Aaron continue to cut planks, while Lionel and I collect lianas, a woody vine that can be made into rope. All you have to do is carefully remove the bark and then split the vine in the middle with your fingernails, separating it into two pieces. Voila, you have bush rope. It's flexible, malleable and, most importantly, it's strong.

There's something very romantic about building a raft, especially with bamboo and bush rope. It's got that old-school adventure feeling, the sort of thing you'd play imaginary games of when you were young . . . or at least I did, anyway.

The planks keep coming, and Lionel and I tirelessly tie them up with our cordage in a crisscross to create a solid structure. It needs to be sturdy enough to carry five people and our bags.

We are one plank away from having all the materials. Vivian and Aaron head off into the bush to find that final bamboo piece.

And then, disaster strikes.

I hear the sound of the bamboo falling to the ground. *Great,* I think, *they've got it.*

Aaron appears out of the forest and comes to where I'm sat on the riverbank. He leans down and gently whispers in my ear, 'Vivian is hurt.'

Then I see Vivian walk out. At first it seems like nothing has happened. He doesn't look hurt, he looks stoic as usual, but he's holding his right arm with the other.

When the bamboo fell, it ricocheted off something else, changing the projection so that it headed towards Vivian. Vivian raised his arms to protect his head but this meant the bamboo landed on his forearm. One of the lethal spikes that grow out of the joins of bamboo pierced Vivian's arm and is now stuck in there.

Vivian is now unable to close his hand, signalling this spike of bamboo is in deep, and potentially touching a nerve.

I have never seen Vivian look so concerned. This isn't the look of anger, like he had when he almost met his match with the bushmaster. This is genuine worry.

Just like the cut on my thigh a few weeks ago, this small injury could lead to much worse – sepsis, especially since it is inside his flesh. The other issue is it's his right arm – his working, machete-cutting arm. Not only does he, and to be honest, we as a team, rely on his strong biceps and forearm, but his livelihood back home does, too.

After sitting down with him with the medical kit, cleaning the wound and attempting to get the spike out with tweezers and a squeezing technique, it still won't budge.

'Can you move your fingers at all?' I ask.

He shakes his head, his jaw tight. 'No.' He glances up at me. 'It's in deep.'

I try again with the tweezers, squeezing gently to see if I can ease the shard out. He barely flinches but I can tell it's hurting. And not just the pain. He's scared. I've never seen that in Vivian before.

'This isn't coming out here,' I say quietly. 'Not without cutting you open.'

The good news is that it couldn't have happened in a better place. We have our resupplies, and we're on a riverbank, which means we have the delight of sunshine and blue skies – this means I should be able to contact a doctor for advice on the sat phone.

'I'm going to make a call,' I say. He gives a short nod, as if he knew it already. I need to get advice.

I dig the sat phone out of the dry bag and go in search of a clearer signal. It takes a few tries but then, on a cracked line, a voice crackles through, our emergency medical contact in the UK. I explain what's happened as clearly as I can.

'He can't grip with the hand, and the spike's not shifting with first aid. We're worried it's on a nerve.'

There's a pause. Then: 'You'll need to get him out. The risk of infection and long-term damage is too high. He needs proper medical attention.'

I close my eyes for a beat.

They have confirmed what I feared: Vivian needs to be

evacuated and seen to. I'm heartbroken, not just for me but for Vivian too.

I wrack my brain for any other solutions, of which there are none. I have to get him out.

When I hang up, I walk straight over to Aaron and Lionel, who've been hovering a few paces back. 'I've spoken to the doc. Vivian needs to be evacuated. We're not taking any chances with nerve damage or infection.'

'Shit,' Lionel mutters. 'What do we do?'

'Anders must still be in the roundabout area,' I say. 'He's only just done the resupply drop. I'm calling him now. If we're lucky, he's not far and can turn around.'

I go back to my sat phone spot and dial again, heart thumping. I never wanted to make these calls. Anders picks up. Once again I can't believe it's happened here, one of the only places we're able to get sat phone reception.

'Lucy! You get to the resupply OK?' he says. 'We're at the village, about to head back further downriver.'

'Yes, got the resupply. But don't keep going. I need you to come get Vivian.'

There's a pause. 'What's happened?'

I fill him in quickly. He doesn't ask questions. 'We'll be there tomorrow morning,' he confirms. 'Tell him to sit tight.' I hang up and walk back to Vivian.

He's sitting quietly, watching the river.

'You're going out tomorrow,' I say. 'Anders is on his way.'

He doesn't say anything for a second, then quietly, 'I might be OK to continue—'

'I wish that was the case. But it's too much of an infection risk. And, you're not out,' I tell him. 'You're just going to get fixed up. Then, you come back to us, OK?'

He nods slowly. 'All right.'

I give his shoulder a tap. 'We'll finish the raft while you're gone. You know I need you. You're my Vivian.'

I latch on to the positive side. If this had happened in the forest, any rescue would be way more complicated and could take weeks. Vivian should be able to get this taken out at the nearest medical centre, which will be about a three-day boat journey, and then come back.

The sounds of the boat carrying Anders is unsettling. We didn't expect to see him until the end and this feels like it's disrupting the whole journey. Anders and I have a quick catch-up and we both know that this evacuation will have a ripple effect on the whole expedition. The extra fuel cost to get Anders here and then bring Vivian back once he's been seen to will be significant, plus we have to pay for the boat captain's and bow boys' time. We're already cutting it fine with the budget, but this will mean we're over quite significantly. It'll mean we'll struggle to cover our second resupply drop, and even our pick-up if we make it to the end.

As the engine starts up to take Vivian away, my eyes fill with water. Vivian is looking right at me, supporting his injured arm; he too has teary eyes.

'Go get fixed up, and don't forget to come back,' I say from the riverbank.

'I will. Watch out for jaguars,' he replies. 'Stay safe.' As he says those last two words his voice cracks. I can feel the enormity of them.

I watch the rest of the team carefully. I get the feeling they have a desire to also join Vivian for the boat ride back to civilization, and not return, but thankfully, they wave goodbye to it and remain by my side, for now.

*

The next few days of waiting become a blur. I'm stressed out waiting for news, but soon I'll have my own health to worry about.

Our camp by Rewa River, although idyllic to begin with, with the sunshine beaming down and a sandy bank, is getting smaller and smaller by the day. The water is rising rapidly from heavy rainfall in the south, forcing us to move our hammocks higher. We pay close attention to our raft and regularly need to re-secure it.

One afternoon, as I lay in the hammock, wearing my sleeping bag liner as a sarong to air my thigh wound, which is finally healing now that my body is getting some rest from the damp conditions, I feel my stomach turn. At first, I think it might just be hunger; it's that hollow ache I've become so familiar with. A few seconds later and I know this is different. Sharp and sinister. A slow build-up with a nauseating twist that feels like something tightening from the inside. I bolt up, holding my side, grimacing. Is it the water I've been drinking?

I swallow hard, trying to breathe through it, but dread creeps in. I am getting sick.

The forty-eight hours that follow involve the worst sickness that I have ever experienced. Liquid comes out of everywhere it can, including my nose. In the middle of the night.

I'm up every half an hour, urgently waddling to get to a small bit of undergrowth to, well, errr, evacuate, shall we say. On one horrible occasion, I drop the loo roll. Loo roll is gold here. It's something to be cherished and preserved, even more so when you're facing this sort of thing. The roll bounces, unravels and rolls down the sandy bank and into the river. I am screwed. It is dark, with just the moonlight illuminating my surroundings. I am desperate.

I have no choice but to crouch and go where I am. Afterwards, I go into the river to clean off, not advised in the dark by the way, but as I splash water on myself, I feel my stomach cramp again, and turn to vomit. As I retch, I start to feel little flicks and nudges around my legs, sudden darting movements brushing my shins. Then I see the telltale ripples and flashes under the surface. Piranhas. Now I am feeding the fishes. The piranhas are overjoyed as they rush to gobble up any drop of sick they can. I'm not bothered by piranhas too much; they tend to ignore you, unless of course you've got a fresh bloody wound. They are everywhere in the rivers here, tiny ones to large black piranhas, and are the most common thing we catch. They are tasty. What I'm not a fan of are the nibbling fish. These are like the garra rufa doctor fish, found in Thailand, known for their use in fish pedicures. They are a different species here, but do the same thing; they nibble your skin, eating the dead flesh and in this river, they seem to be everywhere. I can feel several of them now, biting my feet and legs.

So here I am. Trying to clean myself after a severe case of diarrhoea, vomiting as I go with piranhas eating my sick and nibbling fish making me squirm.

All that is going through my head is: *at least this is happening now, while we are next to a river, with nowhere to go tomorrow*. It must be food poisoning from something that was in the resupply or, more likely, from the unfiltered water we've been drinking. *I'll get over this soon. The sooner it is all out of my system, the better*, I think.

'Lucy?' Aaron says sheepishly. 'My oh my. How are you feeling?'

It's the morning.

Poor Aaron, he heard my antics last night and called up during one of my many vomits, but I managed to reply in-between throw-ups with, 'I'm OK, all good.' I don't want him to waste energy worrying for my wellbeing. The team don't need any extra doubts in their mind.

The only thing I can handle eating are biscuits. I eat a packet a day along with as many litres of Dioralyte as I can manage. It's funny how on any other occasion, Dioralyte tastes absolutely foul, but when you need it most, it's the tastiest beverage there is!

As I'm polishing off today's packet of sugary carbs goodness, I get a message on the inReach. It's Anders with news about Vivian:

They were not able to find and get out the piece of bamboo. They cut him up a lot so he will not be able to get back for now.

'Oh fuckety fuck,' I say out loud. I feel like I've been kicked in the stomach. Any energy that I have left from this sickness melts away from me in an instant. I remove myself from camp, taking the camera with me.

I flip the camera around and film myself. I find it helpful to talk to the camera in these moments of trouble; it's like therapy. Only me, trying to articulate my thoughts and let it all out. 'He was like my lucky charm,' I say. I mean it. There was something about Vivian that felt like a magical gemstone, keeping us safe from danger. I am all of a sudden talking about him in the past tense, like he's dead. I used to criticize reality TV shows – you know, when a contestant leaves the Love Island Villa, Traitor Castle or Big Brother House, and everyone is crying like they'll never see them again? I get it now . . . My life is this and only this right now, and it's everything to me – nothing else outside of this exists, really. The only thing we know for sure is the only time we have right now is now.

How could this happen? Out of everyone, Vivian was my rock. We were going to finish this together.

I don't even know if any of the other team will stick by me

until the end. At the moment, it doesn't seem like it. With Vivian gone, we're down our strongest man. Who will cut line now? Vivian's sixth sense was the only thing keeping us from a deadly snake bite. The other thought that floods my mind is what if all the team *does* leave? Even if we find replacements to meet me at the next river in a few weeks' time, it will mean no one will complete this journey except for me. I hate that idea. This is our expedition, I don't want it to be just me, an outsider, doing this as a first. It doesn't sit well with me. I always counted on Vivian, and internally even thought, *Well even if every single member bails on me, at least I have Vivian.* I even sent a message on the inReach saying exactly that to Tim.

I burst into tears and as the beads roll down my face it feels like a relief. I let the emotions flow and think about the toll the past few weeks have taken on me. The responsibility for safety, the navigation, the morale booster, the agony of my open wound, the money concerns, the sickness and now this. Crying in the jungle isn't like curling up into a duvet, forgetting all of the surroundings. I'm bawling my eyes out but I'm suddenly alert as trees above me move and debris falls down to the ground beside me. I look up.

It's a small troop of spider monkeys, I think five or six of them. They're bouncing between the branches, watching me with those curious little eyes. One of them pauses and stares. I stare back at it. Its head tilts, just slightly, and then another one swings down to a lower branch and hangs by its tail for a second. They chatter softly as they swing through the canopy. It all looks like a game to them. It makes me laugh through my tears and I'm suddenly aware of how ridiculous I must look to them! I'm some large hairless monkey, crouched in the dirt and crying into an inanimate object. They're not scared. They're just there. Watching.

BAMBOO

I know I'll get through this. This is just another test to overcome . . . I look up, making out some sky through the tops of the trees. Is Ian doing this deliberately now? I've caught myself thinking that more than once out here. Like he's always testing us, making sure we're sharp by sending little signs. Not like he's messing with us, but to make sure we are at our best to keep us going. I think about it: the monkeys showing up right as I fall apart. A rare bit of sunlight just when I need it. Probably a coincidence, but either way, I'll take it. It feels like something to hold on to. It's a reminder that we're just a part of this ecosystem, that the jungle's watching . . . and hey, maybe Ian is too.

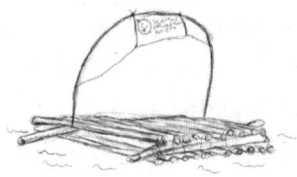

30. Setting Sail

We're standing on the raft, ready to launch it into the water. Our team is back to five people, with new addition Carlos replacing Vivian. Carlos was found by Anders and arrived yesterday. On Carlos's arrival, he shook my hand but then went straight to Lionel, Mikey and Aaron. He hasn't looked me in the eye once since he arrived.

He was in the Brazilian army and apparently works hard, so this, combined with him being fresh, should bode well for cutting line.

I get the feeling he isn't used to being in the jungle with people like me, not only because I'm an outsider, but because I'm a woman. I can't help but find it frustrating; it's like the whole slate has been cleaned and I've got to start again with building up the dynamics and everyone's place in the team. What I mustn't do is allow Lionel to act as if he's the one in charge and making the decisions, because that'll just belittle anything I say. Carlos should be able to observe the friendship Mikey, Aaron and I have developed over the past three weeks. This dynamic should show him what operating in the jungle with this team is really like.

*

SETTING SAIL

The day comes to set sail and with a last touch of adding a flag to the raft – the Scientific Exploration Society flag, one of our sponsors – we are set to go. Will she hold? That's the question on everyone's mind.

We don't have oars but we do have two pieces of bamboo that we will use to push the raft away from the bank. These pieces of bamboo will also make a handy weapon if the caiman come to say hello.

Although the past few days have been upsetting with the loss of Vivian, and tedious and frustrating with the waiting and sickness, it has also had some upsides. The time out and exposure to the sun has allowed Mikey's and Lionel's feet to heal. Their feet have hardened up just as my wound on my thigh has. The body is incredible. It just needed some time to repair itself, allow the antibiotics to kick in and now the skin on my thigh is tougher than ever. The sickness may have knocked the wind out of my sails a little but, like I said before, it couldn't have happened in a better place or at a better time.

I think we often take for granted what our bodies are capable of. There's so much untapped potential in each of us, but we tend to become what we perceive. It's a bit of a nasty trap. The brain is a funny place; it tries to trick us into choosing the safer, more secure route. While that's great from an evolutionary standpoint, in our comfortable and abundant lives, I think that it does us a disservice. We need to push past what our brain naturally wants to do and give ourselves the chance to go further.

I'm the first on the raft, followed by Mikey, then Lionel and Carlos. Aaron gives us a push from the bank and carefully balances his weight as he steps on to the back of the raft. We've got all our gear packed in large dry bags within our rucksacks, essential for keeping everything dry. I even pull out my machete, as Aaron instructed, in case a caiman attacks; I'm supposed to fend it off. Not sure how that would go, but a girl can dream, right?

The good news is that the raft is holding up. The bush rope that Lionel and I rigged is keeping everything secure and as long as we don't hit too much white water, I think we'll manage just fine.

Steering, however, is another story. We didn't put too much thought into that. At first, it's a struggle to keep from going backwards, but Mikey and Aaron manage to manoeuvre us with their bamboo poles. Eventually, we get the raft facing front and drift beautifully down the current, making our way north so that we can pick up Mapari Mouth and begin leg two of our journey.

The sun's warmth is intense but welcome. We rotate steering duties, which gives everyone the chance to relax. Those off-duty soak up the views of the dense forest on either side. I think we're all thinking the same thing – we're grateful to not be fighting our way through it. We are covering so much distance and quickly. As we drift, it's easy to see why so many Amazon expeditions opt for waterways. Travelling by boat isn't just tradition, and useful because you're by a food source (the river), it's a necessity in these parts. It's faster, and having the sun and sky in view really does wonders for the soul.

As we glide past, we can spot giant river otters playing, capybaras swimming, and caimans watching us closely. It feels like a childhood dream, being on this raft with these men, and I'm incredibly grateful to each of them. This is exactly the team morale boost we need after everything we've been through.

After just five hours on the river, we see it split in two, which marks our destination, and remarkably we've managed to stay dry for the entire voyage . . . My day clothes are the driest they've been since we left Rewa village! But, as the jungle always keeps us guessing, the heavens open up just as we approach our stop.

SETTING SAIL

Within the last five minutes on the raft, we're completely soaked, but none of us mind. We've made it to our camp in record time and probably saved ourselves five days of walking north to this point.

31. Balata Bleeders

THE MAPARI MOUNTAINS ARE TUCKED away in the remote stretches of Guyana. We are now in the middle section of our journey and this is where the terrain changes from swamp and lowlands to hills and mountains, or bumps, as my team like to call them, which I have affectionately adopted too – it makes them sound less intimidating!

The area we are in is cloaked in mystery and lush green canopies that could hide any natural secret that the world has left. The vegetation is thick and layered, a messy tangle of foliage that looks stitched together over centuries and centuries. The leaves are bigger and glossier here. They catch what little light makes it through. Vines dangle all around us and even the tree bark is covered in mossy greenery. Hey, even the air has changed; it's still humid but feels cooler, like it's flowing in and out of the trees and plants, which of course, it is.

There's an obvious difference between here and where we set sail on our raft. It's far more biodiverse. On the last leg, it felt like we were in one thick bush, with just bushmasters for company. Here, I can almost feel the forest like one living and breathing being. There's also a sense that the stories passed down through generations surround us. Each tree, river and cliff face holds a whisper of the past. This is helped by the fact that Aaron and Lionel keep telling me stories their elders told them when they were younger.

Not far from where we arrived on the raft, we pass what would have been an old camp settlement. The untrained eye wouldn't be able to spot it; I certainly found it hard to. Lionel stops and points. 'This used to be a balata camp,' he says, almost casually. 'Balata bleeders stayed here. Long, long time ago, maybe late 1800s, early 1900s. They come to tap the bullet trees.'

Balata bleeders were the people who harvested the latex from the wood of balata trees, also known as bullet trees or rubber trees. Often these people were indigenous Amerindians and it is estimated that almost half of the indigenous male population were hired as balata bleeders by the 1930s. This boosted the economy for Guyana as it was a sought-after commodity. There was a high demand for rubber in the industrial revolution and motor industry but the work was brutal. People were often coerced into working as bleeders in poor conditions and men would toil in the forest for months at a time. The bleeders would not cut the trees down but slice them and make a V shape. This would make the tree bleed a white, milky liquid that they'd collect. After a few minutes the tree would essentially clot up and be otherwise unharmed.

It makes sense that there's evidence of the bleeders' presence here. We're by the river and due to the heavy weight of the latex, the balata bleeders could only go a few days away from each major river as they transported the latex back to civilization on boats. That's why once you go further into the forest and weeks away from rivers, there's no sign of any human activity – it's just too far from the water. It will be interesting to see if there are untouched balata trees where we are headed.

Aaron tells me that if there was a balata tree in the area

bleeders were operating in, they would have found it. Lionel then points out a towering balata tree just near to where we stand; its bark is weathered and rugged, and I can spot old scars some ten metres up. Those scars would have been below my height at the time of bleeding. Lionel stops to bleed it to demonstrate, using his machete to make precise cuts that release the thick, milky latex. The sap cries down, resembling something once that was so valuable to this country, a resource these trees have provided for generations. The quest for rubber catapulted the indigenous population into a global industry and some say that this really disrupted the indigenous communities' cultural practices and way of life.

The story of balata, like so many elements of our 'modern' discoveries, began long before the West claimed its existence. This rich, rubber-like material was not a newfound resource; it was already embedded in the fabric of indigenous life. These communities were of course the original stewards of the forests and had been tapping into the versatile properties of balata far beyond the memory of any colonial record. Yet as we so frequently see, our historical accounts often commence at the point of Western intervention. It's a glaring reminder of how the world too often overlooks the wisdom of indigenous peoples, assuming that the beginning of 'our' story marks the start of 'the' story. There are so many health practices and even 'fads' that come into our modern lives as if they are brand-new and new research has proved it, but if you look a little closer, I bet you'll see that historically indigenous people did these.

This land, like many others with ancient histories, carries lessons that we have yet to fully appreciate or understand. For example, how my team look at the world. Indigenous communities have long embraced a relationship with nature that is both sustainable and symbiotic, recognizing the intrinsic value of biodiversity long before such terms entered the global vocabulary. As we face some of the world's most daunting challenges to date, from climate change to the loss of biodiversity, I think we would do well to take a leaf out of their playbook. The profound connection to the environment might just hold the secrets to overcoming these crises, offering us a path forward that respects and preserves the natural world we all depend on.

With that thought, we leave the balata tree and begin making camp. Tomorrow, we officially start leg two of our journey.

32. Marksmen

I WAKE UP STILL SMILING AFTER such a successful raft journey. Maybe leg two is going to be different.

Our day begins early – packing up camp and setting off by 7.30 a.m. Lionel's at the front, machete in hand, leading the way with an actual spring in his step that I haven't seen before.

He turns back briefly and grins. 'Let's go, man! This is nice now: clean bush, clean air, nothing like the last leg,' he says, swiping through a hanging vine with flair. Carlos chuckles behind me.

Lionel pauses and looks back at us. 'We gonna make good time today, I can feel it. Let's catch a fish and make a pepper pot tonight!'

Who is this and what have they done with Lionel?! He's got a new-found energy! Perhaps he's trying to impress Carlos and suggest he's been like this all the way?

Where was this when we needed it in leg one? It would have given Vivian some much-needed respite. Oh well, it's very welcome now and I appreciate everyone's enthusiasm.

Lionel moves efficiently, his machete swinging rhythmically, cutting through vines with effortless precision. Behind him is Carlos, and to my relief, he's proving good at following my compass directions and not questioning my ability. It's just a small victory but one that gives me a little boost. It's like the whole team wants to show Carlos that we're the real deal, me included. As usual, I'm third in line and for the first time, I'm feeling the pace, but I'm not complaining... We're flying, moving faster than we have in days or really, the entire trip. It's a beautiful feeling seeing the light filtering through the canopy and the path ahead not looking like the usual messy bush to problem-solve through.

In my head I say, *And we're back!* It's great not to be sick any more. I couldn't have imagined carrying this 35 kg rucksack a couple of days ago! But here we are, back in the embrace of the forest, and for now, it feels kind. Lionel keeps saying 'for now' in his calm, knowing tone, which feels more like a warning than reassurance. Still, the terrain surprises us and I'm thankful to the jungle. It's flat, the brush is sparse, and the oppressive and claustrophobic density that defined the first leg of the journey seems to have lifted, if only temporarily. We take full advantage of this rare mercy and I find myself not wanting to upset delicate mother nature. I've even taken off the gloves I was wearing during the first leg; I feel confident that my senses are getting on the same page as the jungle and I want to feel the earth on the palms of my hands and the bark as I hoist myself up and over trees.

And as predicted, all good things must come to an end. We hit a creek.

It's big. Wider and deeper than anything we've encountered so far. The water is dark and murky, the surface broken by clusters of floating vegetation. Aaron looks at it and points: 'Electric eels.' There are three of them.

The electric eels in Guyana are not ones to mess with. There's recently been a new species discovered, capable of giving a shock of more than 800 volts! That's three times more power than our home power points . . . I know Aaron is quite used to getting the odd shock to top up his adrenaline, but it's not something I fancy . . . especially if it gets you in the chest. There's also a smaller caiman lurking on the bank, suggesting there could be more underneath the water. Because we're not far from the main river, there could even be some black caiman. With all these nasties, it would be great if I could just look at the map and say we find a way around, but I know that crossing it is non-negotiable.

Stepping into the water with our packs means everything will get soaked and weigh down our bags. Aaron, ever the problem-solver, suggests using the rope to ferry the gear across. But first, we have to get the rope to the other side.

'I'll just climb a tree,' Aaron says casually.

I assume he means climbing low to cut a tree for a makeshift bridge. But no. He looks up, gauges the height of a massive tree leaning over the creek, and starts climbing like it's nothing. He's wearing wellington boots for goodness' sake! Higher and higher he goes, his wellies somehow gripping the bark. He must be up a good twenty metres or more. My heart clenches as I watch him ascend with the agility of a monkey, the drop below him getting larger and larger. He seems to have suddenly got a burst of his old self back. He's a whole different person and it's like he's embodied his younger self, both in confidence and in physicality.

'Aaron!' I call, half in awe, half in panic. 'You don't need to go that high!'

But he's already there, his silhouette a tiny figure against the green expanse. My mouth is dry, my heart pounding in my chest, but he makes it across, somehow. I'm impressed! He stands on the far side, shouting for us to toss the rope. If we can get the rope across, we can use a pulley system to pull the bags over the water without them being submerged, and then use the rope to safely pull ourselves across quickly, without splashing and attracting the nasties.

Easier said than done. Mikey takes the first attempt, but his throws barely make it past the bank. Lionel and Carlos, watching the scene, shrug and opt for the wet route instead, a little further upstream. With machetes in hand, they wade into the creek, using long sticks to probe for anacondas or anything else lurking in the depths.

'When you reach the other side, drop your bags and start to cut trail while we catch up!' I shout.

They nod and get to work, while Aaron cheers Mikey on. Finally, we manage to get the rope across using a fishing line that we throw first. The bags follow, attached to the bush rope, bobbing slightly in the water but making it to the other side mostly unscathed.

Now it's our turn.

I brace myself and slide into the deep water. The coolness shocks my overheated and itchy skin, but to be honest, it feels lovely! Every second we move through this jungle, I crave to be submerged in water to wash away the ticks and tree dust... Oh to be clean! I move quickly, pulling myself along the rope with my eyes fixed on Aaron. I'm not looking around, I don't need to worry myself with how close the eels are. The jungle really makes you act on your instincts. It's something we lose so easily in our modern world; in fact, we really lose touch with ourselves with all the distractions. We get so used to having every need met effortlessly, and our instincts become obsolete. But here, instincts are what keep you alive. Every instinct screams at me to hurry as I imagine caimans gliding silently below or an electric eel ready to jolt me. My hands grip the rope tightly, the muscles in my arms straining as I reach the far bank.

Mikey's crossing, on the other hand, is a spectacle. He tries to gracefully slide in but instead makes a giant splash and in the process loses his cap. 'Your cap, your cap!' Aaron shouts. 'Never leave your cap behind!' It sounds like a throwaway comment, but he has a point. Caps are very useful in the thick bush because they prevent little insects and flesh-burrowing creatures that fall from the vegetation getting on your head, and into your skin.

Mikey grabs his hat and Aaron, with a grin, pulls him along the rope like he's towing an otter. Mikey flails slightly but manages to hold on. 'This is not fish, this is human!' Aaron laughs, breaking the tension. We're across and it's like Aaron has crossed some sort of a threshold. What a transformation.

We press on, energized by the puzzle of the day . . . In a way it was fun, but so time-consuming and we definitely don't want any more of those today.

As we approach our camp for the night, the landscape opens up. It's a flat expanse next to a narrow stream, and looks like a seasonal flooding area. Trees are sparsely dispersed. Great for moving through, but Lionel takes off his bag and comes to address everyone: 'This is prime big-cat territory, look—' He points to a tree that has several claw marks on the bark. 'Marking their territory.'

'Do you think it's safe to stop here?' I ask.

'Well actually, they won't be able to surprise us. We'll hear them moving through these dry leaves.' Somehow, that feels comforting.

Later, Mikey and Aaron sit behind me at camp. I'm writing my journal in my hammock when I pause to listen. Mikey, ever patient, is teaching Aaron how to use the GPS, explaining how the arrow on the screen points the way. It's a tender scene, and cross-generational. It's funny to think of Aaron learning a new use for an arrow, even if it's in digital form. It's nice to see Mikey feeling empowered to pass on his tech knowledge and Aaron is soaking it up in the moment, but I'm not sure how much is going in.

We settle into the familiar rhythm of the evening. Dinner is, predictably, sardines and farine. Lionel, with his usual dry humour, speaks to himself as he's rustling through his ration pack: 'What flavour noodles today? Chicken?' as if we have an endless menu to choose from. His comment gets a chuckle out of me, even though my body feels like it's ready to collapse. Food is food – well, food is fuel!

I get a message from Anders: Vivian is healing well and should join for the final leg. It feels like a promise of positive things to come.

Lying in my hammock, I reflect on the day. Each step brings us closer to the end of this journey, and the thought stirs conflicting emotions. I'll miss this life, chaotic as it is. The jungle has a way of seeping into your soul. For now, though, I let the jungle's hum lull me to sleep, grateful for the small triumphs of the day and on guard in case I hear the sound of paw prints on dry leaves.

The next day, exhaustion drapes over us like a humid, unshakable fog. Every muscle protests as we trudge through the terrain, but at least today's ground is kinder, firm and forgiving, allowing us to cover more distance than usual.

We've stopped for a water break when Lionel turns to Mikey. 'You take the lead?' he says, gesturing ahead with his cutlass. 'Go on, big man. Take front.'

'Yes, Lionel,' Mikey says, adjusting his pack. He's clearly flattered, maybe even excited, but I can sense some nerves behind his eyes. I can't deny a knot of unease tightening in my stomach. I love Mikey, but he's not a bushman in the way Vivian, Lionel or Aaron are.

I step closer, voicing my concerns. 'Are we sure this is a good idea, guys?'

Lionel shrugs. 'Big man got to learn somehow.'

I hesitate. 'Mikey, seriously, if it gets thicker than it is now, stop. Aaron or Lionel can take the lead again.' I say Aaron or Lionel because I know they're actively looking for threats and potential dangers in every direction; it's a skill and takes a long time to learn. What if Mikey had been leading the day of the bushmaster? We may not have spotted it.

He gives a quick nod. 'I'm good, I'm good, Lucy,' he says. He's trying to play it cool but I notice the stiffness in his posture as he walks ahead. I don't know if Mikey is ready, but Lionel is right, he's got to get used to the responsibility somehow . . . I'm just not sure if now is the best time to put that to the test.

We move like a loose train, single file, the sound of each step muffled by the leaf litter. I can't shake the unease.

The jungle feels alive today, buzzing with an energy that is almost tangible. The air carries an earthy, damp smell, mingled with the sweetness of warm, overripe fruit decaying somewhere unseen. Vines hang like curtains and shafts of sunlight break through the canopy in golden beams, lighting up pockets of emerald green.

We're moving steadily when a shout, sharp and urgent, splits the air.

'Wasps!'

I don't know who said it. I freeze for half a second, then instinct takes over. Aaron and I sprint back the way we came, but it's already too late. They're aware of us and before we know it, they're following us. A black cloud and loud buzz fills the air.

These aren't just any wasps; they're marksmen wasps. They don't just sting; they aim. You see, there are a few different types of wasps in the jungle and you really need to know them. We're constantly coming across wasp nests and they're devilishly difficult to spot, like most things in this dense jungle. Every leaf and branch is laden with some sort of life here and wasp nests are the most common occurrence – they seamlessly blend into their surroundings. The nests often look like extensions of the trees or leaves themselves, and can even be inconspicuous mounds on the forest floor.

Up to now, the wasps we've been spotting are the ones where you might disturb the nest; you freeze, they swarm you and maybe sting you a little, but after a few seconds they leave you alone. Then there's another type of wasp when you run as fast as you can – these wasps look exactly the same (to me anyway) as the former wasp.

These wasps we've just disturbed, though, are not the type where you freeze – instead, you leg it.

They're known to hunt you down and keep swarming you for a mile, essentially to get you as far away as possible from their nest.

Zing, zing, zing! The first sting is sharp and electric, landing on my head. Then another, a searing jab on my neck. My ears burn as if they've been lit on fire. Stings rain down on my arms, back and elbow. The pain is intense and unrelenting.

We run as fast as the uneven terrain allows, dodging roots, vines and low branches. The wasps chase us, their angry hum filling the air as I try my best to cover my throat and eyes, but I can feel them getting stuck in my hair. When you try to rush in the jungle, it works against you, at least for the non-Amerindian. Being tall gives absolutely no advantages here. A vine catches on my bag. I'm stuck as the wasps continue to swarm me. I shout to Aaron. If I take off my bag to free myself, they'll swarm my back and things could get really bad. Aaron, the hero that he is, hears my call and, with his cap placed over his neck, he turns back to me. He takes one clean slice of the vine I'm attached to with his machete, freeing me. We both continue to move as fast as possible.

After a few minutes, the wasps finally retreat. We're far enough away from their nest now. 'I think we're good,' I say to Aaron. He looks around and nods. We allow ourselves to pause, panting with our hands on our knees. The adrenaline did its job!

There's also another type of wasp to be aware of, which is hard to miss: the tarantula hawk wasp. This wasp is huge, two-and-a-half inches long, so it's not one you want to mess with. As the name suggests, it hunts tarantulas and has one of the most potent (painful!) stings in the world, only beaten by the infamous bullet ant. We've already seen some on the forest floor dragging their prey to their burrow.

They have striking blue-black bodies and the way they hunt the tarantulas is truly something else . . . Get this: they divebomb the spiders and sting in-between their legs, which paralyses the spider. It then drags its immobilized eight-legged meal to its burrow, lays a single egg on it and then seals the entrance to the self-made larder. The egg then hatches into a larva that eats the still-living tarantula from the inside out. It even carefully avoids the vital organs to keep it fresh as long as possible – nature is incredible! This grim nursery tale ends with the larva hatching and eventually emerging as an adult wasp. Now tell me that isn't impressive! Thankfully the tarantula hawk wasps don't work in swarms and are lonesome wasps; they're also not really bothered by humans and won't attack unless you get really unlucky.

Aaron's face squirms in pain. My own skin feels like it's crawling with fire. Sharp, electric pulses run across my scalp. I grit my teeth, trying to stay calm, to not give in to the panic knocking at the edge of my chest. I try to control my breathing, pushing the ever-present element of 'what if it leads to anaphylactic shock' out of my head.

We regroup with the others, who haven't fared much better.

'I still feel like I'm being stung,' I say, trying not to scratch at my scalp. 'Lionel, is there one still on my head?'

He leans in, squinting as he parts my tangled, sweat-drenched hair. 'Oh . . . there are hundreds. Hundreds.'

I give a nervous laugh. I'm feeling the heat rise to my face as Lionel searches through my hair, while at the same time I crouch by my pack looking for antihistamines. My fingers are clumsy as I fumble around in my bag. My head throbs.

Aaron hunches over, wincing. 'Very painful Lucy,' he says, sympathizing. 'Very, very painful.'

Lionel squeezes at something in my hair, then another. He lets out a low chuckle, shaking his head. 'They can be the real marksmen, those ones. They just go for you. You can be a mile away and then *whoosh*. They get you. Got me all on my bald head here.' He gestures with an exaggerated rub of his scalp. I finally find the tablets and toss a couple into my mouth. 'There's going to be a lot of swelling on my head, I think,' I say through gritted teeth, already leaning over my open bag, searching for water to wash them down.

'Normal day. Normal Amerindian stuff,' Lionel says. He's right, it's just another moment to learn from, but I can't help feeling frustrated that it came to this. I want to give everyone more responsibility, of course, but not at the expense of safety.

What happened wasn't down to bad luck, not really. It was avoidable. An experienced bushman – like Lionel or Carlos or Aaron – knows how to read the signs, how to move through the jungle carefully, scanning not just for where *they* are stepping, but for what their movement might disturb for those following.

Mikey doesn't yet have that awareness. It's not his fault exactly, but it *was* his lead. And we all paid the price.

I suspect Lionel handed him the lead not because Mikey was ready, but because Lionel didn't fancy being upfront any more, cutting line.

'All right,' I say, half to Mikey, half to everyone, 'from tomorrow, I'm going to reshuffle the order. I want either Carlos, Lionel or Aaron up in front.'

Mikey looks at me, caught off guard. 'Wait, why?'

'It's just . . . this proved we've got – I just think this might not have happened if we'd had more experienced eyes up front . . .' I say.

Mikey doesn't argue. Just nods slowly, jaw tight. 'Yeah. Fair enough.'

I keep my voice level. 'This isn't about blame. It's obvious you didn't want that to happen! But I need you with me for a while with the camera, it makes sense to be near me. You're getting so good with it! Cameraman Mikey.'

He gives me a half-smile. 'Guess I've got a new job then.'

'You're a born natural!' I say, smiling back. 'And don't worry, you'll be leading again soon enough. Just need to ease into it.'

Lionel stretches, wincing from a sting on his arm. 'Well, at least now you know what it's like,' he says to Mikey, with a grin that's only half a tease.

Aaron just grunts in agreement. Carlos gives him a pat on the back.

Today has really shown how the jungle offers no sympathy! It's exhausting but it's what we signed up for. We push on, sweat slicking our bodies as the afternoon heat intensifies. I have my eyes on the clock: 2 p.m. I get the feeling that bushmasters will make themselves known soon enough with the way this day is going.

33. Bush Cow

For fuck's sake, I can't wait to feel safe again. After one of the mini creeks we kept passing we stopped for a water break like we normally do; there were some nice inviting rocks to sit on. I was going to sit on one that didn't have moss on, as Lionel had warned me about getting leishmaniasis, a flesh-eating disease that comes from sandflies that can live on the wet moss. But the top rock with the moss looked comfier, so I got some leaves to put on it and sat down. I sat for five to ten minutes then I left to go get my bag.

'Snake, Lucy!' Carlos said. I froze, getting ready to flee; I thought there must be a little snake in the water below us all of a sudden. No. It was a mashed-up tiny labaria right next to my boot. Labaria snakes are deadly, and the tiny ones are often worse as they have less control of their venom. I'd never seen one before, they're so well-camouflaged.

Lionel crouched to get a closer look. 'You must've stepped on it.'

I blinked. 'I stepped on that?'

He nodded. 'Maybe even tried to get you.'

Thank goodness I was wearing my snake gaiters – useful for a snake of this size, nothing bigger. Snake gaiters are protective covers worn around the lower leg, made out of a tough, puncture-resistant material . . . Tested on rattlesnakes, they are unlikely to stop the two-inch fangs of a bushmaster.

Honestly if I'd have sat there, where the snake was, that could've, well . . . you know. It shook me up. How are you meant to spot those? I'm not a praying person but I think tonight I will be. Gosh. Now I'm nervous to use my hands at all for balance.

It's not long after that the whistles of the bushmaster begin. Carlos is leading and seems a little cavalier in the way he is cutting line. He's swinging his cutlass like he's in a rush and charging forward with big, confident slashes. It looks impressive but he's not stopping to properly scan ahead, or check what's around the vines and branches before stepping through. I'm worried it's going to lead to another Mikey wasp incident. That's the risk. You go too fast, you miss things.

'Carlos,' I call out over the whistles. He looks back. 'Let's ease the pace a bit.'

'All good, Lucy,' he says, half-smiling. 'I've got this.'

'I know. It's just . . .' Another whistle; I signal the direction I think it's coming from. 'We're super remote, rescue is not an option. Better we take a little longer scanning the area to stay safe.'

While trying to locate the whistles, we stop. And then . . .

A crash comes out of nowhere. A massive tapir (bush cow in Amerindian slang!), explodes from the undergrowth. Right now, it's more like a thunderous beast than anything resembling a cow. Its sheer size is staggering, a creature that seems too big for this jungle. It moves with alarming speed, its hooves pounding the earth.

I instinctively leap behind Lionel, my heart in my throat. The creature barrels past us, a blur of muscle and power, before disappearing back into the dense foliage. My pulse thunders in my ears, and I exhale shakily. First the wasps, the labaria and now this? These animals are like a mix of bull and horse, their presence both awe-inspiring and terrifying, but within a few seconds, it's gone and we're on our way again.

Camp feels intimidating today – whistles surround us and Aaron has the pure look of fear in his eyes. I feel trapped. Every sound makes me tense. I'm in fight-or-flight mode. I keep telling myself that we just need to get through this patch. That maybe tomorrow will bring light and some kind of reprieve. But right now it's hard to believe it. I just have to roll with it. It's funny, there's a strange loneliness in leadership when you can't show how unnerved you are.

34. Roses

WE ARE ALL THE SUM TOTAL of our life experiences, whether good or bad. We believe what we perceive and become what we think about.

During these expeditions, it's a chance to really live in the moment. I don't wake up every morning and look at the bad news. I'm not bombarded by a constant stream of issues that aren't directly mine to fix. These issues seem to seep into our lives, staining our moods and outlook for the rest of the day, whether we realize it or not. Here, I wake up and get on with my day, I am in charge of my actions and the dangers are immediate. At least I can prepare for them and when I get to the end of each day, I feel fulfilled.

While I'm getting my hammock ready, the familiar bushmaster whistles echo around us.

Mikey comes over. 'You know,' he points out, 'every time things get a bit scary out here, you flash that smile.'

He's not wrong.

I look over at Mikey, still with a smile on my face. 'Honestly though . . . I think smiling helps. If I smile, I can keep moving and it makes me think of ways to find a solution. But if I stop and don't smile, I stagnate. That's when you're in trouble. Just like if anything stagnates, water for example . . . But if I keep moving, we're good.'

Mikey nods. 'Yeah, Lucy, I guess that makes sense.'

'It's either smile or cry my head off into that termite mound,' I add, pointing to the termite mound next to Mikey. We both laugh.

Mikey is barefoot and holding his towel; he looks like he's about to go and wash.

'Mikey, make sure to cut a clearing when you go to the creek,' I say, concerned for the wildlife that his bare feet might encounter.

'Oh yes, yes, Lucy. I was actually thinking I might wait a little bit before I bathe.'

I've noticed Mikey's a bit self-conscious about bathing, often skipping it or opting for the darkness of the night, which I'm not keen on.

'Please, don't wash during the dark hours,' I urge. 'It's too risky out here.'

I catch Aaron's eye and realize he's been following our conversation. 'If you're not going to wash now, which by the way you should, maybe it's safer to skip it today, just to avoid any risks,' I suggest.

'Maybe, Lucy,' Mikey concedes.

'Hey, Mikey, you smell like roses anyway!' I throw in with a grin, trying to lighten the mood.

Mikey blushes, and echoes, 'Smell like roses, huh?'

Aaron chuckles, joining in. 'Yeah, Mikey boy, you smell like roses!' I look at Aaron, seeking his support on the no-night-washing rule, and he nods in agreement.

'Yes, Lucy, this camp is very dangerous. Very, very dangerous. We shouldn't wander off after dark and should stay in our hammocks like you say. And if I really need to go, I'll use a ziplock bag!'

Everyone howls with laughter.

*

Something that is really weighing heavy on my mind is our money situation, or lack thereof. I've spent the last few days composing multiple messages on my Garmin inReach, each one carefully crafted to fit the device's letter count, sending updates to Anders to relay to our sponsors. Without additional support, I don't know how we're going to be able to afford to have the next resupply dropped off, let alone be extracted if we make our end point. This is a grassroots expedition. Everything we've done so far has been with the absolute bare bones . . . people power, favours, borrowed kit and good will. We've hit the stage where we're cornered . . . Things would go south if anything went wrong and without that next drop of food and fuel, we can't continue.

The weight of that responsibility is suffocating me, especially when we're already stretched thin on every front.

It's devastating that even in the middle of the wilderness, money is on my mind. I've done everything I can for now; I'm really trying to think if there's a way I can get a credit card loan from the middle of the jungle, but no, that's pushing it too far. All I can do now is wait.

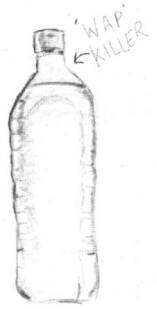

35. Wap Killer

It's Aaron's turn to lead today. While getting into my disgusting, wet day clothes, I glance over at him and can see he's obviously nervous. Our camp last night wasn't nice, it's dark and dense here. Camps really vary in how safe they make you feel. This one isn't helped by the fact we woke up to the sound of whistles this morning. Everyone knows that whoever is first in line puts themselves most at danger of stepping on a snake. Aaron is right now trying to locate where the whistles are coming from and we all simultaneously point whenever we hear one to indicate where we think it might be. This time it sounds like it's coming from exactly where we're headed and we won't be able to avoid it.

As we set off, Aaron makes extra loud noises with his cutlass. He bangs every large tree we pass and we all do the same, hoping that the vibrations from the noise penetrate the ground and scare any slithering creatures away. But it's not long before a whistle is heard, right in front of us. 'The evils are out,' Aaron says. He couldn't have put it better. We cautiously take each step at a time and move further into the Mapari mountains.

We're not even a hundred metres from our camp when Aaron shouts, 'Bushmaster!'

My immediate reaction is to think he's hurt, but he's not. He's just seen one slither past him. We're all trying to see if we can find it, but what's on my mind is are there others? Carlos then calls out. He's spotted it going into a small, rocky cave. Bushmasters like rocky terrain, it gives them protection from the likes of peccary – yes, wild boar eat bushmaster snakes!

I try to spot it but can only see a faint silhouette. But then, I catch the eerie glint of eyes, fixed directly on us. Watching.

'Leave it,' I say to Carlos, aware that Carlos didn't experience our close call last week with the bushmaster and Vivian.

'There will be more,' Aaron mutters. We leave the snake and once again my senses are heightened.

The bushes rustle and our attention switches from the snake to the noise on our right. Lionel stands upright from crouching down and his body language changes from wary to alert and focused. His gaze settles on something I can't see. Of course my mind jumps to the worst: *Is it a jaguar?* I grip my machete that bit tighter in anticipation of what might happen next. My team's eyesight is impeccable, I feel almost blind in comparison. All I see is undergrowth.

'What is it?' I ask, not sure if I want to hear the answer.

Lionel begins making a deep sound: 'Oh O H,' he calls, 'oh O H,' trying to communicate with the mysterious creature.

Aaron whispers, 'Trumpeter.' Ah, a trumpeter bird. These black, ground-based birds have plump bodies and are about the size of a chicken, just with long legs. They're of the genus *Psophia*, and they're named trumpeters because they make a loud sound like a trumpet. Often used as 'guard birds' in Amerindian villages – yes, there is such a thing – they provide an early warning for things like snakes or intruders because when in distress they call out in threat. They also make for a tasty meal.

Lionel stays focused on it, as he gets his silencer ready. I then realize that there's not just one trumpeter, there are probably around half a dozen. Mikey puts his hands together and rubs them while smiling. He whispers, 'Oh yeah, man. Come on, Lionel, we want bird tonight.'

I can't help but feel something primal within me when I watch the guys go into hunting mode. It's a mixture of adrenaline and nerves.

Our rations are not looking healthy; we're eating into our snacks and will run out of calories by next week. A bird of this size could really ease the pressure.

Lionel pulls back his arrow. Aaron instructs, 'No, not yet, left, left. Now.' With that, Lionel releases the arrow, the birds become startled and an eruption of trumpeter noises begins as they flee the scene. Lionel breaks the tension with a laugh. 'No no, didn't get it.' Blast! That would have made the day for us.

Better luck next time!

I see an open area ahead and don't need to look at my watch to know that we've gone way over our one hour moving time.

'Water break!' I shout so that that Aaron, who's cutting line, can hear me.

Before unclipping my bag, I scan the ground for any nasties. I'm looking for ants, scorpions or snakes. There's a line of ants marching to the side of me, but they look like they're moving home and they're too busy with that to bother me.

My bag thuds to the ground and I see Lionel giving me his cheeky grin. I know a day is going smoothly when there's laughter around this strange and bizarre situation that we find ourselves in!

I've always thought that if you've done everything you can but still find yourself in a sticky situation then sometimes the best thing that you can do to help is smile.

I look again at my watch: 10.27 a.m. and note the time. We have fifteen minutes until we should be on the move again; 10.42 is our go time. I go into break mode; I've got it down to a T now. Every second counts! I take my water bladder pipe, unzip the side pocket of my bag, grab one sweet and a bag of crushed biscuits. Biscuits, by the way, are not a good idea to take on expeditions; they essentially become sugar and carb dust, but, finding decent sweet and savoury snacks in Guyana is a challenging task and we have to work with what is on offer. I say we – Anders was the one who picked our food. In fact, looking back, I put my stomach trust in his choosing of our sustenance and was incredibly relaxed about that. I just gave a rough daily calorie goal and asked for sweet and savoury. Tip: salt is king on expeditions.

Anyway, I'm resting on my bag and after a few sips of my sugary-flavoured water I pour some biscuit dust into my hand and with one swift movement, I chuck it into my mouth.

Aaron is also sipping his drink, flavoured with a powder by a brand called Max-C. It's been entertaining to watch him do this every day. He has a two-litre plastic water bottle that's tied to the back of his pack but he never undoes it to drink, which means that every break he's crouched next to his bag with the bottom of the bottle pointing up into the air as he takes gulps. Because the bottle is see-through, every day we see what different colour and flavour of Max-C is on the menu. It's either bright red, blue, orange or purple. It's so bright that it looks as if you could use it as a torch to see in the dark!

The guys have been using the term 'wap killer' to refer to this drink. At first, I thought they were saying wasp killer – maybe because it's so sugary that it would attract wasps and slowly kill them as they got stuck to the sludge – but now that I've realized it's *wap*, I have no idea what the meaning is.

I do have a feeling that it's an inside joke they're keeping from me. They have a few of those, but as time goes on, I'm being less of the leader and more 'one of the lads', so to speak. My next mission is to figure out what this 'wap' means.

Once everyone is sat down and taking advantage of the rest I know it's time for me to put my plan into action. 'I'm just going to help myself to some of my wap killer.'

Mikey bursts out laughing. I don't know if the others heard what I said.

'Lucy, what did you say?'

'I said I'm going to help myself to some wap killer.'

'Oh man, oh man!' Mikey is cracking up laughing and shaking his head. He turns to Aaron, 'Oi, big man, Lucy just said,' he interrupts himself with laughter, 'she said she's having her wap killer.'

Aaron laughs too. 'Oh my, Lucy, oh my.'

Lionel and Carlos are giggling too. Carlos is being shyer on the matter, which hints to me that what we are talking about is a little rude and most definitely an inside joke. Carlos is far more reserved than everyone else. Admittedly he hasn't known me for as long, but he's also held back from me far more than anyone else did.

'What? You're going to have to tell me what it means!'

Mikey is in hysterics and falling all over the place. It's like I've just told the funniest joke in the world.

'Tell you what, Lucy, what do you want to know?'

Mikey knows exactly what I want to know.

'Wap!' I raise my eyebrows, smile and look at Aaron. 'Go on, you can't leave me out on this one! What does wap mean?'

Aaron starts to talk a bit of gibberish. 'Well, Lucy, wap in Amerindian means an old drink but not drink—'

Lionel stops him there. 'Go on, tell her the real meaning.'

Mikey is still giggling like a school boy.

Aaron is clearly nervous to be the one to spill the beans on this secret.

'Well, Lucy, it means . . .' – there's a pause – 'it means penis, Lucy.'

'Ohhh.' But in my head it still doesn't make sense. Why is wap, penis? 'OK – why would you want to be drinking so much penis killer?'

Carlos is watching from afar, smiling. I can tell he's eager to see how this conversation will pan out!

'Lionel, tell Lucy what the boat captain said.' Aaron is also smiling; I think he's relieved I don't think less of him!

I look to Lionel. 'So what's the story?' I love asking Lionel that; he's a very good story teller and I know that now he'll reveal all.

'Well actually, the story is based on the truth. The boat captain told me. You see us Amerindian people, we don't really drink these sugary, processed drinks like Coca-Cola and so on, but the boat captain would go on trips along the river, you know, with guests and things, and he'd get these Max-C rations. Us Amerindians, when we get these drinks we normally take too much.'

Lionel is referring to the diabetes crisis that indigenous communities are currently facing.

He continues, 'The boat captains wouldn't put the Max-C into water, but would pour it into their hand and chuck it into their mouths.'

I think back to how I've been eating my crushed, dusty biscuits. Just the same, I think.

'They wouldn't dilute it with water,' Lionel says, 'just straight into their mouths for a hit while they waited in the sun all lazy, lazy, and not moving or sweating.'

I'm still confused as to where this is going. 'OK but where does the penis come in?' I figure the more I say penis, or shocking words in general, the more OK everyone will feel about including me in their silly jokes!

'Well what the boat captain told me is that when they got home to their wives, they couldn't get their nature up and it was because of the Max-C. It wasn't good for their nature.'

Nature. I don't think I've heard it called that before!

It all makes sense now but I still can't work out why everyone continues to drink it – except for Mikey, he stopped some weeks back.

Aaron butts in, 'It's OK for us because we are moving, not like the captain; we are sweating so it won't affect us. It's only wap killer if you don't sweat it out. They would sit in the boat and just keep eating it and eating it, and get another pack and eat it and eat it, and go nowhere and they cannot get no erection!'

'I see,' I say, 'but I have noticed that Mikey is being extra careful, he definitely doesn't want to take that risk!'

Lionel laughs, 'Mikey is young man and thinking of returning to his baby mother too much!'

'Mikey is frightened of it!' chuckles Aaron.

Everyone laughs and then Mikey says, 'Lucy I am fine with normal water, I don't need it.'

'I think you've got another concern on your mind,' I laugh as I pop my sweet into my mouth.

I catch a glance at my watch: 10.42. 'Right, everyone, take your last sip of your wap killer, time to go!'

36. Bush Dai Dai

AS WE GROW CLOSER AS FRIENDS, we are becoming more vulnerable with one another. Carlos is still a little wary of me but I think that's just in his nature and it's offset by the bond everyone else is developing together. He maintains a professional manner when I'm instructing him left or right during the day so that's all that I ask from him. Lionel and I have grown closer too. He's told me how much he misses Ian and was distraught when the authorities wouldn't allow him to see Ian's body or go to the funeral. Lionel's world has really been turned upside down since his passing but I hope that this expedition opens doors for him. Anders has hinted that he will stay in Guyana if we complete this, and possibly begin a business that takes on a lot of the responsibility that Ian's Bushmasters did.

The vulnerability didn't stop there. As I finish putting up my hammock, Lionel takes me to one side.

'So actually, Lucy, I am sorry to say that I think I will need to end my journey at the next resupply.' He says it with a broken voice, a tear in his eye. 'I will be sorry to leave you and the guys.'

I expected this was coming with the way he frequently referred to his 'poor knee' – it was an exit and insurance strategy. I sympathize with Lionel enormously. He came on this as a nod to Ian's memory and I think he probably presumed the terrain was going to be a little more predictable than it has been, but we all know just how brutal it has turned out to be. This has been more than anyone signed up for, and Lionel is in his early fifties. To get this far is inspirational in itself. I think he has also accepted that Aaron will continue. At first, I really think he wanted to bring down Aaron with him, uncomfortable with the fact that Aaron, who's a very similar age to him, may be able to keep going.

For his whole life, Lionel has been the number one man. He was Ian's right-hand man, was always the lead guide, the main character when television shows came to town. He was even picked to swap lives with a British man for a BBC production! When telling the team about that experience – a week where he was put up in a hotel in London, working in an office, while the other person went to Surama village to farm – what he recounted to the team wasn't what you'd think. He didn't talk about the skyscrapers, shops or escalators. He joked, 'You wouldn't believe it, when I visited the countryside, they put blankets on horses!' Everyone rolled around in hysterics; they could neither believe nor understand it. That was what he remembered most? Well I guess horses definitely don't get cold in Guyana! Wait until he finds out what I do with Sami and her outfits! Lionel also told us how he had a tuna fish sandwich but said that it tasted like 'old fish' – again, fair point. It would have been canned tuna, which is a world away from catching an aimara in a pristine creek.

Now that Lionel has allowed himself a way out and told me his plan to leave, I can tell there's a weight off his shoulders. He's accepted it and seems to be looking at the experience with positivity now.

'Lionel, I completely understand. Thank you for coming to

me first with this news.' His posture relaxes. 'It's been an honour to share this part of the journey with you,' I say, smiling.

'It has been my greatest honour, Lucy.'

There's never silence any more in camp. It's really lovely. Everyone's smiling, sharing what little rations we have and telling stories. A frequent story that comes up is the team's encounters with jungle spirits. I'm the only one who's never heard of the Little Red Man. Aaron's the one who brings it up again tonight around the fire. 'You hear that whistle last night?' he mutters as he tosses a stick into the flames.

I shake my head. 'You mean the bushmasters?'

He smirks. 'Could be. Or could be the *Little Red Man*, Lucy.'

I laugh, assuming it's a joke. 'Sorry, the what?'

Mikey pipes up, a little cautiously. 'Oh yeah yeah, Chiny – tiny guy, red hair. My uncle used to say if you follow him, you're never seen again.'

Aaron nods. 'Oh yes. He don't just kill you, he just takes you. Lures you to him with his whistles and also steals your food. Oh yes.'

'Wait, have any of you seen it?' I look around for responses.

'I saw one once,' Lionel says calmly. 'On a solo trip. Just for a second. Little fella, red, walking fast through the trees. Actually he stole my food that night, my fish. I didn't follow. I'm still here.'

Aaron pokes the fire. 'Vivian saw one too, you know. He said it made his blood run cold. Very dangerous, Lucy.'

I sit back, trying to take it in. 'And what . . . you just don't follow the sound if you hear it?'

Aaron shrugs. 'Don't answer. Don't follow. Don't even look curious. It's a trap.'

'Right,' I say. 'Good to know! Just another thing to add to the list of what not to do in the jungle!'

Mikey leans towards me. 'If you hear a whistle and feel something's off . . . just walk the other way. Fast.'

'Oh I do anyway . . . I just presume it's bushmaster territory!'

We all go quiet for a moment, the forest humming around us.

Then Lionel says, 'Don't worry. If the Little Red Man wanted you, he'd have taken you already.'

'Comforting!' I say.

Another spirit that I know of already is the Bush Dai Dai, which is a Yeti-like creature, half man, half human. Sometimes with hooves and horns, it can shape-shift into other forest animals. The Bush Dai Dai is the guardian of the forest and if you mistreat the jungle, it will come after you. There are certain rules you must follow so as not to upset this creature but these rules translate into good jungle drills too so it's clear why the knowledge is passed down from generation to generation. These go back centuries and are widespread across the whole of South American communities. It's like a road map for how to act in the forest. For example, one must always cut a line in the jungle, and if you're not cutting trees then you must slightly mark the tree so that if you happen to stumble across the creature, you can run away. The other rule is not to shout in the jungle; if you do, it will know where you are – this of course is also a good lesson to avoid scaring animals that you may want to hunt. The final rule is don't take more than you need. The Bush Dai Dai likes mountainous areas, so these Mapari mountains and Kanuku Mountains are where we'd expect to find it. The team are truly frightened of these spirits and so far, the jungle plays out exactly how they see it, so I have no qualms in also believing that we share this area with these spirits and must be cautious . . . and it is a reminder to not go chasing the sound of *any* whistles!

We are really feeling gratitude for every day we spend

here – finally – and taking peace in the little things like washing, even if it is in a muddy puddle.

When returning from my wash today, carefully placing my feet on the least sludgy pieces of ground on my way back to my hammock, so as not to sink into muddy bogs and dirty my feet and legs again, I pass Lionel. He's carefully shaving his face. 'You're looking very dapper!' I say.

Lionel looks around. He's wearing just a towel around his hips while holding the razor; he may as well be in a spa! 'Well, actually Lucy, I am shaving but leaving some hair.' He points to the beard goatee he's neatly created. 'I am leaving it because you see, Lucy, one of us has to have facial hair.'

I scrunch up my face. 'Why does one of us have to have facial hair?'

'In case the Bush Dai Dai comes a-peeping. If at night the Bush Dai Dai makes a visit to our camp and sees one of us with facial hair, it will leave us alone.'

This seems a little far-fetched, keeping a beard to lure off a jungle spirit, but like I said before, if that's the way things are done then I've got no problem following it. 'Well it's a good job we've got you, Lionel – I can light fires, cut line and navigate, but I think I'd struggle to grow facial hair! Even with the best will in the world!' I imagine what this Bush Dai Dai might look like if it came here tonight, peeking over Lionel's hammock, seeing his goatee and leaving in a huff.

I received a message from Anders on the Garmin; it was sent two days ago but has only just been received. *Some progress with funding. Stay safe out there.* This is good news. I feel a weight lifted off my shoulders and loosen up immediately. I close my hands together and whisper, 'Thank you.' I feel a rush of gratitude towards all of the sponsors of this expedition then look up,

Before the expedition, planning with the 50-year-old maps laid out – a lot of jungle to get through!

Anders Andersen – the best operations manager you can get! Anders now lives in Guyana and runs The Wild Tales.

Lionel, Mikey and me during a break early on in the expedition.

The terrain was unforgiving – no wonder we only covered 2km on most days!

Washing is crucial in the jungle. We'd go weeks without being by a river (or even sunlight) – this was a fairly nice water source, but very shallow, so it was a case of chucking water over ourselves with our food containers!

Vivian and Aaron after catching our first proper meal: wolf fish (aimara).

River crossing. We had to go quick because the waters were rising, fast.

Vivian peeping through the relentless bamboo bush.

Camp life.

Mikey took this without me knowing I had a giant tick stuck to me!

Me and Aaron on the raft.

I got very used to being soaking wet, all of the time!

Around the fire in my
dry night-time clothes.

Captain Aaron!

Me taking control of the steering.

Mikey posing with his 'mosquito worm' after we'd squeezed it out!

After the tarantula hawk wasp sting.

Always alert in the jungle.

Aaron after a close bushmaster encounter.

Throughout the expedition, I tried my best to improve my target practice. Never as precise as the team though!

Working my way through the vines.

A few hours before we finished, celebrating as we could see Lethem! Max, me, Aaron, Mikey, and Vivian crouched in front.

hoping to see the sky to pass on my grateful thoughts through the atmosphere and down to all the supporters, but of course there is no blue sky above me, just thick canopy.

As I lay in my hammock I can't help but think that we're all standing on the shoulders of giants. None of us can achieve anything alone and there's something so beautiful in that. We must all strive to lift one another up. People who have come before us, those who dared to dream and venture into the unknown. People like Ian, whose legacy has paved the way for explorers like me to keep exploring. And people like Neil, whose belief in me propelled me forward and changed how I dreamed. My mind drifts to my childhood, running through the fields behind our house, pretending they were the farthest reaches of unexplored jungles. It was there in my imagination in Suffolk, in those seemingly endless afternoons, that my love of adventure was born. Lying here, I think of just how isolated we are, but it doesn't feel lonely. We have one another in a way that is hard to replicate in our modern world. There's a romance in these expeditions that helps you push past the uncomfortable and scary thoughts.

As I close my eyes, the howler monkeys begin to call. Their calls are a distinctive sound of the jungle, not to be mistaken for a deep-yelling man. It creates an eerie echo that travels for miles, bouncing off the trees in the forest. It's the monkeys communicating in their troops, asserting territory with a guttural, roaring chorus that builds in intensity.

I smile, finally feeling at ease with the jungle. I'll be safe tonight because after all, Lionel has his goatee.

37. Aaron

Today, our Bush Dai Dai stories feel less like legends and no longer seem so outlandish. Aaron has stopped us all in our tracks and looks noticeably worried. 'Bush Dai Dai,' he says and gestures with his machete at two snapped trees in front of us.

'Yes, this is the sign of the Bush Dai Dai,' Lionel intercepts. 'You can see it went from here, all over here.' He points to the path of the creature. Closer inspection reveals multiple trees broken at waist height, snapped away methodically and evenly spaced about a metre apart. 'No other animal could do this and we know it is not human, there would be other signs, so it is the Dai Dai.' He's right; what other creature could snap trees so perfectly and rhythmically? Lionel continues, 'It has gone into the mountains. We must be careful, Lucy.'

We are nearing resupply two now, which marks two-thirds of our journey complete. I estimate we have another four days and we'll be there. It can't come soon enough; I have one more full day of rations left and my energy is starting to dip. The final leg will push us to our limit because it will involve the Kanuku

Mountains. These mountains are 3,000 feet high, covered in trees, and we have dozens of them to cross.

We've managed the Mapari mountains well, finding some respite on their flat, long ridges. But what goes up must come down, and some descents have required us to use ropes. As we prepare for today's final descent, we hear that familiar whistle and nod to each other, trying to pinpoint its source. We all nod and attempt to locate the position. I look at my watch: it's nearing 3 p.m. 'We have to go. Come on, everyone.' We swing our bags on our back and begin to use gravity to our advantage as we go down. Because our bags are so heavy, it's harder work to put on the brakes because it puts all the force through our knees. Instead, we allow ourselves to controllably fall and use our hands to swing from one tree to another. The whistles get louder and more frequent. Are we entering bushmaster territory?

Mikey calls, 'Go go, I just saw a bushmaster!' We can't go any faster. We hurl ourselves to the bottom of the mountain.

I reach for the camera once we get to the base. 'We just ran down that mountain!' The correct thing to say was 'we just fell with style down that mountain'. The unexpected waterfall, not marked on any of our maps, is both a marvel and a mystery, and is the perfect place for a camp. The loud sound of the crashing white water means we can no longer hear the whistles.

'That was very close, Lucy,' Aaron says as he high-fives me.

'Well done for getting us safely down, Aaron!' I pat his shoulder.

'Oh well, Lucy, that was very dangerous but we made it, Lucy.' His charming smile makes everything seem OK.

The jungle decides she wants to continue with the snake theme tonight. Mikey calls, 'Snake! Snake!' It's pitch black, but

I grab my head torch and walk over, as does everyone else. The light illuminates a bright-red and black coral snake slithering around in his gear. Out of the whole team, Mikey is the one who hasn't been following strict jungle protocol. In the jungle it's standard practice not to leave anything on the ground but Mikey acts like it's his teenage bedroom. This obviously has dangerous implications. He's already had scorpions crawl into it but this is the first time a snake has tried to make it home. We manage to get the snake to find another place to curl up and, as I return to my hammock, I see Mikey hastily organizing his equipment. He's tidying his kit and begins to cut some pieces of wood, which he then makes into a platform seven feet in the air.

'What are you building, Mikey?' I ask from my hammock.

'I want to be higher off the ground tonight, in case the bushmasters come to curl up under me and I don't hear them! So I'm making a high place to sleep.'

Suddenly, Mikey's gone from the least organized to the safest. It only took a coral snake.

As the days go on and we push deeper into the jungle and closer to the Rupununi River, our second resupply, I notice Aaron getting stronger. Thankfully Lionel's constant complaints have subsided and stopped holding him back; it's like Aaron is free to really show what he can do. With every morning that breaks over the jungle, he seems more confident, almost as if the jungle itself is changing him, showing us a new side to him day by day. Aaron's really coming into his own. Like the rest of us, he's shed some weight, but more importantly, he's also shed any lingering effects of alcohol. There's a newfound childlike enthusiasm in him; he's taking charge and making decisions, which is both inspiring and a great comfort to me. I am so happy to have him by my side; he is a wonderful man. This expedition is for him to remind himself of who he is and what he's capable of.

When we get to resupply two, we're hoping to reconnect with Vivian, assuming his wound has healed well. With Carlos scheduled to leave with Vivian's return, and because I already anticipated Lionel's early departure, Anders has arranged for a new team member to join us at that point as well as Vivian, so that we remain a five-person team.

After briefing the team on today's route and while packing up my bag, I let out a cry and jump back. I feel as though something has suddenly set fire to my finger – a sting. Out from my bag strap crawls a black scorpion. My finger is throbbing. After all that time looking at Mikey's disorganized pack, here I am, the one who gets stung. I can't stop my eyes from streaming with the tears. It hurts like hell, and I immediately go to the creek and submerge my finger, hoping the cool water will give some relief. Between the hunger, exhaustion and now this sharp pain, I can't help but take a moment alone, overwhelmed and sobbing quietly, feeling like a hurt child.

I don't have much time to feel sorry for myself before the rain begins. This rain could lead to problems because we have a river to cross that is already high and raging. I hold my finger in pity and go back to the team. 'Are you OK, Lucy?' Aaron asks, concerned. 'It was one of the really painful ones. I have had it, it really hurts. It'll start to feel better in a few hours.'

We get our bags on and I presume we should go upstream and try to find a narrower part of the river to cross, but before I say anything Carlos is ahead. He throws his bag and balances it on his head, and begins to wade into the water. That's the plan? Lionel and I watch in disbelief, but then Aaron and Mikey follow suit. Within a few metres they are swallowed by the depths of the water with just their heads and bags visible. The current is strong and they are clearly struggling, trying desperately not to be whisked away from below. They will be taken far downstream into powerful rapids if they make one wrong footing.

'You see, Lucy, the problem with Amerindian people is we are small people! So we have a problem!' Lionel giggles, balancing his bag on his head with one hand; in the other he holds his silencer. I swear it's only humour that gets us through these situations.

Lionel takes the lead, stepping cautiously into the river. He takes a slightly different line to the others, and suddenly the current surges, snatching at his legs and pulling him off-balance. From the opposite bank, Mikey spots the danger. Dropping his pack without a second thought, he dives into the turbulent water, Aaron right behind him. They plunge through the swirling currents and reach Lionel just as he's being swept downstream. Mikey grabs hold of Lionel's rucksack while Aaron anchors him down, stabilizing his footing against the rocky riverbed. Together they fight the river's pull, inching their way to safety with Lionel in tow. It's a narrow escape for Lionel, and the tension is palpable.

Now it's my turn. I hope that my height is of an advantage on this occasion. Heart pounding, I struggle to hoist my heavy bag over my head – although no food left, it's filled with camera gear. I swear mine is the heaviest; no one else batted an eyelid when they put their bags on their heads.

I step into the river but after just three steps, the cold water is swiftly up to my neck. It's hard to keep my balance as I tiptoe across the slippery stones and riverbed, because the weight of the bag threatens to fall and tip me into the water with it.

My mouth is just above the water now; I'm conscious to take a breath in case it gets deeper. Seeing my struggle, Aaron swims over and positions himself in front of me, ready to catch my

AARON

bag if I fall. His determined gaze comforts me and, with a deep breath, I step forward. Just as I reach my limit, the water at my nose, the riverbed rises beneath my feet, and I stumble out of the water and on to the bank. We've got through yet another challenge, and resupply two is finally within our sights.

38. Resupply Two

'We're fifty metres out!' I shout, clutching the GPS that tracks our progress towards the resupply waypoint Anders set. We're finally breaking free from the dense jungle and approaching the open stretch near the Rupununi River.

I can't believe it. We've actually got to the next resupply. It's been almost three weeks since we left the river, and our raft. Our bodies have collectively powered through and we might do this. We're not in any way out of danger yet. The Kanukus are not to be underestimated, as I know from our expedition last year. I can only hope that our bloody-mindedness and our dogged determination will get us through – and that the spirits and wildlife let us pass.

The coordinates are spot on, and there waiting for us are blue barrels and two figures. One is Vivian, all smiles despite his ordeal, and the other has to be Maximus. We all rush to greet them, thrilled at the reunion. Vivian's arm bears a rough star-shaped scar from an unsuccessful attempt to remove the bamboo spike, but he's managing. The spike is still somewhere deep in there, but so far not causing any issues. I can't help but think that it looks far worse than it did when he left us! At least we know it's been properly cleaned and monitored for the few weeks he's been away. He can grip a machete again, so that's something.

Maximus, Max for short, is noticeably tall and from the Macushi tribe. His outfit seems somewhat out of place in the extreme jungle and he looks like he's going to the fairground instead of the untouched wilderness. He wears a bucket hat, a loose, red vest top with black Adidas tracks and a small rucksack that has a bright-yellow rain cover over it. My immediate thought is that he'll need to take Lionel or Carlos's rucksack because he won't be able to carry any team equipment with that teeny thing. I'm told that Max grew up in the forest and is a dab hand at hunting. Yesterday, when asking Mikey if he knew Max, Mikey was very vague with his answers and I sensed there was a feud between them, but couldn't work out how serious it was. His reply was, 'Oh yes, Lucy, I know Maximus.' And he left it at that.

What I do know is that at twenty-one, Max is younger than Mikey, knocking Mikey off the youngest member top spot. Could there be some jealousy because of that?

I shake Max's hand and, as I'm filming the introduction, I say, 'You don't mind a camera do you? Looking forward to this leg of the journey?'

'I am very happy to be joining you for this part of the expedition.' Max's response is polite and at least he looks me straight in the eyes, unlike Carlos. 'I don't want to be on camera so much,' he then says. It's a little difficult to hear that when we're such a close-knit team. You can't really help but be on camera, but I respect his wishes and, to be honest, I think his mind might change. At the end of the day, many people warm to the camera upon familiarity with the person holding it and then find that they want to feature, so I will give it time.

There's no time to waste so after filling our bags with rations – the new noteworthy items being peanut butter, jam and wraps – it's time to say goodbye to Lionel and Carlos.

Carlos goes to shake my hand but I head straight in for a hug. Carlos is a good guy and hard-working; I managed to get him out of his shell a little and after a week with us, he slotted into the team nicely. Not the most talkative guy, but one willing to slog it out and join in with the silly jokes we shared.

Lionel's departure is not just a physical exit but a symbolic one, for a number of reasons. It's Lionel accepting that he can't go on and that he isn't the strongest guide in the team, something that with Ian became his identity. Ian passed on knowledge to Lionel but now he's also passing the torch, acknowledging that it's time for Aaron to step up as the lead guide, a role he's never held before. Aaron is ready but I know he is nervous about the responsibility. All I can do is encourage and support him. It'll be up to him to converse with me about big safety concerns and I'll need Aaron to be present if any heads bash with any other team members.

I hug Lionel and it feels like a part of me is leaving with him. He's been a constant in my jungle life, just like Ian, over the past seven years. Lionel was there when I first stepped into the jungle, naive and uncertain, and he's played a crucial role in teaching me how to survive out here.

I step back, and Aaron moves forward. We all watch as he embraces Lionel, their exchange formal yet heavy with so many unspoken emotions.

'Make sure to stay safe, step by step, and you'll be all right,' Lionel advises, his voice tinged with confidence and a hint of self-consciousness.

'Oh, yes. Thank you, Lionel,' Aaron replies.

The importance of this moment is palpable and I feel

RESUPPLY TWO

honoured to be a part of the journey that both these men are on. Now, our route is further west into the jungle and across the Kanuku Mountains, but first, we have the Rupununi River to cross.

39. Peccary

THE RUPUNUNI RIVER IS A WIDE and powerful swath that cuts through the wilds of Guyana. It's much more than just a river, it's the jungle's main water artery. Yesterday, we trekked a few kilometres upstream from where we left Carlos and Lionel (who'll be collected by Anders and taken home; they've probably already gone) and made camp here. It's the place that looks the narrowest, but it's still a good fifty metres or so in width.

We've decided we'll need to swim across this time. There's no suitable bamboo around and we just don't have the time to make another raft.

Standing here, about to cross, I can't help but feel daunted by the life this river supports. Like Rewa River, it is teeming with wildlife. It's a hub for giant otters who dart playfully in the water, tapirs come for a drink and the banks are prime bathing spots for caimans, which we've spotted a few of. I've seen a number of spectacled caimans sunning themselves on the riverbanks. Spectacled caimans are on the smaller side for crocodilians, usually measuring about six to eight feet long. They get their name from the distinctive bony ridge between their eyes, which looks a bit like a pair of spectacles. They're not as aggressive as their relative, the black caiman.

It's the black caiman that's got me really worried about this crossing. I've seen a few on the bank, their dark scales blending eerily into the mud, but last night I saw the biggest black caiman that I've ever seen – this thing was huge. I think it was between sixteen and twenty feet. It appeared out of the water, and I was mesmerized but also horrified . . . It swam silently, using its powerful long tail to propel itself forward, barely disturbing the surface of the calm Rupununi water.

The guys have reassured me that we will have the best chance in crossing – meaning the best chance of not being chomped down by one of these crocs – if we go when the sun is at its highest in the day. That is because the black caiman's hunting hours are dawn and dusk. If we go at midday, they shouldn't be too peckish.

I find myself wishing for X-ray vision so that I can peer through the murky brown waters and spot any lurking predators. They tend to rest on the riverbed, and I imagine them seizing the opportunity if they see five tasty humans taking a dip.

Aaron, being the 'water dog', volunteers to lead. He and Vivian will go first, swimming across with the rope but without their bags to make it faster.

Aaron doesn't look nervous, instead he just looks focused. He's got a job to do and he's taken on the responsibility, just as Lionel asked him to.

Before they dive in, I catch Aaron's eye and ask, 'Anything I need to know?'

'Just don't splash, Lucy, go very smoothly. Go smooth and fast,' he instructs.

Mikey interrupts, 'Yes, Lucy, the caiman are drawn to splashing.'

I think Aaron was trying to calm my nerves by not adding the reason why, but Mikey went and blew it. Oh well. *Smooth and fast, no splashing*, I repeat in my head so that my body takes in every one of those words.

Then Aaron is in, followed by Vivian. He is fast – I won't be able to go that fast! I watch Vivian swimming with his machete in hand; he is clearly the one keeping an eye out for any silhouettes rising from the water.

They make it to the other side, clambering up a large rock and securing the rope. Now it's my turn. I want to get it over with and just let my body go into automatic. This has to be done so there's no point fretting about it; I have the team on both banks who'll be able to look around for anything suspicious and I know how accurate they are with the silencer, so I feel like they'll have my back . . . and hopefully my limbs.

I strap on my heavy bag. It weighs a ton but is buoyed slightly by the inflated dry bags inside. I take a deep breath and prepare to step into the river, silently hoping the caimans are content to just watch us all pass. Gripping the rope tightly, I step into the water. I'm ready to glide across as smoothly and quickly as possible.

The rope stretches as soon as I'm submerged and I have to rearrange it so that I can pull myself along at ease. My bag drags me down, but my jungle boots buoyantly push up, helping me float and stabilize the bag's bottom. I find a rhythm, my hands methodically pulling along the rope, knowing the eyes of caimans might be tracking every ripple. That thought sends a chill up my spine.

I then hear Aaron's voice, 'Just keep it going, Lucy, just take your time, Lucy.' He's being very thoughtful; he knows I'm not so keen on this swim.

I focus intensely on my hand placement; I don't want to

fumble the rope because it will make a splash. After a couple of minutes, I see Vivian's hand and he hoists me up. Water pours from me.

'That was behind you!' Vivian points to my worst fear. There it is, a long, black caiman, the length showing above the water. My heart pounds. Thank goodness I didn't know that had appeared while I was in there, I might have frozen!

'What about the other guys?' I ask, concerned.

'They will have to wait a bit before we can go. I'll try to entice it downstream.'

If Vivian can catch some fish and generate some splashing, he will draw any predators to one area . . . I then question why we didn't do this before the three of us had our dip but it's too late for regrets. I'm just relieved to be on the edge of the Kanuku Mountains.

Vivian's plan works. The visible caiman heads downstream and the rest of the team, and the extra bags, make it over safely.

I stare up at the dusk sky and spot the Milky Way. I'm trying to get some moon shots on camera before we're back in the thick canopy again. We've camped right where we crossed the river, ready for tomorrow's leg. While I'm filming, Max joins me, stepping out to take in the night sky alongside me. Without prompting, he opens up.

'I like to sleep outside,' he says.

I glance at him. 'I only really do it on expedition now.'

He nods. 'I do it all the time. I grew up like that.'

There's a small pause. He kicks at the dirt with his boot.

'You excited to join us?' I ask.

'Yes,' he says quickly. He nods again. 'Is big thing for me. I want to do well.' He stutters slightly, eyes darting as he searches for the words. 'I work hard. I'm not scared.'

He glances over. I get the sense he's trying to show me something, maybe prove something.

'I have a kid,' he adds in a shy manner.

I'm surprised but smile. 'That's a good reason to be out here.'

Max nods again, proudly. 'I'm happy to be here.'

He's only twenty-one. A young dad, just like Mikey. I find it hard to imagine the two of them as fathers. I can't yet imagine myself as a parent; I'm nowhere near ready to dedicate everything I have to a tiny little human. I want to and hopefully I will be lucky enough to be able to in the years to come, but not yet. I guess it's a little different here, plus I'm sure (and hope) they step up to fatherhood when they're home.

Max unloads his thoughts, eager for me to understand his life. I can tell he's a little sweet on me. I get the feeling he's trying to charm me. Maybe this is why Mikey was a little reserved to speak about Max . . . because Mikey wants to be number one . . . Either way, the fact he's being so attentive and kind suggests he'll slot nicely into the team.

He then surprises me. 'Can you film me here?' he asks. I'm taken aback.

'I thought you didn't want to be filmed.'

'Ah, I do,' he admits.

I knew I'd get there but I didn't think it would happen this quickly!

Vivian is in great spirits. He's so happy to be back. Before I got into my hammock, he came over and gave me something that his wife had given him for me. It is an appreciation necklace and will keep us safe during our final leg of the journey.

'She wasn't worried about the cut on my arm,' Vivian says as he looks at his scar.

'Oh, she wasn't?'

'No. She said that it would be a memory of you and this expedition.' He smiles.

I blush. 'What a sweet way of looking at it.'

I'm so glad he's back and ready – together we can finish this.

I gathered the team just before we set off this morning. We were all packed and ready, but I could feel the shift in energy: Vivian was back, Max was new and full of beans, and those of us who'd been here since the start – me, Aaron and Mikey – were worn down.

'All right,' I said, standing in front of them. 'This is the final stretch . . . the last leg. But don't be fooled. Just because technically it feels like we're almost there, we still have a huge expedition to complete. We are not safe yet. In fact, this is when people start slipping up. Getting close to the finish line makes people sloppy. We cannot let that happen.'

I looked around at each of them, trying to ensure they were taking in what I was saying.

'Aaron, Mikey . . . we've been here since day one. I know how tired you are. Well, even if you don't show it, Mikey, you must be! I feel it too. Now's the time we double down and get this done. Remember though, it could be another few weeks before we are finished and safe.'

I turned to Vivian. 'Vivian! I'm so glad you're back. We've missed you. If anything doesn't feel right in your arm, tell me. We move together.'

Then I looked at Max and Mikey. They'd been joking this morning, a bit of that young competitive edge showing.

'Max. I get it, you're new and you've got fresh young energy, which is great. But don't try to prove anything. Mikey, I know it might feel tempting to match him or one-up him . . . but now is not the time.' I knew that would make Mikey feel awkward.

He gave me a smirk. 'I'm not trying to prove anything. I'm just faster than him.'

Max grinned back. 'We'll see, big man.'

I smiled but this is what I was talking about. 'We've made it this far because we've looked out for each other. We need to do that now more than ever. Keep the pace sensible, stay alert, we know how dangerous the jungle can be.'

Aaron nodded. 'No point rushing now.'

'Exactly,' I said. 'One step at a time. We can do this.'

I know that because this is the last section, they will feel like we are nearing the end and may not be as cautious as a result, but the jungle doesn't work like that. There's a lot of responsibility on me and I feel like I've got to maintain the level of safety and caution we have had throughout . . . but it feels like it could get harder, especially with Max and Mikey together.

I think the team is strong. We have to just maintain our strength, our morale, and navigate through these mountains. I've been looking at maps and the navigation is going to be hard on this one. I'm a little nervous but I'll be learning the mountains as we go.

As I lay in my hammock I think back to the little girl I once was. So often labelled 'shy', I was never the traditionally born leader. I could never raise my voice or order others around me.

What would that shy little girl think of where I am now? I think she'd be excited and want to be here too. She probably wouldn't be surprised that I'm here.

The term 'imposter syndrome' comes up a lot when I give interviews. It's a term that's been used more widely in recent years. It's linked more often than not with women in male-dominated jobs. I've been thinking hard on whether or not I feel it out here and, really, I don't know if I do. Imposter syndrome suggests that I feel I don't belong here, or that I've got here by accident or that I think I don't deserve to be here. But I've worked incredibly hard to get here. This didn't just happen. I had to swim against the tide and keep getting up when the odds were stacked against me. I did that. Me. I need to remind myself that I have this capability in me and not be sucked into societal pressure to feel grateful for everything, as if I am just lucky. I am lucky too: I grew up with loving parents whose greatest gift to me was always giving me the benefit of the doubt in whatever phase I was in – including when I declared that I wanted to be an explorer all those years ago. But luck doesn't lift you back up or push you on when nothing you've tried has worked. Resilience and dogged determination does that. Relentless optimism takes work. There have been so many dead ends and hurdles on this expedition, and in my life so far. I could've given up on my dream to be an explorer years ago, but I didn't. So I've got this far, I think. I can keep going and get to the end of this expedition. We, as a team, deserve it. So no, I don't feel imposter syndrome. I am exactly where I need, want and deserve to be.

We all wake up simultaneously before sunrise and there is a feeling of positive energy that reaches all of us.

There is a unanimous eagerness to tackle these Kanuku Mountains and discover what awaits us. Bags on our back again and the familiar ache settles into our shoulders. We all stand around our now empty campsite as I brief everyone on the day ahead.

'Right, guys, this is our final leg but it will also be the most physically challenging. These Kanuku Mountains will be hard to move through. I know you will all be eager to get to the end, but we have to stay focused and alert. This is when things can go wrong.'

Aaron is nodding. He looks anxious about what lies ahead.

'Aaron, Mikey and I have been on this expedition for almost six weeks. We are not as strong as you, Max, and you, Vivian, who has been at home resting.' Mikey looks up when I mention his name. I continue, 'We need to go as a team, support one another. Now, who wants to cut line today?'

'I will,' Max says with his arm raised, silencer in hand.

'Great. Now, Max, just make sure you keep looking behind you. We stay as a unit and look for all dangers ahead.'

Being at the front and cutting line is the most physically demanding job, and Max is the youngest and freshest. Although I was worried about young Mikey cutting line, Max is a true bushman and, unlike Mikey, he grew up deep in the jungle. His way of life has been to hunt, survive and move through forest. Plus, he rejected my idea of him using Lionel's bag instead of his little one, so he's also got the smallest and least heavy. I've seen this before. When people think it's their prerogative to take less kit because they choose to have less. I've no problem with that, but what I do have a problem with is a small bag that can't fit any team kit or take kit if someone is struggling.

Max sets off at a pace that is, frankly, too fast. I feel OK, but Aaron and Mikey both seem slower and in discomfort. I don't want to draw attention to it yet, maybe they are just finding their feet and getting used to the extra bag weight.

As I'm thinking this, my thought is disrupted when there's a shriek in the distance. Vivian is in front of me and pauses to listen. I can't see Max, he's gone too far ahead. 'Peccary,' Vivian identifies with a note of caution in his voice.

'How many do you think there are?' I ask, tension mounting as more shrieks and rustles fill the air.

'Hundreds.'

Peccary, or wild pigs, might sound harmless, but they are

anything but. While I was planning for my 2020 south to north expedition, I asked Ian what to do about jaguars, and his reply was, 'Take a picture. What you really need to worry about are the peccary.'

White-lipped peccary are the ones to be cautious of. They are stocky, muscular and have coarse black hairs. They have tusks and a white band around their strong, powerful jaws. They are known to be aggressive, especially when they have young, and they travel in squadrons of up to 500 and take down anything in their path. We've seen evidence of them trampling through large areas of the forest before but luckily, not come across them.

The male peccary tend to be on the outside of the squadron, with the females and young protected on the inside. You can hear them coming because the young yell or shriek, and they grind their teeth together. If you find yourself in the path of the peccary, the only thing you can do is climb a tree and wait for them to pass.

As the reality of our situation sinks in, I scan for climbable trees, then Aaron catches up. He looks around. 'Where's Max?'

I still can't see him. 'Shit.' I'm worried that Max has deliberately gone to them and is aggravating them.

'Shhhh,' Vivian hisses, putting his finger to his mouth. He's crouched behind a fallen tree and signalling towards the peccary's location. Aaron readies his bow as Mikey points out a nearby tree, its vine making it a viable escape route.

Then, the underbrush rustles ominously, and a solitary black boar bursts through, just metres away. Vivian's voice is urgent. 'There will be more, go!'

Time to act: we have to climb. I dash to the tree Mikey pointed out. I undo my bag, aware that there are more peccary on the way. If the bag is leaned up against the tree, it shouldn't be trodden too much by their hooves and tusks.

I begin to climb. It's awkward in the jungle boots but I squeeze hard with my thighs wrapped around the tree. I am literally hugging it for dear life and get six feet off the ground. The sounds of the peccary squadron are growing louder. Mikey's clambering up a tree in my field of view; I am not sure where Vivian or Aaron have got to. The shrieking gets even louder and the ground vibrates. Another boar, another and another. They run past, seemingly unaware of my presence above. Hundreds of black peccary fill the forest floor, the smaller vegetation being trampled as they pass, small trees ripped from the ground, termite nests destroyed. As I hold myself up, a sea of black moving beneath me, I picture that moment in *The Lion King*, where Mufasa falls dramatically into the wildebeests stampeding below – I do not want to end up like poor Mufasa.

Hundreds pass, but after a few minutes they're nowhere to be seen. I jump down, arms sore from gripping the trunk so tight. We reconvene and Mikey is chirpy. 'Ah, we could have had pork for dinner!'

'Maybe the pork had Max for dinner. Let's find him,' I reply.

Max comes running out from the bushes, holding his silencer. He's out of breath and looks stunned.

'What happened, boy?' Aaron asks.

Max is now bent over, his hands on his knees as he tries to catch his breath. He looks up and points to where he's just come from. 'Puma. There was a puma,' he says between breaths. A puma isn't to be mistaken for a jaguar; a puma here is known as a mountain lion, and is much smaller and more slender than a jaguar. They can be dangerous because they are naturally very curious, especially the younger ones. He goes on, 'I was hiding and waiting for the pigs. I wanted to try to get one of the weaker ones at the back.' I'm wondering whether young Max is a liability. It seems like my safety briefing went completely over his head.

'I didn't realize the cat was also waiting for the last weaker ones, in the tree above me . . . But then it saw me and turned to me.'

'What happened?' I ask.

'It tried to attack me! I had to fire an arrow near it to make it go away!'

Great. Now there's an angry puma around. I hope it managed to get its planned pig in the end.

'Don't run off, Max,' I say, with conviction. 'We have to stay as a team. If you're leading, you have to understand you're leading with all of us. We have been out here for over a month and our bodies are not as strong as yours. You may be used to flying through the forest but there's no backup here. One wrong step and we are in trouble.'

Vivian intercepts, 'Yeah, you don't realize how many bushmasters there are here, boy.'

Aaron is nodding intently.

And with that, it's time to go. It was a mistake to ever think that this last leg would be uneventful.

40. Mosquito Worm

These mountains are so steep that I'm hallucinating. I keep thinking I'm seeing things that are most definitely not there. Things like sofas and suitcases. My mind is making them up in the foreground and it's not until I'm right up in front of them that I realize they're not there. Sweat has dripped out of every pore. I don't think I have any fluid left to give. Because of the humidity, the sweat just sits on my skin, suffocating me. I haul myself up the mountain. I grab the tree trunks as I go for stability but I have to check every hand placement, not just for spikes but to see if the tree is secure. The trees are not as rooted in on the side of the mountains – they sometimes break completely from the ground when I put my weight on them, threatening to send me plummeting down.

When I glance down the mountain face, Aaron and Mikey are a long way behind. I've never seen Mikey so exhausted and Aaron looks physically sick. I call to Max and Vivian, who have both got something I call 'leader's legs'. It's not a medical term, just something I've noticed during expeditions. It's all in the head but it definitely happens! When you're up front, cutting line or setting the pace, it's like you tap into a different energy.

You feel stronger, more capable and almost invincible. You move fast and it gives you this weird boost. You get to decide the pace, you're not matching anyone else's, and that control brings confidence. That's leader's legs, and Vivian and Max have them right now.

But drop to the back and everything changes. That's 'loser's legs'. This isn't because you've failed, but because that strength just seems to drain away more quickly as you watch the people in front go faster and faster. You're slower, maybe even stumbling. Your mind slips a little too easily into doubt – 'what's the point?'. It's psychological. Being up front makes you feel like you've got something to prove, or something to protect – your position – and it gives you that extra power. At the back, there's no momentum to ride. Just the drag of everyone else's pace and your own tired thoughts.

I signal to them to stop and wait when I see a point ahead that isn't as steep. The three of us wait there for Aaron and Mikey. Mikey catches up first and isn't his normal, smiley self. I feel for him; I imagine he doesn't want to show weakness in front of newcomer Max but he clearly can't hide it. Highlighting just how much he's feeling it, he dumps his bag and collapses on the floor. Aaron is next to arrive and he is as pale as a ghost.

'Aaron, seriously, are you OK?' I ask. He can't even get his words out. He too collapses in a pile and then looks as if he is about to retch. 'Our bodies are just getting used to the steep ascent. We need to drink more than we have been and take it step by step,' I say, hoping my words are of some comfort. Aaron turns his head to the side and throws up. He is showing signs of heat exhaustion, possibly heat stroke. I open my bag, pick out two sachets and ask for his water bottle. 'I'm filling your water with Dioralyte. It has salts in it that will make you feel better. I need you to drink this whole bottle in front of me right now.' He follows the orders and laps up the water. When people enjoy the taste of Dioralyte, it means they need it. On regular occasions, that stuff tastes like crap.

Internally I am thinking that we need to stop and make camp early, at the first creek we reach after we've ascended this mountain. The thing about the mountains in the jungle is we are unlikely to find any water source while we are on them. Even though the creeks are not on the map, they are likely to be down the valleys or at the bottom of the mountains and from the last expedition in 2020, I have a good idea of how to read the map and guess where the water will be.

Aaron is starting to look a little more alive again when Mikey asks for some of the sachets too, which makes me realize that I need to hand them out to everyone, which I do, and I have one for myself too.

Stopping early was a good decision. It means we get a little more of the sunlight through the trees, which boosts spirits and immune systems. The creek we've found is large enough to submerge in and has rocks at the side, which means you don't have to get really muddy when you get out after washing. With the fire alight and the smoke filtering the sun rays in a beautiful way, you'd be forgiven if you mistook this for heaven. It seems heavenly on the surface. Max is in the creek, catching fish. I watch him as he takes aim with the bow and manages to spearhead with his arrow. His aim is remarkable; these fish are no longer than the size of my thumb. He even takes account of refraction, although when I ask him how he makes allowances for it, he has no idea what I'm on about. He just knows it's different to shoot things in the water than it is on land.

We eat well, and the extra rest does Aaron and Mikey good.

We needed today as a break-in and to reset the team dynamics . . . again.

The next few days we begin to settle into going up the 'bumps', as the mountains have come to be known. Lionel started calling them 'bumps' whenever we were referring to the mountains on the map, and it's stuck. I tried to correct everyone initially when they called the mountains that, as it suggests they are small hills that just require a hop, skip and a jump to get over, but now I kind of like it. It makes the endless mountains we have to climb seem innocent and less daunting. 'Just two bumps today,' I've been saying.

There's nothing like downplaying our situation.

Tonight, we're camped in between two steep mountains and our camp is small because of the limited flat space and sturdy trees. Max asked if he could share a tree tonight, meaning he wanted to put his hammock and his tarp on the same tree as mine. Sharing a tree for hammocks is normally fine but sharing tarps can be tricky as it stops them from being streamlined and letting water flow down them. I accept it today, because of the trees available, but it means that we are going to be sleeping very close together and I also can't say that the tree looks super strong.

During the night I'm so tired that I feel almost paralyzed. It begins to pour with rain. Normally, this would bother me as I'd have to get up and take in my clothing that hangs outside (yes, even though it's wet already, we still take in our clothes – don't ask why) but everything is under my tarp tonight. I'm going in and out of consciousness when I feel like there's a tapir or another large animal moving around underneath me. I don't properly register it to begin with but then, after a little while, I wake up with the movement. It's pitch black and I can't work out which way I'm facing. It's only then that I realize I'm no longer hanging in the air in my hammock, I'm on the floor in the mud. The tree that Max and I were sharing has given way because the tarp that's also sharing it has sagged with water and added extra weight to it, and I'm the one who's fallen down. I switch on my head torch and see Max's hammock is also on its way to the floor, but for now he's still in the air. I untangle myself and climb out of the saggy hammock, which is awkward to unzip without the tension. The rest of the night is spent trying to find a reasonable place to tie my hammock. Thanks, Max. I really need to stick with my instincts more. Nothing quite like a night in the bush.

As the days go on, my navigation through the forested ridges, or up and down the right 'bumps', improves. We make decent progress and we're able to pick good routes up the mountains. Each day, my confidence with navigation grows.

The best part comes when we reach the top of one of the higher ridges. For a few blissful minutes, we can walk upright, shoulders relaxed, and it gives us a respite because we barely have to duck under vines. The canopy thins just enough to let the light in and the ground is soft, not a swamp in sight. We move quietly and at speed, across the crown of the forest.

Suddenly, to our side the trees open in a small break. We all freeze, instinctively sensing it's worth checking out. There it is, a window across the wild. It's a compromised view but more than we've seen before. We can see for miles, dozens after dozens of tree-covered mountains. It's a glimpse of the distance we've covered. The peaks roll off into the horizon like a sea of green waves. Low clouds drift between them at the base like a silk blanket.

'Wow,' Mikey whispers behind me.

We all stand still. It's one of those rare moments that feels cosmic. I look at everyone's faces. We are mud-splattered, tired and sweaty, but right now, we are all awestruck. There's nowhere we'd rather be.

Vivian steps closer to the edge of the break, squinting at the horizon. 'I never dreamed of climbing this high in the Kanukus,' he says quietly, almost like he's speaking to himself. 'But now, here I am.' He's smiling with his eyes wide, taking everything in. I nod, heart full. His face beams with delight. So does mine. Every pain, ache, insect bite, every struggle that has led to this point has disappeared in an instant. This is medicine for us. Views can do that for you – every one of us is filled to the brim with endorphins and gratitude for this landscape, this planet, and one another.

We stand for another minute, each of us taking it in in our own way.

Then . . . *CRACK!*

A thunderous crash breaks through the stillness below us. We all jolt backwards, away from the ridge.

'What the hell was that!' Mikey blurts.

We cautiously peer down the slope in time to see a huge towering tree topple through the canopy. It's dragging vines and branches as it descends. A deep rumble shakes the ground beneath our feet and then more trees fall with it.

'Deadfall,' Vivian says, adjusting his pack.

We all look at each other. The peaceful moment is broken with excitement from the jungle once again. We shoulder our bags and move on.

We've been taking it in turns to pick off ticks from one another's backs in the evening. I'll go up, most often to Aaron, and say, 'Please can you de-tick me?' Then turn around, lean down and lift my shirt up to reveal my tick-ridden back. He'll then use a head torch to study my back for the ticks. It's odd to say but I enjoy this process, either because of the physical touch or pulling the ticks out! I've been in the jungle without any touch for months now and so the ritual of tick removal is quite therapeutic. The critters get everywhere, and especially like creases on the skin because it's nice and warm. This means you'll even find them in your undies (don't worry, I get those ones off myself!). Their size ranges from hardly visible to the size of a large ladybird. At the start of this expedition I found them rather gross, but now I have a newfound respect for them!

Tonight, Mikey complains of some sores on his arms. He shows us and they look like pimples, but upon further inspection, they seem to have something in them. 'I thought it was a simple pimple, but then I squeezed and squeezed, and I think there's things living in there. It hurts real bad at different points during the night.' He winces while studying his arm.

What he's describing is botfly larvae, something that I've been trying my best to avoid with my hygiene routines. I suspect that Mikey has got these because he hasn't been washing as much as everyone else. My team call them 'mosquito worms' and say that you can prevent yourself from getting them if you stay as clean as possible (not sure how this stands up scientifically but it seems to have worked for the rest of us). They've got this sneaky way of getting under your skin, quite literally. Here's how they pull off this creepy feat – a botfly attaches her eggs to the underside of a mosquito. Then, when this mosquito bites you, the eggs get transferred to your skin. Warmth from your skin triggers these eggs to hatch. After a few weeks these grow into a proper larva, breaking through the skin each night to breathe, and then, they grow hairs, wings and finally, fly out. It seems like Mikey has a few of them and they are causing quite some pain. We have to suffocate them and then try to get them out after that.

Vivian tries cigarette ash, but that doesn't seem enough to

me, so I suggest as well as this we use some of my super industrial plaster tape. We'll leave it on there for twenty-four hours and see what happens.

Later that night, I write in my diary:

> This morning the whistles were all around us but Mikey said to Vivian, 'This is nothing compared to Mapari mountains in leg two.' Vivian was surprised. 'Really?' Mikey responded with, 'Yeah everywhere, even at camp.'
>
> It's so grubby in the rain and mud. We have had to climb steep, with all body parts in mud for traction. Everything is so wet and unsteady. My feet are starting to give in; wet and hills – not a great combo.
>
> We got to a creek, more like falls on rocks. Had a freezing-cold wash, all of us on our rock throwing water over ourselves using our food containers, covering ourselves in soap and trying not to let the bush cow flies eat us while our flesh is out.
>
> I forgot myself earlier when I was getting changed. Vivian said, 'Lucy?'
>
> I answered, 'Yeah?' forgetting I didn't have a top on, then as I made eye contact with him I realized and covered myself immediately.
>
> 'Hot water is ready if you want some,' he replied. Too much time here? I'm becoming at one with nature it seems...
>
> I'm also at the stage where I could just eat and eat and eat. I want all my snacks. I had my noodles for lunch by making them up in the morning then putting them in my food container. It seemed to work well and gave me those vital salts needed for these mountains, but despite this, I still dived into more of my snacks. I'll be out of snacks in the next

day or so and hungry then. Mikey is the same, we can't seem to be satisfied now. We need food!

The next day I'm struggling, but I'm not the only one. Max is also beginning to flag and so with that, Vivian decides he's ready to take the lead. It will be his first time putting his injured arm to the test.

After a couple of hours I hear Vivian say calmly, 'I think I've cut my leg.' In a split second my mind is jumping to the worst. My mind has already gone into what I do next – bag down, medical kit out, tourniquet out, bandages at the ready . . .

'Stop,' I say, keeping with the calm tone. 'Let's take a look.'

Vivian looks worried. The jungle is a dangerous place with its jaguars, bushmasters and deadfall, but really, the most dangerous thing out here is us. Every day we hold the one thing that could end our expedition immediately, but that same thing is the very thing we need to make this expedition possible: the machete. Machetes would have no qualms about going through an artery and unfortunately they are swung at the perfect height for the leg artery. We sharpen them every day and take thousands of swings of them, day and night. There's a right and wrong way to use a machete – cutting away from you – but the problem is, we are out here with limited food, water, sweating and exhausted. It's easy to make a mistake and Vivian has done just that.

Because the machete is so sharp, it's hard to tell how much damage it may have done; it slices right through without leaving much surface damage. Vivian's trousers are torn ever so slightly, which makes me fear the worst, but I don't show it on my face and remain ready to deal with what's in front of me.

I go to Vivian and crouch down. He looks away as I roll up his trouser leg . . . 'Phew.' I breathe a sigh of relief. 'Its a very small cut. There's no blood squirting out, we're good.'

Vivian takes one breath, 'Ahh phew.'

'Don't scare me like that. I was all ready to go full emergency on you,' I say with a smile. 'Me too, I thought that was me done!'

I can tell you this, there's never a dull moment on this expedition.

As we set off again there's an extremely loud noise. We've been hearing it all through these mountains. Imagine a piercing, metallic clang, like a hammer striking steel, echoing through the dense forest; it's sharp and short. 'What is that?' I ask Vivian, who's the bird expert.

'White bellbird,' he answers. The white bellbird is the loudest bird to have ever been recorded. It's an incredibly forceful sound and can be heard from great distances. It slices through the cacophony of the jungle with surprising clarity. Maybe it's laughing at us.

I wake up the next day really feeling the weight of the expedition. The good news is we only have around 30 km, as the crow flies, to go. We could be done next week if the terrain is forgiving... which it never is.

Navigation has been getting continuously harder. Aaron's been great as he uses his X-ray vision to see where the mountain ridges begin. I can't spot them through the trees like he can.

As we make our way to the top of the second and hopefully final mountain of the day, the most frustrating thing happens. There's bloody bamboo on the top of it. Bamboo – of all the things, bamboo at the mountain's summit! Throughout this journey, bamboo has been the bane of our existence, except for that one time we used it to build a raft. Otherwise, it's just a nightmare. It forms a thick, sharp, tangled wall that's a chore to get through. We thought we'd left it behind in the lower terrains, yet here it is, right at the top. Today, it's more than an inconvenience, it could really screw us over. It's 2 p.m. and we need to find a way through it and then get down and find water and set up camp, all before our cut-off time of 3 p.m.

Max goes ahead and with force he just barges into the wall of bamboo. That doesn't really do much because within half a metre he's tangled up in the many vines. This isn't about brute force; it's about cutting a path methodically. We have no idea how extensive this bamboo patch is, and with our drone batteries dead, we're blind to what's ahead.

After thirty minutes of futile cutting at the mountain's peak, I decide we need a new plan. We backtrack, searching for another route along the mountain's flank. Luckily, Mikey spots a less dense area and we manage to cover some ground. We're headed in the right direction and finally get to where the mountain descends. Everything is going great, the downhill is steep and we'll be at the bottom in no time, but then we're faced with our next problem.

We all come to a standstill and stare at what's beneath us: a steep ravine. We stand there at the top of what must be a 300m drop, down to a raging river. This ravine was not on the map, and it's lucky we saw it and didn't follow our usual method of descending mountains, which is to effectively fall with style.

We each look down, feeling trapped. The hill we've just come down was so steep that it'll be very hard to get back up, but we have to find a way. There's no time to waste. I look at my watch: it's about to hit 3 p.m . . . Shit. I'm careful as to where I place my hands as the trees are just popping out of this steep ground. Equally, my feet are trying to grip the loose soil; one slip and I'll be a goner.

'We have to go back,' I say. 'We've no choice.'

There's not much more to be said than that. We have to try another route. I can't tell you how demoralizing it feels to retrace our steps here. It is like being punched in the stomach, all energy sapped from every inch of our bodies.

We turn around, being very careful with each handhold and step. Our rucksacks want to pull us back and down the ravine, so it takes our utmost concentration to fight gravity, which results in our calves burning.

Once at the top, it's time to recalibrate and try another route down. Every second counts and although it's light up here, when we glance down to the valley, the light is already fading. This means that the wildlife is beginning to come out. My heart pounds and I have a rush of anxiety. We have to get down, set camp up, wash and get our feet off the ground, quickly.

We take a new route and begin to descend. It's looking promising. We move fast, hoping for the best and allowing our instincts to kick in as to where we place each hand and foot. Suddenly, as I'm trying to keep pace, something slams into the side of my eyelid. 'Ow!' I cry out, feeling like I've been hit by a stone, but it quickly escalates into a bolt of electricity. 'Owwww!' I shout.

I immediately know that I've been stung. There's a sharp shooting and blinding pain that wipes out any other sensation, but I keep moving. The pain is excruciating, and then I look down on to my chest and see the culprit – a tarantula hawk wasp. I swipe it away and on to the ground, but the pain radiates through my entire head while my tears stream from both eyes. It's stung me on my eyelid. The most painful and intense sting (after the bullet ant) has entered the side of my eye. There's no time to contemplate what's just happened. In agony, I continue the descent. I'm worried that if I panic, it could lead to the venom going to my neck and swelling on my throat, restricting my breathing. This could be fatal. I don't know how my body reacts to this venom. With everything I have left, I focus on controlling the rhythm of my lungs – taking air in and out – and allow the pain to take over my skull, without fighting it. Already, I can feel it swelling and my eyesight begins to get compromised, but I have to get down.

We make it to the bottom of the mountain just as the light begins to fade, urging us to set up camp quickly as nightfall in the jungle brings its own set of dangers. The problem is, we haven't found any water yet and are all in need of it desperately. We're all on edge, our senses heightened by the encroaching darkness and the day's exertions. Vivian volunteers to lead us through this last section. We will need to stop regardless within the next few minutes. It's getting too dangerous to push on.

Suddenly, the calm of getting to the bottom shatters. Vivian jumps back with a start, Aaron and I see his reaction and begin to run in the other direction. We both think he's spotted peccary, until someone shouts, 'Snake!'

It's another bushmaster. I catch my breath and ask Vivian if he's OK as my mind is racing through emergency scenarios. 'No,' he snaps. I fear he's been bitten.

'Did it get you?' I press, ready to spring into action.

He shakes his head. 'No.'

Thank goodness. He nearly stepped on it while trying to avoid the thicker bush where we always assume the bushmasters lurk. He saw it just in time to avoid a disastrous misstep, propelled forward by a bending branch that almost threw him on to the snake. He once again dropped his machete and silencer. How could this have happened to Vivian again? I can't help but think he has once again saved us – lucky charm Vivian. Equally though, how many close calls have we had that we haven't known about?

This bushmaster is bigger and darker than the last, blending almost perfectly with the decayed leaves and underbrush. 'How did you spot it?' I ask, still in disbelief.

Vivian's response is laced with irony. 'Will of God. I don't know.'

The tension breaks momentarily as I ask about what we're supposed to do with it, hoping we can leave this one.

Vivian replies with his characteristic dry humour: 'We're going to put it in bags and take it as a souvenir.'

But the moment of levity passes quickly. Aaron has already taken decisive action. Without hesitation he tells us to move back and he shoots the snake in the head. The sound of other bushmasters whistling nearby sends a chill down our spines – they seem to sense the death of one of their own. I feel once again a rush of pity for this creature; it didn't choose this encounter any more than we did. I feel powerless.

Aaron doesn't hesitate after shooting; he charges at the snake and begins beating it with a stick to ensure it's passed quickly. It's a raw, primal reaction to the immediate threat. Max watches from the side, taken aback by the ferocity of the response, his usual hunter's composure shaken by the violence. He looks as uncomfortable as me, which I find surprising.

We examine the snake afterwards. It's huge. Its tail, with bone exposed like a needle, makes its final movement feebly. The sight of its large fangs, especially the prominent one on the lower jaw, is chilling. We're reminded yet again of the perils that lurk in this wilderness, the constant dance with danger that defines this journey.

Just ahead there's a small swamp so we hastily set up camp. There are more bushmasters in the area but we have no choice, darkness is falling. The urgency is palpable; we need to get off the ground, to find safety from the jungle floor's hazards. Tonight, when we set up camp, it's quiet, the day's events weighing heavily on us

I feel the need to have some separation from the team and

take my camera to go just out of sight, making a line to get back safely and watching every step. I crouch down, begin filming myself. I need to unload my thoughts from the day. I start talking to the camera, almost using it like therapy, but within a few seconds I break down. I can't stop the tears. 'I can't wait to be finished now. I just want to be safe,' I say to the camera. I'm exhausted. The pressure of getting everyone back safe is so much, I have to rely on the luck of the jungle. My mind is tired of the responsibility and constantly playing this dance with death. We are so close to the finish now but still anything could happen. Rescue is still out of the question, there's not even a helicopter in the country at this moment in time. We're on our own and I'm just not sure that the jungle will let us finish this.

I let it all go and for a few minutes tears stream down my face, snot pours out my nose and I weep into my arm with the camera still rolling. I say all I need to say and I know I have to get back. I stand up, wipe myself down, take deep breaths and go back to the team. I think I got away with it and no one suspects that I've had a cry. I just needed that, it's hard to keep the emotions in. I have to be strong here because there's no other choice, but equally it's so important to have an outlet for emotion, when the time is right. I think that with today's obstacles – the bamboo, ravine, wasp sting and snake – it just came at me like a tonne of bricks.

We gather around the fire, each lost in thought about the narrow escape and the relentless challenges of the jungle. I look worse for wear: my eye is beginning to swell a lot – it still burns – and my body is covered in marks and bites. It just has to last another few days.

41. Cheerfulness in the Face of Adversity

WAKING UP IS A SHOCK. My body aches and the side of my face is tender. I peel my good, left eye open, unable to see anything out of my right eye. I get my camera, flip the screen around and look back at my swollen face. War wounds. I look like that picture of Bear Grylls after he was stung by a swarm of African bees on one of his programmes. I suppose I always fancied myself as the female Bear Grylls, but this wasn't exactly what I had in mind . . . I guess it looks good for the camera, silver lining and all. I only hope that it eases up by the time we finish – I want those celebratory images of us, preferably where I don't look like I've been punched in the face.

All the team laugh at me in a concerned way; it is funny. 'Oh my, Lucy,' Aaron laughs.

I love these guys; it's great that we can laugh in adversity. That's it, isn't it? Cheerfulness in the face of adversity. A value that the Marines hold deeply and probably the main trait that I look for in a team . . . and a partner, like Tim. Wow, the thought that I'll be back in his arms with Sami by our side so soon is something that makes me grin from ear to ear. We've just got to get through these last few days.

I snap a twig from a nearby branch and crouch down beside the map, spreading the final section on the forest floor. From the looks of it, we've cleared the worst of the complicated nav. The ridgelines ahead are clean. The terrain looks, dare I say it, almost straightforward.

I use the twig to trace the first stretch.

'We'll hold this bearing along the ridge here,' I say.

I set the bearing for the first part of the day, and show the map to Max, pointing out the ridge line and the natural handrails that will guide us. He nods, quietly taking it in. A few weeks ago, this would've gone over his head. Now, he's getting to grips with it. We pack up the map and then we're on our way.

During our lunch break, I decide we all need to discuss what happened yesterday. I want to understand the team's reasoning behind killing the bushmaster, and let Max have his say too. I start the conversation.

'Vivian and Aaron, it would be good to know your thoughts and reasons for killing the snake. Max, I'd also like to know your take on it. I know that you looked unsure.'

'If it wasn't bothering us, we could have just walked around it. But if it was me, in Vivian's shoes, surely I would have killed it too. I would have been worried it would come after us. But I still think we could have discussed not killing,' Max says.

'If it had bitten Vivian, my my, that would have been very bad. We had to kill it, it was on his tools too,' Aaron says sombrely.

'We don't know how many bushmasters we passed. Probably hundreds. We saw a few but we heard many,' Vivian says.

I can't help but feel that the bushmasters represent more to the team than just a snake. They've become the embodiment of our fear and of the unknown. They are a symbol of not being in control, of the wildness that surrounds us. Killing it gave some of the team a sense of security, a moment of control in a place that constantly reminds us we're not in charge here. We have always been at the mercy of the jungle.

But the truth is, the bushmaster isn't the biggest threat in this jungle. We are. Human beings as a whole. With our short-term thinking and our greed. It's the endless appetite for more. Our species poses the greatest danger to this forest and every other like it. The jungle, or nature itself, is never purposefully malicious. It's never cruel for the sake of it. It simply is. It does what it needs to survive. But our species, when driven by profit over protection, can be devastating. It's clear that we're not acting in the interest of survival, we're actually doing the opposite.

Deforestation, the burning of fossil fuels, the stripping of our vital ecosystems – these aren't acts of necessity. They're decisions made by those in power to turn a quick profit, no matter the cost. This is about corporations levelling forests for short-term gain, governments turning a blind eye and a global system that rewards destruction over stewardship. It's not about survival, it's about making a buck. It's costing us the very world we rely on.

This expedition has revealed the true wonder of this place: its complexity, its generosity, its breathtaking beauty. It's not just home to snakes and jaguars and towering trees, it's a vital system that supports every lifeform on earth.

We need these ecosystems. For our air. For our water. For our food. For our health.

The killing of the bushmaster wasn't just a moment of fear, it was a reminder. A reminder of who the real threat is.

And a question: What are we going to do to stop ourselves from destroying it all?

*

The day goes smoothly and was just what we needed. By 3 p.m. we have found the perfect spot for camp. The pain in my eye has subsided and we are all beginning to feel a little giddy on the idea that we will be finished in a few days. I think of home. Sami, Tim. I cannot express my excitement to be in the frosty British winter. I feel this desire to go for a run in the cold and misty mornings, come back red in the face from the chill and treat myself to a bath and coffee. It feels a world away from where I am now, covered in ticks, sweat, grit and bites.

I pour out the last of my farine into my bowl and scoop boiling water from the pot over the fire to soak it. All of us share what food we have left, knowing that adrenaline and excitement will get us through. 'At least we still have some coffee and wap killer! That's all we need!' says Mikey. We all burst out laughing.

'Awake and ready for your wives!' I declare.

Aaron looks down at his stomach. 'My wife won't be happy.'

'Oh yeah, boy, I'm not in good shape either,' agrees Vivian.

'What do you mean? You guys look great,' I say.

We've all lost a lot of weight and our belts are on their last holes. I was looking at our 'before' photos yesterday and the difference in everyone's faces is phenomenal.

'Amerindians like size. I am out of shape. My wife won't like it. She will feed me well,' Vivian says.

'Yes, Lucy, and you, you have really reduced,' Mikey says, looking me up and down.

'Reduced?' I ask, puzzled. 'Oh, you mean reduced . . . like, literally reduced in size!' I laugh out loud.

It's crazy the cultural differences in what we view as attractive. It also shows how subjective it is and how influenced we are by what everyone else likes. These guys genuinely prefer heavier women and vice versa for the men. It's rather lovely that's the way it is.

CHEERFULNESS IN THE FACE OF ADVERSITY

As we're speaking, I've finished my dinner and placed my bowl temporarily on the ground. When I glance down, I can't believe what I'm seeing. My bowl, my trusty blue bowl that's been with me from the start, is a shambles, half of it literally gone! It's like a scene straight out of a cartoon. Hundreds of leaf cutter ants, in a display of teamwork that is honestly impressive, have claimed it as their own. They've meticulously sliced it into manageable pieces and are now marching off into the bush with their bounty.

These little creatures are incredible, really. Leaf cutter ants can carry pieces up to twenty times their body weight; watching them work is a lesson in efficiency and strength. They're not just muscle, though, there's a whole system at play. Back at their colony, these fragments of my bowl will serve a purpose; they're used to cultivate a special type of fungus that the ants feed on. It's not just about destruction with these guys; it's about sustenance, creating life from what they harvest.

The sight of them, a determined line of tiny workers each hauling a blue fragment, is both frustrating and awe-inspiring. They're certainly resourceful! They navigate the jungle floor with precision, avoiding obstacles and adjusting their paths as needed. Each ant knows its role, whether it's cutting, carrying or defending the line. Their organization is something else. They are a super-organism functioning as one amid the chaos of the jungle. It's a stark reminder of the jungle's rule: adapt and survive. Here we are, fumbling with maps and gear, and these ants have it all figured out. Simple, effective, relentless. Just like the jungle itself.

'I guess I have no bowl now!' I declare. Serves me right for putting the bowl on the ground. I'm out of food anyway so what use do I have for a bowl?

As I'm in my hammock, writing my journal by head torch, I hear noises in the distance. 'Vivian?' I call.

'Yes, Lucy?'

'Do you hear that?'

'I do . . .'

'Does everyone else hear that?' I wait for them to answer but only Aaron confirms. Vivian shines a torch over to Mikey and Max's hammocks, but their hammocks are sagging – they are not there. It must be them. Where on earth have they gone?

Vivian gets up and manages to make out their lights in the distance between the trees.

'They are shining,' he tells me. Shining is when you shine your torch into a creek. Reflecting back at you, you see the fish, and with that, you can take a shot with your silencer and get them. The thing is, this is all very well in the safety of a village or with clear 'get out' points, but we are still without rescue, and they are risking this whole expedition by walking at night. On the other hand, what I do like is the fact that Mikey and Max are spending time together. There was clear opposition to begin with, even jealousy from Mikey, but now they've realized they have a lot in common and have put any beef aside. I think the issue was the fact that Max had begun his job as a ranger and become the 'new kid in town'. It would have stepped on Mikey's toes. The same thing happened when he arrived here.

I wait for them to return and tell them I'm not happy with them doing this – I even use my 'firm' voice. The only other time I've used that voice on this expedition is when I confronted Lionel over the medical kit. Vivian and Aaron back me up, and I get an apology from Max and Mikey. Accidents can happen, and though they're solid in the jungle, we're still on our own and they're still just lads in their twenties, dads or not. I feel like a mum angry with her kids, or even worse, nagging her kids, but I have to make myself heard – it's not over until it's over. We can't make any mistakes at this late stage.

42. Forest Family

I WAKE UP BUZZING WITH EXCITEMENT. We snap a cracking team photo before beginning our route, laughing at the daily frustrations like feet being constantly wet, wading through creeks and mud – all this will soon be a memory.

Mikey really steps up with the filming; he's got a new lease of life and is getting all the shots. He throws me a compliment that sticks: 'When people ask how Lucy did, I will tell them, "Even though she's young, she's like a mum to us."'

This might stem from last night when Max and Mikey got a bit daring, but I also think it's because of my leadership nature. I know I am compassionate. I like to speak to everyone individually to make sure they are feeling well in themselves, and Mikey even said how much he likes the daily check-ins. I think it took him a while to adjust and to open up, but now he has really embraced it and has become a better team member as a result.

Today, Max starts to flag a bit. Vivian mentioned last night that he's been watching Max, impressed by his stamina. 'I was like that on the first leg,' he said. But now Max is feeling the burn. It just goes to show, this expedition doesn't play favourites.

Then, just as the light begins to thin under the canopy, we break out of the dense undergrowth . . . and there it is.

A clearing: wide and quiet. The canopy open above us and the sky clear for once! It takes me a moment to realize I've stopped walking. The others come up behind me, one by one, and we all just stand there, breathing it in.

We didn't plan to camp here, not exactly, but the moment I see it, I know: this is it. Our final camp.

We drop our packs, stretch out our aching limbs with huge smiles. I spin around looking above me. 'Our final camp spot!' I say, beaming. 'For the first time in weeks, we might be able to see the stars!'

It's the clearest camp we've ever had.

Aaron is wearing the biggest smile I've seen him with.

I turn to him. 'It's time to go home now right? I can feel it now!'

'Yes, Lucy, when I come out and into the savannah, I'm going to feel like I'm fifteen years old!' He flexes his muscles in his torn, oversized green T-shirt. 'Yes, like I could walk another trip of these Kanukus!'

'Another?' I ask in disbelief.

'Yes!'

'I couldn't!' Everyone laughs. Aaron has certainly found his spark again. There's the man I was hoping to see.

We all gather around Mikey, who's been dealing with a botfly larva under his skin. It's a grim souvenir that I'd rather he didn't take home. It's finally time to address it; after suffocating the parasite with tobacco and tape, it's ready to be squeezed out. At least the light is better here at this camp.

Mikey braces himself, his face a mix of anticipation and disgust. I reassure him, 'All right, let's get this thing out of you,' trying to keep the mood light despite his obvious discomfort. Vivian positions himself to help, his hands steady as he applies pressure around the swollen area.

As he squeezes, the worm begins to emerge, inching out slowly. 'Ewww!' I say.

It's a bizarre and somewhat nauseating sight, this worm creature that's been living just under his skin. 'It's dead now, we have to get it,' Vivian confirms.

Mikey winces. I'm not surprised; this is a fat thing to come out of your skin. He will never wince at an injection again. He's holding strong, relieved to be getting rid of his unwelcome guest.

'Oh boy, that's a big one,' Aaron observes with great interest. 'Big mosquito worm!'

Vivian is focused on the task and then offers Max a go. Max takes over and squeezes more out, revealing the slug-like length. 'Mikey's a tough boy,' he says. With one final push, revealing the fat tummy that makes it look the shape of a snail, the worm is out. It's white in colour with an obvious mouth that it's been using to munch Mikey's flesh. We all let out a collective sigh, half relief, half revulsion.

'Good riddance,' Mikey mutters, inspecting the worm with a fascinated grimace.

'I'm glad we got that out,' I say, impressed again with the jungle's creations!

Meanwhile, I get a message from Mum and Dad. The clear sky means that they got my message about us finishing soon. They must be so relieved. I reassure them: *We're nearly there.*

I light the fire for our last camp, smiling to myself about the enormity of what tomorrow represents. I feel elated and so proud of all we've done.

Sleeping doesn't last long. I wake up at 2 a.m., unzip my hammock and step out quietly. Mikey's already there, crouched by the flames, poking at a half-burned log.

'Can't sleep?' I ask.

He glances up, eyes open wide with a tired sort of energy.

'I'm just so excited, Lucy!'

I smile and nod, then sit down beside him, stretching my hands out to the fire. The Kanuku nights have surprised us, colder than any of us expected. A few minutes pass before we hear footsteps and see Max, then Aaron, then Vivian, emerging one by one from their hammocks like shadows.

We stand around the fire, warming ourselves. The moon shine is visible and casts a soft light on the forest floor.

'Feels weird, knowing it's our last night out here,' Max finally says.

'Yeah,' Mikey says, rubbing his hands together. 'I don't feel ready to go back.'

Vivian gives a small laugh. 'I thought you were counting down the days?!'

'I was. I just—I feel different now . . . I don't know. It was so, so, so, so wild out there. I love it.'

We go quiet again, each staring into the fire like it holds the answers. There's a peace right now that we all know won't last once we get home. We are all at one. Content with ourselves and life right now, exactly the way it is.

Mikey breaks the silence, 'I've been thinking. I want to start something when I get back . . . a business. Something that involves filming. Oh, and I want to build a home of my own.'

Aaron leans on his knees, eyes locked on the flames. 'I want to spend more time in the forest. Work as a guide. Learn more from senior guides too.'

Vivian nods slowly. 'I want to inspire more young people to learn the old ways, the proper skills. Not just know them, but respect them. I want young people to carry the silencer with pride, have pride in our traditions. Maybe then they'll care more about protecting this place.'

Max shifts his weight. 'I want to do more expeditions.'

They all look at me like I'm supposed to have a big answer too. I let the silence hang before speaking.

'I want to tell our story. Properly. Not just the adventure aspect or the snakes or the slog, but what this journey really was, us and this spectacular jungle. I want to see if it can stir something, even if it's just a small shift in one person's attitude towards the environment. Maybe even real change. Behaviour, policy, whatever. If it makes someone stop and think, then it's worth it. I want to try to spark a little of what we all feel when we are here – the need to protect these ancient forests.'

We sit like that for a long while, passing back memories. We reminisce the close calls with wildlife, the days we thought we couldn't go on, the pain and the laughter – it was killer! The way the jungle broke us down and rebuilt us all in different ways.

Of course it's not just competence and experience that has allowed us to pass through here. It is also luck. Luck has been a huge factor and we've been close to the wrong side of luck many times, which has reminded us all of our own mortality. There's electric energy; no one can take away what we've been through together. We all hold a special connection and will always be part of one another's lives.

After two hours of chatting and getting giddy with excitement, it's clear we're not going back to bed. We decide it's time to pack up our bags and our hammocks for the last time, and make our way up our final mountains in the darkness. This part of the mountain is different. We're out of the thick jungle now, where the wildlife thins out and predators aren't an issue. The path is clearer, safer, and for once, moving at night feels like the right call. We might even get to the top for sunrise.

We march up the mountain in a line, head torches on. We are silent, all deep in our own thoughts. I suspect we are all thinking the same way, quietly going over this time together and what it will feel like to get home.

Our climb up the mountain, Schomburgk's Peak, only takes a few hours. When we reach the top, it's still only 5 a.m.; it won't get light for another hour. As we get to the top, the clouds come in, the wind starts up, the heavens open and it begins to pour with rain, stopping any visibility. We are all freezing, but want to wait for the light before we make our way down to the savannah – marking our finish point. The summit is exposed and our wet, exhausted bodies feel every bit of weather. Aaron curls up under a bush, rocking side to side. Our energetic 2 a.m. bodies have had the fun sapped out of us, reminded of the pressure and physical exhaustion we've been under this whole time.

We can't end like this. I have to keep spirits up, even if it is this one last time. I encourage Mikey to jump up and down. We dance and do star jumps. 'Jungle bootcamp!' I say. 'Come on, Aaron! It'll keep you warm!' He gets up from out of the bush, his clothes in soaking-wet tatters, and joins in. It's not too dissimilar to Stair Club at ITN! Vivian and Max also step in, and we dance and prance around in the rain.

'Please, jungle weather god!' I shout to the sky. 'Please stop the rain for us!'

'Yes, weather gods, end the rain!' Aaron yells.

The movement gets us all laughing again. Vivian points in the distance, 'Look!' It's beginning to get light and there's a break in the grey clouds. Our dance may have just worked!

The rain stops and the light reveals the most gorgeous view that I've ever seen. We are at the high point, on the edge of the jungle. On either side of us are dozens of jungle-covered mountains with a beautiful layer of mist blanketing the bottom, leaving the top of the peaks showing. Until now, we've not had anything like this.

On one side, these mountains are the same ones we've spent so long going across; on the other side is Brazil. Directly in front of us, there is no jungle: instead it is the savannah. Then, located on the savannah, there's the most unusual sight of all. Civilization: Lethem. The cluster of lights shines bright. The air feels different too. It's refreshing and still cool. Why is it that even the biggest storms are followed by such calm conditions? That goes for life events as well. In this moment of peace, all of us individually choose to go off and take some time to ourselves as we stare at what lies ahead.

It's an odd feeling, seeing the world that we left behind. Below us is society, its running water, food, toilets, electricity . . . safety. Suddenly there's a desire to pull away from that; I don't know if I want to go back. I feel conflicted. Our jungle expedition life that we've created is so pure, down there doesn't feel like the 'real' world – this does. Will I be a changed person? Will the lessons I've learned last forever or will they gradually fade out of existence and I'll lose this incredible lust for life that I've found by being here? That's what the wild does: it rekindles a sense of awe for the planet; it shows our strengths, our weaknesses. It reminds us who we really are, which is something that most of us, in adult life, lose. We lose track of what makes us tick and what our North Star is. The jungle doesn't care who you are or what you look like. It doesn't judge or have laws but what it does have is an indescribable force. A force so great that you feel it in every inch of your body. Even on the days where the piha birds are singing and the sun rays scatter the forest floor, there is still this silent force present. It reminds you of the power that mother nature has and reminds you of your own vulnerabilities. In the wild, you have no choice but to be brutally honest with yourself, and it means you get things done and are a better person all round. I hope I can continue to live my life like that in one way or another.

Leading these men has been the greatest honour of my life. We are more than team mates; we have become what Mikey affectionately calls us: a forest family.

I knew during all the times it was painful and uncomfortable that I'd look back at this fondly. We may not have always felt welcome in this wilderness, but we have always been a part of it. After all, we ourselves are nature, we have just lost sight of that along the way.

Before descending down to the savannah, I bring everyone together. I get them to gather around, and I bring out my notebook and begin reading them the words I have written over the last week as we near the end of our journey.

I just want to take this moment to say a few words.

When I started to plan this expedition, I knew it would be long, I knew it would be hard but I didn't know how long or how hard. Some people thought it would be impossible, some thought we wouldn't come back. But here we are, having moved through such untouched jungle. I think we can all agree that this has been one almighty undertaking.

Every single one of you, and of course Lionel and Carlos, should be so so proud. What we have achieved here is huge. I have seen not only myself but every single one of you grow as individuals, as people.

This is an important expedition and I hope you will continue to spread the word of the importance of protecting this forest, your forest, and the need to protect everything related to it.

I will miss you all dearly. You have become my forest family, my friends, my brothers if you like.

So as we go home from this pioneering expedition, I hope you will remember this fondly because no matter what anyone says, ever, no one can take this away from you. These memories we have created will last forever.

We will share this experience and bond together, which is something truly special.

So thank you for teaching me so much, for being so kind, for being such fantastic human beings and for saying yes in the first place to come on this hell of an adventure.

The reading brings tears, not just from me but from the team. Aaron has to go off to collect himself and Mikey also wipes his eyes. I meant every word of what I said.

The time has come.

'Shall we get out of this crazy jungle?' I ask.

It's followed by a big 'Yeah!' and everyone fist bumps in the air.

Rucksacks on our backs, down we go for the last 2 km.

After fifty days and 400 km (253 miles), we finally emerge from the deep, damp and dark jungle, and into the heat of the savannah, at the border of Brazil. The air is dry. The ground is cracked. The sunlight bounces off the parched earth, a harsh contrast to the constant shadow and saturation we've lived in for weeks. The heat hits us like a wall. We just stand there for a moment, blinking in the brightness, like animals surfacing from a long hibernation.

'Here,' I say, pointing to a patch of scorched grass. 'We can wait for Anders here.' And with that, our journey is over.

We hear the 4x4s long before we see them, their rumble rising through the silence like something so alien to us. The hairs on the back of my neck stand on end and when they finally appear, kicking up a plume of dust, none of us move. We just watch. We are hesitant about what's ahead. After so long in isolation, the sight of 'other' people feels almost invasive. We've become a tribe, tightly bound, and suddenly the outside world feels like a threat.

'Yeah, man!' Anders calls from the car. He jumps out and pulls me in for a hug. 'Oh, man, I can't believe what you guys have done. You actually fucking did it. Ian would be so proud.'

Then he smiles mischievously, and waves to the second vehicle. The door opens and out steps Aaron's wife. Aaron tears up when he sees her and they embrace. I can't help but think about what Aaron and Vivian said – that Amerindians prefer their partners with a bit of 'chub' on them. She won't know what to make of Aaron, who has 'reduced', as Mikey would say!

After celebratory photos spraying a bottle of suspicious sparkling wine over one another, Anders hands us some food; real food. We eat like the wild things we are. My request was simple: an apple. Just one apple. It tastes like the best thing I've ever eaten. (I love apples and have been craving fresh fruit!)

And with that, it's time to go back. This expedition is complete. We are now safe. We've done it. It's going to take some time to get my head around that and to loosen the grip of my senses being alert. To believe we're no longer at the mercy of the jungle.

Look at what's possible when you apply your mind. When optimism is your compass, when you believe, truly believe, that there's always a way. And you don't stop until you find it.

Direction is everything. And this . . . this has been one of the most defining, magnificent chapters of my life.

Somewhere in that clearing, I can still feel the presence of the girl I used to be. I haven't swerved far from her. The one with callused hands and a wild imagination, climbing trees and pretending to be Tarzan. She would have loved this moment. She dreamed of it before she even knew how.

And Ian? I carry him with me too. Ian has been with me every step of this journey. Not just in memory, but I can feel him in the trees and in the firelight. His presence has lingered in the air, reminding me to keep going. To go with my gut, to do it my way. Not just on this expedition, but in life.

I just hope that stepping out of the jungle doesn't mean leaving that feeling behind.

He never needed to spell it out, but he believed in me, not just as an explorer, but as a storyteller. I hope I've made him proud. I hope we – Lionel, Vivian, Aaron, Mikey, Max, Carlos and Anders – have made him proud.

But it's not the end. The best is always yet to come.

The only way to get there is to keep stepping into the wild.

Epilogue

When I came back from the Kanukus in 2021, I thought the hard part was over. But in truth, the journey was really only just beginning.

The press reception when I got home was immense . . . it was interview after interview. There was so much promise and excitement about the fact I'd filmed the whole expedition myself. But those promises fell short. Weeks turned into months with no broadcaster biting. Still, I persevered. I knew the story was strong, that audiences would connect with adventure in a way they hadn't before: raw, emotional and with real risk.

I was living the life, though: explorer, full time. No plan B. Even without the TV side of things, I managed to pay my bills through public speaking. But I knew that couldn't be the only thing I relied on and my heart was in making films. It always had been. I could see the vision clearly. I just needed others to see it too.

That meant pulling together everything I'd learned so far: filming, storytelling, public speaking, producing, hustling. It meant taking rejection after rejection and still showing up the next day.

When Channel 4 finally said yes to making the show that

EPILOGUE

would become *Secret Amazon: Into the Wild*, it felt like all the battles had led to that one moment. Though if I'm honest, even that nearly slipped through my fingers.

It had been just under a year since returning home that I decided enough was enough. I needed to take things into my own hands and go straight to the top. No more relying on others. I had never done that before, why was I doing it now? No one cared more about telling this story than me. It was up to me to make it happen and cut out any BS in between. Channel 4 had always been the dream. I'd grown up on their documentaries and adventure shows. It felt like the perfect home for my debut. Risk-taking. Different.

I managed to persuade the one commissioner I'd had my eye on from years before to have coffee with me. (When I was working at ITN Productions, I used to note down the names of people who made the shows I enjoyed, with the intention of one day meeting them.)

It was late afternoon, not the ideal time for meetings. The day has worn you down by then. Channel 4 was having renovations so he suggested when I met him in the lobby that we go find a place for coffee. Immediately, precious time was being wasted, no time for small talk. We found a small place nearby and sat outside.

I went into full pitch mode very quickly, and he listed every reason why it wouldn't work. He was kind, but his job was to say no, really – to filter out the endless stream of 'crazy' ideas that landed on his desk, especially expedition ones. For a moment, I thought that was it. I had an out-of-body experience, as if future me was looking down on the scene.

I could not let this opportunity go. The reason he was saying no was because he wasn't getting it. I needed to make him get it. I'd been waiting for this chance for ten years. I wasn't about to walk out of that room empty-handed.

Something inside me flipped.

I fought for it, turned every obstacle over, found another way through. Not the industry way. My way. And to his credit, that commissioner, who could so easily have said no, became one of my biggest supporters and I love working with him. His willingness to back something different, something risky, allowed *Secret Amazon* to exist.

When it finally went out into the world in October 2024, I braced myself – I wasn't sure how it would be received, expecting some kind of backlash. Instead, I was flooded with messages. Parents telling me they'd watched it with their kids. Older viewers saying it reminded them of the adventures they thought had vanished from television. Across generations, people wrote to say the series had touched them. I really hadn't expected that.

But here's the thing about this industry. One success doesn't mean the battles are over. If anything, it resets the clock. After *Secret Amazon*, I thought the next commission would come easier. Foolish, really. Television doesn't work like that. It's a rollercoaster! Knockbacks, false starts, dead ends, doors slamming shut. But I've learned something vital along the way: when one door closes, another opens. The industry isn't dead. It's evolving! And if you're brave enough to disrupt it, to find new ways through, there are endless possibilities.

You see, disruption doesn't just mean breaking things. It means creators taking control and making the shows they want to make – finding alternative ways to make that happen. It means collaboration. It means working with passion. It means more ownership.

Budgets are shrinking, yes, but that gives power back to those who can do more with less. This suits our time. We've grown up creating. I've spent my whole life making films; producing them,

EPILOGUE

filming and directing them. Lean, personal, real. That's how I work best.

Television often mistakes bigger for better. The problem is, bigger usually just means more expensive. Strip out the costs, prove the story is strong and worthwhile without all the extra bells and whistles, and the risk then shrinks. Take the risks yourself and you get something better: freedom and creative control. In a world where online platforms can cut through just as much as traditional TV, those risks are definitely worth taking.

With *Secret Amazon*, I'd learned how to make something real with limited means and how important it is to protect the story at all costs. The next step wasn't about starting over, it was about building on that foundation.

That's what *Secret Africa* represented for me.

For the first time, I had a three-part series commissioned from the start. A dream come true. Bigger and bolder, but still holding on to what mattered most: a raw and unpolished adventure, self-filmed again with the human story at its heart.

Getting it commissioned was another expedition in itself.

After a few months of false starts, the idea was born. I knew immediately this would be the next Channel 4 series – I just needed to put things in place to bring it about in the easiest and quickest way, and work my socks off to make it happen. There were endless hurdles but with the right team of disruptors around me, we made it a reality.

Since the expedition, the team's story has continued to unfold in ways that make me deeply proud. We all stay in touch. Anders stayed on in Guyana and built The Wild Tales, a small but brilliant company that now takes people deep into the forest to learn jungle survival and experience real expeditions. Vivian, Lionel and Carlos work with him regularly as guides, keeping the same spirit and humour alive in the forest – and I'm fairly sure that wap killer is nowhere to be seen!

Mikey's talent for photography and videography was so impressive that I sent him an iPhone so he could keep shooting, and he's been creating some wonderful videos ever since. Max has taken to rodeo, keeping up a long-standing Guyanese tradition. And Aaron? He's already keen for the next adventure.

Once Tim was better, we flew back out and spent a few weeks in the jungle with Aaron and Vivian. We swung from vines, fished with our bows and arrows, and shared stories around the fire. It meant a lot to have him finally see that world for himself after hearing so much about it. We will be back again soon. The bonds we formed out there will never disappear.

There were many people who helped make both *Secret Amazon* and *Secret Africa* possible. Firstly, the audiences that chose to spend their time watching *Secret Amazon.* Then there were those who believed in it when it was just an idea, from funding to guidance to sheer cheerleading. I wouldn't be here without them. It has taken so many people to get here and I owe them more than words can say.

This is what I've come to realize: being an explorer today isn't just about trekking through jungles or crossing deserts. It's about collaboration, surrounding yourself with those who also thrive on adapting in an ever-changing world. It's about learning how to tell stories in a shifting landscape and about fighting for them to be seen. At the end, stories are what matter.

A new friend of mine, Oisín Rogers, put it perfectly: 'Stories are the currency of our time.' They outlast everything else and they're worth fighting for.

That's why I do what I do. It's not just about the thrill of

EPILOGUE

adventure. It's about the awe, the perspective, the reminder that we're part of something bigger. It's about protecting the last wild places and making sure their stories are told so they don't vanish. It's about proving that exploration, like storytelling, isn't dead. It's exciting, it's urgent and it's evolving. Storytelling and exploration aren't going anywhere, you see – they'll exist for as long as we do.

The Kanukus gave me the confidence. *Secret Amazon* gave me the platform. *Secret Africa* is giving me the momentum. Where it goes next will be shaped by the same force that carried me through those jungles and across those city meetings: perseverance, disruption and a refusal to let go of a story worth telling.

Because if we lose the wild, we lose more than landscapes. We lose the stories that bind us to this planet and to each other. And if we lose those, we lose ourselves.

Afterword

THE WILD IS CHANGING FAST. I've seen it. Forests thinning, rivers shrinking, seasons shifting. Yet, somehow it fights to hold on.

Every expedition I take, every story I tell, reminds me of how we are not separate to nature, we are nature. We've now pushed things too far. Protecting what's left isn't a choice any more, it's a responsibility.

We're spending less and less time outside, let alone in wild places. Three quarters of children in the UK now spend less time outdoors each day than a UK prisoner. I think it's time to rethink our priorities. It's no surprise so many people feel detached from the natural world.

We can't protect what we don't value and we can't value what we don't understand.

That's what the purpose of exploration is, for me – not to conquer, but to connect. To see the world with fresh eyes. To feel that sense of awe and wonder again. It's there, we just need to see it through all of the noise. Because awe is where it all starts; it changes how we treat the planet and how we treat each other.

The world will keep evolving, and we'll never reach the end of learning. That's the beauty of it: every discovery only reveals

AFTERWORD

how much more there is left to understand. But as long as there are people willing to care, to take risks, to keep telling stories that make others stop and look closer, there will always be exploration, and there will always be something wild worth fighting for.

The wild is still out there. And so are we.

Acknowledgements

Aaron Bernadine
Altberg Bootmakers
Anders Andersen
Ashley Holland
Bento
Carlos Honorio
Chris Parker
Chris Shaw
Christopher Wright
Courtneay Mann
Dan and Emelie Marsh
Darren Cook
Eggy Fredricks
Guy Fredricks
Iain Anderson
Jon Naylor
Jonah Weston
John Hesler
Joe Fredricks
Larry Walford
Lionel James
Louisa and Charles Taylor
Luke Radcliff
Major General Joseph Singh
Marty Stalker
Matt and Kate Jones
Maximus Griffith
Michael McDonald
Ministry of Amerindian Affairs
Monique Stephens
Neil Laughton
Neptune Infrastructure Associates
Oisín Rogers
Peter and June Felix
Peter Chappell
Protected Areas Commission
Rachel Evans
Richard Collins
Sarah Sands
Scientific Exploration Society
Sharron Holland
Sid Kamalakara
Steve Backshall
Stuart and Jean Mackintosh
The Jellicoes
Tom Platts
Tony Taylor
Una Maclean
Vivian Smith
Ian Craddock
Mum and Dad
And my rock, Tim Taylor

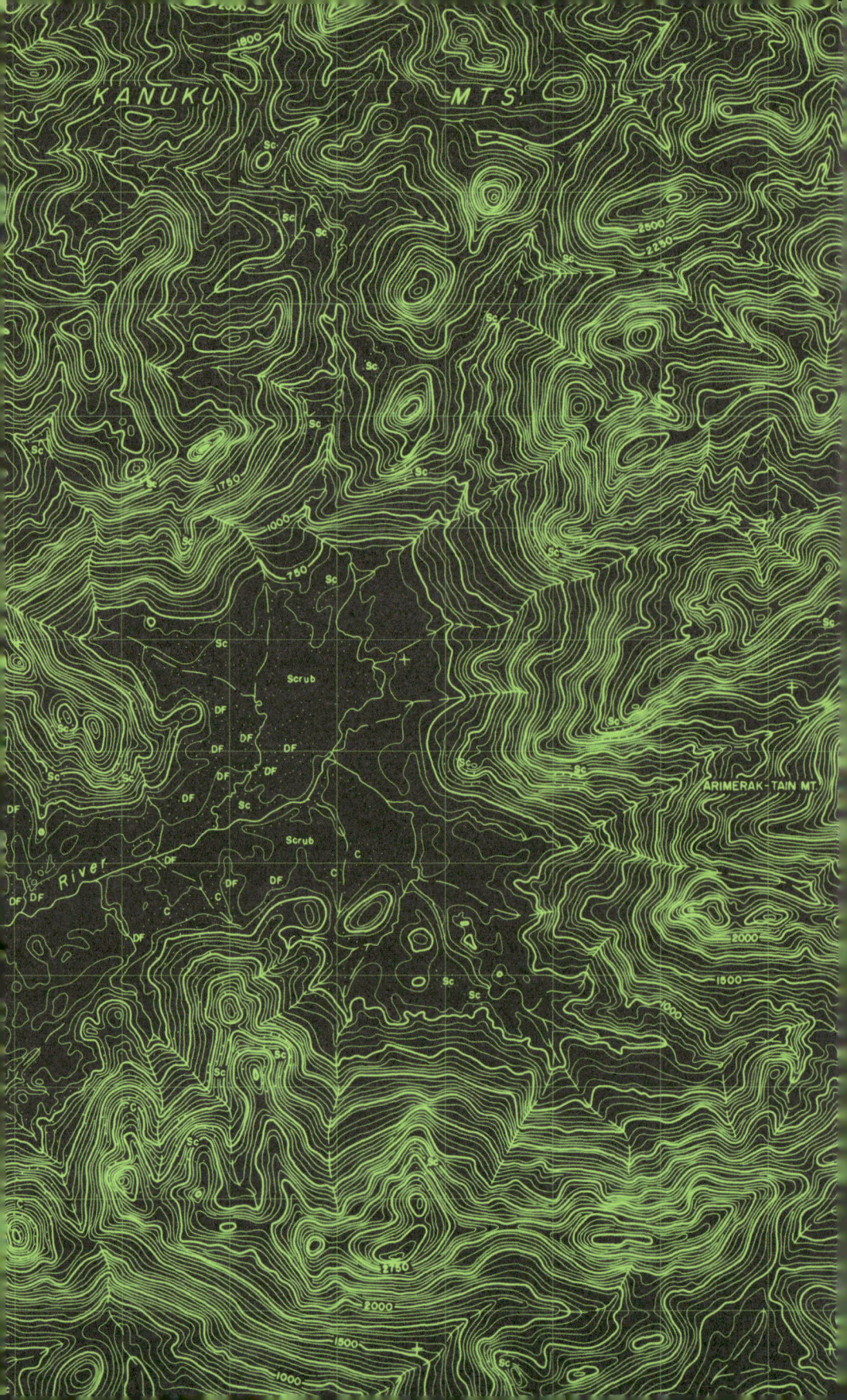